That's A Lot of Bulletin: The Lehigh World According to Ray Armstrong

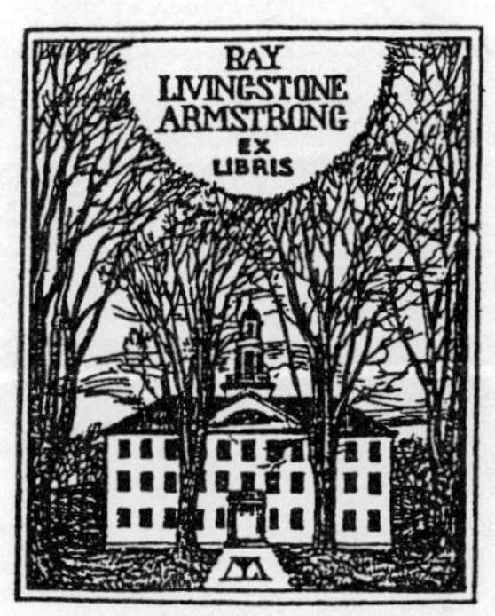

That's A Lot of Bulletin: The Lehigh World According to Ray Armstrong

By Ray Armstrong

Published by Lehigh University
Bethlehem, Pa.

Lehigh University, Bethlehem, Pa. 18015

Published by the Department of English
Lehigh University

Published 1989
Printed in the United States of America
ISBN 0-9624866-0-4

To Harry Ramsey:
It's Really His Fault

Photography and illustration credits:

Photo by Driver 128
API photo 104
Christmas City Studio 70, 93, 94, 221, 262, 279
Photo by Harvan 60, 61
Photo by Bernard J. Suess 214
Yale University Athletic Association 43
Shutterbug photography 61
Douglas Wiltraut 139
Oxford University Press 167, 194

Book design by Marvin H. Simmons

Contents

That's A Lot of Bulletin:

Foreword

In the fall, 1988, Wighty Martindale called to ask if anyone had thought about collecting the essays Ray Armstrong had written for the *Alumni Bulletin.* The idea was irresistible. Here for leisurely delight alumni could re-read the warm profiles of Lehigh luminaries and be jostled again into chuckles by witty observations about the campus. Once again sparkling phrases, delightful turns of thought, and comic footnotes would be available for impromptu diversion. With Wighty's generous support the idea became reality: Ray's fugitive pieces have come home. Read them in the joy with which they were written. I promise you a good cruise in a worthy ship.

Keeping a ship afloat requires the ingenuity and teamwork of several hands. It is a pleasure to acknowledge their sturdy and cheerful help in bringing *That's A Lot of Bulletin* into safe harbor.

Captain: Wighty Martindale [Senior Vice President, Shearson Lehman Hutton], conceiver of the voyage. Bright-eyed in fog, a pillar of good humor when committee winds blew.

First Mate: Glenn Airgood [Director of University Communications] whose ability to fathom new seas was invaluable to the Captain.

Second Mate: Jack Fulton [Assistant Vice-President for Development], expert communicator with far-flung natives friendly to our cause.

Sergeant-at-Arms: Ed Gallagher [Chairman of the English Department], who kept us on the level.

Dorothy Jones, typist, who navigated arcane maps and kept the computer log ship-shape.

Durrae Johanek, proofreader, who purified the ship's log.

Jack De Bellis [English Department], your humble Helmsman,

proud to steer this happy enterprise.

The owner of the ship is Ray Armstrong. The happy cruise you sail in this bark results from Ray's masterly knowledge of how to make a vessel float in strange waters, and how to keep it trim across the years.

Bon voyage.

Jack De Bellis
Lehigh University
September, 1989

The Man Inside

Ray Armstrong's great professional gifts were his teaching, his breadth of reading, and his writing. The writing which makes up this volume allows us to hear his humor, to marvel at his learning, and share the warmth he felt toward those he worked with.

I consider Ray to be conservative in the best sense. After graduating from Williams College, he attended Oxford and not only met but was examined by J. R. R. Tolkien and C. S. Lewis—an honor for any aspiring scholar. Perhaps influenced by them, he taught by asking questions about specific passages, considering accuracy in understanding to be a prerequisite for any scholarship. Ray always addressed students formally, listening to them with respect. He seldom read his notes.

Most students encountered Armstrong in freshman and sophomore courses, perhaps even in English Zero, a course once reserved for those freshmen who failed the proficiency exam given during orientation week. [1]As his composition students soon learned, he believed in Samuel Johnson's dictum that, "What is written without effort is read without pleasure." But he could demand a great deal because he believed intensely in what he was doing. Students will forgive almost anything if they sense that the instructor is prepared for class and cares about the material. I was to witness Ray's intensity early one Saturday morning during a class on John Bunyan. The class period was just ending and Ray had decided to read to us from the concluding pages of Part Two of *Pilgrim's*

[1]Yes, in the dark ages (the 1950's), students not only wrote nearly a dozen themes in each of two freshman semesters, but students had to "try out" to get into an ordinary class. But enough of this. If you want footnotes, Armstrong turns the footnote into an art form.

Progress, a moving passage in which the heroic Standfast crosses from this world to the next. Ray is a fine reader, but this time he got tangled in the passage and then read so rapidly he was nearly unintelligible. Slamming the book shut, he said, "This is one of the most beautiful passages in the English language, and I have butchered it miserably." His eye moist, he gathered his books and abruptly left the room.

I had Ray as my senior advisor on T. S. Eliot's *Murder in the Cathedral.* It was in this class that I learned about Ray's enormous range of reading. He showed how Eliot had appropriated some dialog directly from Doyle's *The Musgrave Ritual.* This converted me on the spot to a life-long Sherlockian. Over the years he has recommended such nonscholarly authors as H. Rider Haggard, John Buchan, Will Cuppy, George S. Chappell, Edmund Pearson, Stephen Leacock, Jean Shepherd, Edmund Crispin, and Bob and Ray.

As a student of Ray's, I recall how he often emphasized what was real rather than what was famous. Ray believed in the humanistic tradition of learning, beginning with the classics, the Bible, and the great literary works of Western culture. Indeed, his casual classical allusions in his generally goofy footnotes in no way disguise his real knowledge. "The stigma of being an educated human being is to know what the *Iliad* is about," he remarked recently. He would not consider *The Great Gatsby* an adequate substitute. Although his career took him through a number of critical approaches to literature—new criticism, structuralism, Marxism, feminism, deconstructionism—he went his own way. "I carry no banner with a strange device on it," he declared.

Ray saw the bright side of energetic Samuel Pepys. He cheerfully recited passages from *The Compleat Angler*, in which Izaak Walton describes "the poor despised chub," and the "bold and lusty trout," and Ray preferred Ben Jonson's *Timber*, a collection of critical and gossipy observations, to his more famous lyrics. He admired John Dryden because Dryden had solid professional skills, excelling as a poet, satirist, dramatist, prose writer, translator of Plutarch and Virgil, and as a religious apologist. Edmund Wilson once wrote that "The style of Walton's *Lives* or Dryden's prefaces was [a very] personal thing; it fitted the author like a suit of clothes and molded itself to the natural contours of his temperament and mind; one is always aware that there is a man inside."

Ray once told a class that if they had only three books to take to a deserted island, one of them should be Richard Burton's *Anatomy of Melancholy*, a rambling thousand-page encyclopedia of health and ancient legend. Ray never claimed that it was one of the world's three greatest books, but he believed Burton's book should be chosen because its various parts could be read and re-read many times over, an endless source of amusement for idle moments. Ray's own writing does the same thing. He recently told me, "Learning sixty years ago that writing is—for me anyway—very hard work, I have done as little of it as I could get by with." The warmth and wit of these collected pieces make me happy that he so often made the effort to amuse us. May you be happy with this book on your own deserted island.

Wight Martindale, Jr.

Professor Armstrong

Pauca optima, as R. Burton[1] wrote in a book where he says everything at least twice and often innumerably. When I composed these studies of "Laurigeres Lehighenses," I saw them as nothing but ephemerae, footsteps on the sand at low tide. Had I supposed that they might reappear in the immortality of a *volume,* I would have taken more trouble as I wrote, weighing the movement of my sentences, purging my diction of colloquialism, verifying my references, and eliminating every passage that I thought especially fine.

It's too late now.

[1]I *think* I mean Burton, but it may have been Fuller or even Glanvill.

Foreword

Some years ago one morning I was approached by a rather flashily dressed young man who told me that his name was Ramsey and that I had been mentioned to him by some authority—the Syndics of Phi Beta Kappa, the Governors of the College Board, or some outfit like that—as a writer who could rescue the *Lehigh Alumni Bulletin* from the doldrums into which it had drifted during his administration. Ill at ease and even furtive, Ramsey enlisted my sympathy, and for some years thereafter I supplied to the *Bulletin* sharply analytical copy relating to the university and its far-flung concerns.

I think that this venture was successful. Ramsey's morale improved markedly, and even his dress smartened up. The alumni themselves were at least undisturbed—Class Notes are the only copy that most graduates look at—and in all the ten years or whatever, I received a total of only seven letters. Two of these were favorable without getting overheated about it. One, emphatically hostile, berated me for misspelling the name of someone else's nephew. Another accused me of being unfaithful to my wife and of other opprobrious behavior. Two, addressed to someone else, reached me by accident and prove nothing except someone's carelessness. The last, though addressed to me, was intended for Professor Amstutz and doesn't count.

Whether the world will respond kindly or at all to the appearance of this libellus is a matter of some doubt. But I am grateful for the goodwill of the friends who unexpectedly proposed and then encouraged the appearance of these already dated observations. May heaven reward them, for I'm not sure who else will.

For myself I am glad to know that my next year's Christmas shopping is taken care of.

Chronology

1910 Born, Brooklyn.

1916-1920 All the way through my time at PSS 39, 51, and 57 I was marked Deficient in Arithmetic.

1920-1926 And all the way through the private day school where I prepared for college, especially in Plane Geometry. But I did win or almost win a Good Citizenship Prize for being a good citizen, yet although my name appeared on the Commencement program, some enemy had libeled me to the administration and the award was canceled. Since no one told me this, I ascended to the platform at the proper time, to stand there with my hand held out like a mendicant and then to descend awardless, blushing like a Susie Q peony.

1926-1930 I proceeded to Williams College, my story at which I have treated in one of the papers that follow. I had a perfectly wonderful time there except at the Spring Houseparty of 1929.

1930-1932 I resumed undergraduate status at Oxford University. Here my promising career as an oarsman was blighted by the appendicitis that smote me just before the February racing in 1932. . . . Taking advantage of the opportunity of travel on the Continent, I enjoyed many interesting experiences, most notably trying to purchase Christmas tree ornaments in the Munich 5 and 10 in 1931.

1932-1934 My "lost" period.

1934-1938 There was this young woman who, finding her life meaningless without me, offered to get a job at Macy's and support me for three years if I would marry her. Since this plan would make Columbia graduate school possible for me, I consented and became a benedick in June 1938.

1938-1941 I was at Carnegie Tech, as they called it in those days. It is memorable that here I met E.N. Dilworth, for many years a valued friend and even today a Colleague-in-Retirement. And there was the football situation: In those days Carnegie played big time and shared the Pitt Stadium with its owners, the schedules being dovetailed. It was possible for a faculty member to pick out his seat on the big chart and to purchase a season ticket for $11. Beat that for a bargain.

1941-1943 A most pleasant interlude at Pine Manor Junior College, a female institution, where for the first time I was permitted to teach what I wanted to teach, an idyll interrupted by

1943-1945 The Great War. I felt sure that I could serve

my country some way in this crisis, but the Army that I joined thought otherwise. So then I made it my object to become some kind of sergeant, so as at least to pay my own way. But here again I failed, reaching only the rank of corporal and requiring my wife to send me $15 a month so that I might maintain my lifestyle.

1946-1975 Golden years at Lehigh. For one thing, we excitedly bought our first house. It cost $7,500, today the price of a power mower without attachments. It was humble enough, no doubt, but we were very happy there for thirteen years, and I grew asparagus of unrivaled quality. In 1959, needing greater scope, we moved to more luxurious quarters in Bucks County among the *rentiers*. . . . My experiences at Lehigh itself are touched on *passim* in the pages that follow. From the primitive days, when the English department had only one telephone, to these, when it has its own switchboard, my relationship with the university has been one golden challenge after another, and, to put it frankly, I am sort of glad to be retired and free of any challenges at all.

1975-? Again, I have spoken elsewhere of lotos-eating in retirement. More than enough.

That's A Lot of Bulletin

Reunion '78

In a large eastern metropolis on the banks of the Hudson may be found a small social club much frequented by graduates of the Potted Ivy seminary that nurtured my formative years. Established over a cigar store on Eighth Avenue, it offers no *faux luxe,* as they say, but the location is central, the clam juice and Ry-Krisp luncheon is deservedly popular, and at the bar are generally a couple of wastrels ready to roll dice for another round of beers.

On my most recent, or 1978 annual, visit to Fun City I found myself on the premises aforesaid making heavy conversational weather with a classmate. Since we had spent four undergraduate years avoiding each other, the talk flowed like Elmer's Glue-All. In desperation I tried to whip up some spurious camaraderie by alluding to our quarterly *Alumni Review,* where I had recently learned that they were building a new library to accommodate new books, or tearing down the old library to get rid of old books—something like that, one of those things that colleges are always doing at the expense of their alumni.

"I don't know anything about it," said my classmate dully. "Sometimes I read the class notes so I can see if anybody died."

Later on, over the clam juice and Ry-Krisp, he opened up a little.

"My wife reads them too," he said. "That's how she knows that Clancy Smith died last fall. She used to be engaged to him one time. Now she goes around telling everyone how she'd be living her own life today and taking cruises if she married him instead of me."

In other words, far from cementing loyalty, waking nostalgia, and stimulating financial support, the *Review* had done nothing for him but depreciate the quality of his home life.

His experience is perhaps not typical, yet I have gathered

The late Nim Smith and his boatman display deepwater catch.

from many sources that if anyone reads an alumni mag at all, he just brushes quickly through the obituaries before spreading the publication on the kitchen floor for the comfort of the new puppy.

Of course it ought not to be like that, and it's clear that if it's going to grow any better the improvement will begin with the class notes and with the necrology.

I think that three principles, which I shall call A, B, and C, must be borne in mind.[1]

A. Too many of our graduates are uninteresting. I haven't actually run the *Bulletin* through a computer, but I estimate that Mr. Average Lehigh Alumnus produces as follows:

1. He spent two years with Bessie.
2. He spent eight years with Du Pont or Texaco, rising to the grade of second-tier vice president.
3. Then he founded his own flange mill, later taken over by LTV.
4. He lives in Short Hills or Ardmore.
5. He has 3.2 children, of whom 1.5 attended Lehigh. The girl (Bonnie) is still at Sweet Briar.
6. His community good works include ten years on the vestry, Church of the Retribution; chairmanship, annual BSA drive; directorship, 15th National Bank.
7. He plays golf to a handicap of 14 and wishes he had more time to fish.
8. Suffers from arthritis, especially in February and March.

All honor to him! The only trouble is that since everyone else in his class has the same Vita, nobody can get overheated about it.

B. The really interesting people in the world are the eccentric, the picturesque, and, above all, the disreputable. Think of Iago, Satan (Milton version), and Dan Baxter; or, in the spirit of Equal Rights, of Messalina, L. Borgia, and Lizzie Borden. My wife said to me that none of this sextet had gone to college, so far as she knew.[2] All right, but I am simply trying to make a point; indeed, I can't see why with the advantage of higher education a graduate

[1] I had to go out of town for three days, and while I was away I forgot what C was going to be.

shouldn't be able to do still better for himself. Take the Reverend George Burrough, Harvard 1670, for example: He was tried and executed for witchcraft in 1692, and what a godsend to some class correspondent he must have been. Or what about Ridgely Hunt of Yale (1902 S), of whom I learned in the pages of George Chappell's memoirs: ". . . a demented hermit who lives in an abandoned charcoal burner's hut in the Connecticut hinterland, a rather pathetic example of a brilliant mind gone to seed. His passion, harmless though annoying, of sneaking into churches and ringing the bells while services are going on, has earned for him the title of 'the mad Bell-ringer of North Guilford.'"

Then there's Aaron Burr of Princeton (1772), the only graduate of Old Nassau to murder a Secretary of the Treasury.[3] And the Reverend Harold Davidson, famous 45 years ago as the Rector of Stiffkey, was one of the most engaging Oxford graduates of recent times, thanks to his practice of deserting his parish for six days a week in order to proselytise young girls in London; after an ecclesiastical court had tried and deprived him in 1932, he spent some time sitting in a barrel at an amusement park and ultimately met his quietus by entering a lion's cage at a carnival.[4]

And how about Philip Spencer, graduate of Union and a founder of Chi Psi? Later he ill-advisedly joined the Navy, a choice that led to his ruin. For, accused of fomenting mutiny, he was convicted and executed largely through his (quite laudable) refusal to translate the Greek of some fraternity papers in his possession.[5]

I don't suggest that any graduate of Lehigh or whatever

[2]I know that five of them didn't. Last I knew about Baxter, he was flogging cheap jewelry out of Denver, but you don't need a degree for that. Lizzie Borden had a diploma from Fall River High School; 1878, I think.

[3]When Columbia was preparing the Hamilton papers, the cost kept mounting and mounting till the Press thought that they might have to sell Baker Field before they finished. One of the editors proposed to dedicate the project "To Aaron Burr, who made this publication possible."

[4]See T. Cullen, *The Prostitutes' Padre*, Bodley Head, 1975.

other university can voluntarily check in with qualitatively similar performances every year or so; I don't want any Lehigh alumni to be hanged or eaten by a lion.[6] But if we could do something to encourage truly newsworthy achievement, it would be a boon to the *Bulletin*, its correspondents, and its readership.

Older institutions, to be sure, have the advantage of us. A few illustrations will show what I mean.

> Thus from the *Wittenberg Annales* (num. hiemalis mxxi): Had a good if somewhat disturbing letter from "Bud" Horatio about his trip to the northern capitals last year. If I didn't know him as well as I do—we were in Quadrivium together—I'd have thought he was drunk. Anyway, he stopped in Elsinore (Denmark) for a while, he said, to stay with "Prince" Hamlet (Arts mxviii) at the castle, and it turned out to be one hell of a visit. Seems he landed right in the middle of a big family row. I couldn't follow half of it, but I understand that Hamlet is dead some way—the letter is so confused that I can't tell whether he was poisoned or stabbed or what; my own guess is diabetes or hypertension, he was always overweight—also his mother and the king and more besides. I know that his classmates join me in extending sincerest sympathy to his family if any of them are left. Horatio writes me to "absent myself from felicity awhile," whatever that means. Hope we can get the full story when he's back in Saxony next year.[7]
>
> (There is no documentary evidence for this next note, but I can safely extrapolate an excerpt from *Jottings*, Copenhagen Country Day School, somewhere around the

[5]The Navy has another version of this incident. But I would believe Chi Psi a lot sooner than the Navy, the Army, and the Joint Chiefs of Staff all together.

[6](a) Well, I do, really, but only four or five.

(b) My wife, who cannot resist a quibble, says that the danger of being same date. "Address Unknown. Does anyone know the whereabouts of 'Rosy' Rosencrantz and 'Gil' Guildenstern [both mxiv]? Last we knew, they were planning a trip to England and expected to be back in about six months.")

From *Gaietés* (University of Paris) Hiver, 1462: It's a long while since we heard from Frankie Villon, M.A. '52, but we sure heard from him today. Frankie's letter, which came from Angers, is so long that I can't begin to find room for half of it. But his main point is he wants his friends to know that there's hardly a word of truth in all the dirty blague that's being spread around about him. For instance, those two silver cruets he was supposed to have lifted from St. Antoine's—he was just carrying them across town for a friend, and he was never inside St. Antoine's in his life. He admits that he killed Père Chermoye in '55, but he claims the priest came at him with a dagger "and damn near took my upper lip off. What was I supposed to do? Let him dismember me at his convenience?

"Some of you probably heard I got taken up by the *flics* for robbery with violence. [Epithet deleted.] What really happened, I found this *poule* frozen to death in the Clos Macé, and all I got off her was three lousy sols. The *sacré crétin* of a prefect made a big production out of it; *on croirait* I stole the Ste. Chapelle.

"As for the breaking and entering at the Collège de Navarre, I had absolutely nothing to do with it. Those clowns propositioned me about it, but I would no more team up with that gaggle of ham-fisted knuckleheads[8] than let a *maquereau* baby-sit my daughter. That Christmas Eve I spent the whole night at the T'il Est Hault on the Ile St.

hanged by a lion is negligible. Forget it.

[7]Hamlet, then, was registered at Wittenberg in the eleventh century, though the university was not founded till around 1500. This discrepancy is one of the many vexing problems for editors of Shakespeare's play on

Louis, and I could prove it by Big Jennie, the *aubergine* [innkeeper's wife], only she fell off the Petit-Pont and got drowned six weeks before the trial."

Frankie has a lot more to say, and I wish I had room for all of it. "Not a chance of making the reunion," he winds up. "I tried to get that [deleted] Provost of Paris to give me a week's break so it would be safe for me to come into the city, and the big slob didn't even answer the letter. Best regards to all the guys."

While I think of it, could I ask you all to keep your news as concise as possible? We reach over 800 subscribers now, and a letter as long as the above raises pure hell in the scriptorium. If Whatshisname, that Dutchman in Mainz, ever gets his invention on a commercial basis, it may be another story in a few years.

From the St. John's College (Oxford) *Register*, Spring, 1645

Now for the bad news. On January 10 Bill Laud (matric. '89, M.A. '98 &c.) was beheaded at the Tower of London after being "convicted" of high treason. There was a big stir about the trial, and most of you probably heard something of it. I'm not supposed to do much editorializing in this column, just pass on the news, but this is the nastiest deal that those Evangelical creeps in our so-called government have pulled yet. Bill wasn't easy to get along with, maybe—pretty strait-faced, I used to think—but for god sake, high treason! He made a great president of John's, too: look at the new buildings and the endowment.

I think I'm right in saying that Bill is the first John's man to be executed this way; I mean decapitation, I wasn't

[8]Here and elsewhere I have had to clean up the language of Villon's letter. Even today there are limits.

thinking about hanging . . . This kind of thing gives us a bad image. The Admissions crowd tell me applications are 'way down for next fall.

Naturally I can't prescribe the careers of our graduates, and the following suggestions are no more than a hint—perhaps a most inadequate one—toward what we might hope to see in the rejuvenated *Bulletin* of the future. Fill in any classes that suit you.

Jerry Smith writes from Rio de Janeiro that he decided impulsively last year to take early retirement and settle down to enjoy himself for a change and forget the SEC and all that. If anybody deserves a rest, Jerry does; he's been wheeling and dealing as long as we've known him. Do you remember the book he used to run during the football season? Had it straddled so that he couldn't take in less than $150 a week, no matter what.

I'd like to think Jerry would use some of his leisure to write up his life. It'd be interesting to know, for example, how he launched Calamine Products on $1,500 and how that rumor got started that their gargle cured cancer. Calamine went from 5 to over 31 on that. And how did it go *up* every time after Jerry failed to take over Tootsie Roll, Suave Shoe, Crude Shoe, Pneumodynamics, and finally Universal Motors? Smart business!

There's something strange, too, about the failure of Jerry's marriage. I recall the rather unusual settlement that obliged his wife to pay him $2,500 a month for life. More in that than met the eye, a lot of people thought.

Jerry's done well in life, but it hasn't spoiled him. Witness his contribution of 1,000,000 cruzeiros to the Fund Drive this year. Thanks to last fall's collapse in the exchange rate this comes to only around $43 in U.S. currency, but Jerry is hardly responsible for the vagaries of Brazilian monetary policy.

We have heard with deep regret of the death of "Nimrod" Smith last August in Nepal, where he was after giant pandas, one of which got to him first.

A lot of Lehigh graduates have found recreation in blood sports, but I don't think anyone has ever approached Nim in the art of chilling wildlife. It was his boast that no one had had more success in getting specimens of endangered species before it was too late. In the East Indies he helped to bring the pygmy hippopotamus and the orang-utan to the threshold of extinction; in Africa he succeeded in bagging a mountain gorilla "before the game-hogs got in there," as he put it; he took one of the few remaining ivory-billed woodpeckers in the United States—he had some trouble with the authorities over that one—and sharply reduced the ocelot count in Central America. A deep-water fisherman, too, he went after marlin every year, and he's the only man ever to take a blue whale on a rod. He told me once that his chief regret was he was too late to shoot the last pink-headed duck on earth, and his big ambition was to wipe out the two bears remaining in New Jersey.

The class congratulates George J. Smith on the occasion of his marriage to the former Violet Schele at Pride's Crossing on June 17.

This is George's third marriage. The first came to an untimely end when his wife was found drowned in a bathtub in their house in Short Hills. So did his second marriage, when his wife was found drowned in a bathtub in their house in Ardmore. George has certainly had bad luck so far, and we wish him the best in this new matrimonial venture. The Smiths are planning to spend their honeymoon in Baden-Baden.

Fubsy Smith is still in New York, he tells me, in TV

work. After a cameo role in a Safeguard commercial last year, he is now regular understudy to Mr. Cholesterol, and he has some hope of the male lead in a new Nancy Walker episode where he spills coffee so that she can wipe it up with half a sheet of Bounty. In the meantime he keeps working on voice lessons, as he's ambitious to get into the big time some day: a vocal with Chrysler or Löwenbräu. "That's where the prestige is," he says. "And the money."

Gypsy Smith sends me a somewhat unusual letter. He claims he discovered last January that he is the Angel of Death; he is going to walk across Lake Winnipesaukee from Wolfeboro to the Weirs on July 4 in honor of American independence, and he hopes that some of his Lehigh friends will be on hand.

Gyp always was pretty holy. I remember how he was all wrapped up in religious activities when we were in college, and I guess his bent is as strong as ever. One time I know he was expelled from the Methodist Church for demanding clerical celibacy. A few years later the Episcopalians threw him out for aggravated Simony, and another time the Roman Catholics excommunicated him for neo-Pelagianism. I guess he founded the Amorite Brethren so he could find a church home. I don't know much about them, but I heard they practice polygamy during Lent, and for some reason they say the Lord's Prayer backward. I also heard a story about unbaptised babies that I'd just as soon not repeat.

Times like these, it's good to know that some people have a real Commitment. I hope there will be a good turnout to greet Gyp next July.

Wetmore Smith and his wife are planning to set off in September for an extended Mexican trip. Smitty mainly wants to look for Ambrose Bierce, but he hopes to run into

Walter Huston and Humphrey Bogart, as well. Good luck, Smitty![9]

Grosvenor Smith is still with the consular service. He and Flabella want to remind everyone that their latch-string is always out any time you're passing through Vladivostok.

More class notes like these, and then maybe something could be done about the articles and the sports news as well. I look forward to a day when alumni will be binding their old *Bulletins* for an honored place on their library shelves, and the new puppy will have to make out with the *Globe-Times.*

And now that the Lehigh Family is being flooded with girls, the news ought to be bigger and better and maybe even more spectacular every year.

> I have been in the scholastic profession long enough to know that nobody enters it unless he has some very good reason which he is anxious to conceal.
>
> Evelyn Waugh - Decline and Fall

We cannot make the news. Our classmates have to marry or to go to jail or die or something if we are to have anything to write about; and since these things generally take place in Utah, somebody else generally has to let us know about them, and he is generally late in doing it. Furthermore, most of these things are routine and unimaginative; everybody does them. We very seldom, perhaps never, get a big story. Like this: Once upon a time my

[9] (He'll need it. If alive, Bierce has to be about 140 years old; Huston and Bogart, though younger men, are *known* to have died some time ago. Ed.)

college at Oxford had an alumnus, Ralph Sherwine '68—that's 1568—who went to the continent, became a Roman Catholic priest, returned illegally to England, was apprehended, and in 1581, far from returning to Oxford for his 13th reunion, was executed at Tyburn. Just a few years ago, in the sixties (the 1960s), he was canonized. Now there's a story for a class correspondent; but how long will it be before he gets one like that? Our classmates are continually being promoted to vice president in charge of Dixie Cups—that sort of thing — but when will Lehigh come up with its first saint?

—From: "A Few Figs from a Barren Tree" given at Class Correspondence Conference, 10/30/76

From My Garden of Memories

Spring '78

It is strange what a terrible fate overtook the emperor's three worst opponents. Londonderry cut his throat, Ludwig XVIII rotted on his throne, and Professor Saalfeld of Goettingen is still professor in Goettingen—Heine

What things may have been like at Goettingen in Napoleon's day I have no idea, but as applied to life at Lehigh—especially in its English department—in the mid-twentieth century, Heine's bitter irony is little short of libel. My 30 years of active employment here constituted a rich field of fascinating, varicolored, and irresistible experience from beginning to end. And in seeking to revivify those bygone days, I regret only that so many of the colorful personalities, and incidents both newsworthy and sinister, must be omitted from this brief, inadequate sampling.[1]

The chairman of the English department when I first came to Lehigh was Professor Robert M. Smith, a Shakespearean scholar whose dynamic personality will be remembered by anyone who ever came within half a mile of him. I venerate Dr. Smith's memory—indeed, I should be afraid not to, for he was lineally descended from Genghis Khan and not infrequently showed it. Yet he had a softer side, as seen when at a departmental gathering he stood on a chair to sing "Brighten the Corner Where You Are." It was one of his foibles to issue demands and directives to his henchmen for no explicable reason. Thus the only motive for my ever reading *Sister Carrie* was that he told me I had to read it within the week. He never alluded to it again—I read it, of course, within 48 hours—and I still

[1]I have left a good deal of material on deposit with the First Valley Bank, not to be available till 2000.

Gus's first restaurant.

Hartung unloads beer working his way through college (left). Bill Neville at the second Gus's (right).

Bob Johnstone awaits delivery (top, left). The John Hertzes at the horse show. Mrs. Hertz ponders her husband's drinking problem (above, right). Author and sports buff Ray Armstrong warming up for the big game some years ago (left).

don't know why he thought I needed it. Or he would call an incomprehensible staff meeting, apparently for the sheer fun of it.

One spring James Croushore '36 (now long at Mary Washington College) and I posted a notice that on April 1 (1947?) the staff was expected to attend a meeting to hear a visiting pundit discuss the Gothic development of front vowels in stressed syllables or some such foolishness. We contemplated only satire, but we builded better than we knew. Perfectly in the Smith tradition, this ukase caught the imperfect attention of Professor Carl Strauch, who, ignoring the date and the insane subject matter, at great inconvenience came across town—he had no car, and fortunately still doesn't—to attend a nonexistent assembly. Professor Strauch is a man of volcanic mold, and for some long time the building reverberated with his imprecations.[2]

It was at Professor Smith's home—now gone, it stood more or less northeast of Psi U—that Bill Neville, Ph.D. '61, made his inauspicious entrance into the Lehigh Family.[3] A shy youth who had never been away from home before, Neville was demoralised during the evening by the glamor of his new associates, the desire to make a good impression, the unaccustomed warmth—for he came from New Hampshire—and the small glass of sherry that he had sipped. So as he stood at the door bidding good-night, his head in a whirl, he fainted, and came to hours later abed in the Smiths' guest room. Next day he wanted only to go home and kill himself quietly but was persuaded to see it through and is now teaching out around Lake Erie somewhere.

Neville was always making history. He phoned us one winter night to report himself in bed with a headache and two degrees of fever. Could we cover his classes for the next couple of days? Of course we could. But when we called him up the next day to find out where he had put Theme #3, Mrs. Neville told us that Bill couldn't come to the phone just then; he was out in the yard burning trash. He said later that he had waked that morning feeling unaccountably better but was reluctant to upset our substitutionary arrangements.

Neville made good, however. It was to him as he received his doctorate that Dr. Harvey Neville, Sc.D. '65, named President of the

[2]Strauch reads nothing but detective stories, else even after 30 years I would hesitate to call up this episode.

[3]A phrase more apposite than its creator (probably) intended. Have you ever taken a good look at a family?

University on the same day, remarked, "It's a great day for the Nevilles."[4]

Neville spent some years sharing an office with Professor Albert Hartung '47, later chairman. Hartung was and remains another picturesque character: angler, horseman, flautist, yachtsman—you name it—a Renaissance man. An enthusiastic horticulturist, he once developed hernia while in Sayre Park stealing rocks for his garden on Pawnee Street. His avocations, though, did not interfere with his dedication to scholarship. Deep in concentration one day, he had not been moved by my ululations outside his office as I sought to detach him for a cup of coffee. Finally I took a tiny pebble and threw it against his second-floor window, which must have been weakened with age, for it burst into a thousand fragments. It also shattered Hartung's mood, and though he sustained only a trifling flesh wound on one hand, he was rather stuffy about it for two or three days.

It was with Hartung and with Louis Thompson, Ph.D. '59 (now long departed) that I was returning from Gus Glicas's restaurant (also long departed; it stood at the handy corner of New and Packer) when we saw a young woman having a perfectly awful time maneuvering her car in a very tight space. Thompson kindly stopped to advise her on clearance, while Hartung wondered how she could dare to drive at all with a baby on her lap. There was no baby, but Hartung, who had come along without his glasses, mistook the girl's bare knees for the bald head of an infant. In the meantime Thompson was getting nowhere with his generalship, for it turned out that the girl was trying to work out of the tight space, while Thompson was trying to get her into it.

Gerhard Magnus, now of East Lansing, Michigan, won fame in the Placement operation one year. In those days we used to put

[4]That was the day when Dr. Neville won a thousand hearts by making what he himself justly called "the shortest inaugural address in history." It was about 25 words long.

the freshmen through a series of tests comparable to the Civil Service examinations under the Manchus; the idea was to trisect the class into English O, English 1, and English 3a. The examination papers bore the seat numbers appropriate to distribution in Packard Auditorium, and Magnus's feat, after the papers had been collected and graded, was to enter on our records the seat numbers rather than the grades. The placement results, nevertheless, were about as satisfactory as usual.

Professor J. Burke Severs, the Chaucerian who succeeded Professor Smith as chairman, created a departmental stir when one spring (1946 or so) he purchased his first automobile, and not just any automobile but a massive yellow Oldsmobile convertible. Professor Strauch was moved to compose (or adapt) a suitable quatrain:

Whan that Aprille with his shoures sote
The droghte of Marche hath perced to the rote,
Than goth Bourke Severs forth up-on the roade
And makyth al the folk to waxen wode.[5]

Nor were these lines unprophetic, for the very next year Professor Severs was cited by the State Police for furious driving and had his license retired for 90 days—a distinction he shared with Professor G. J. Christensen, the other least likely hot-rodder in the department.[6]

Professor Severs is the kindest and gentlest of men; I have only once seen in him traces of normal, healthy asperity. At the time, I was conducting my clientele through an examination of Wagner's *Ring*, considered as myth; and wishing to add a little musical substance, I undertook to present *Das Rheingold* on records. Only at the last moment did I discover that Room 302 had no

[5]For the unlearned "drives everybody crazy."

[6]Professor Smith was the one who ought to have been arrested every week or so. A windowless monad when behind the wheel, he turned white the hair of innumerable other drivers, to say nothing of his passengers. Yet he told me that his only contact with the constabulary had come as a result of his making a U-turn on the Pulaski Skyway.

electrical outlet and so was forced to use a wall plug in Professor Severs's office next door. Not only did the door have to be open; the brevity of my extension cord required the record player to be but a foot or so within the classroom. *Rheingold*, as you will recall, though brief, is a rather noisy opera: Alberich cursing, giants stomping about, the Nibelungs hammering on anvils. But it really cuts loose with the thunderstorm of Scene 4, and there is no way to present a thunderstorm *pianissimo*. When Donner's hammer split the mountaintop, two of the casement windows were blown open, and several pieces of plaster came down from the ceiling. Professor Severs during all this hullabaloo was trying to concentrate on the department budget. And so when I went in to remove the extension cord, there was—I think—just the least edge to his voice as he suggested that perhaps my next musical illustration might be provided in some other classroom.

Christmas-Saucon Hall, though, was always a noisy building, or at least one ceaselessly assailed by noise. Worst of all was the time when they were getting ready to build the Aspidistra—as Dean Preston Parr '43 wittily called it—next to Fritz Lab and were driving piles a quarter-mile down to the original Cambrian quartzite. That was pure hell, you may be sure. But at any time, if there weren't lawn mowers in the spring there were leafchoppers in the fall, let alone drills operating on the surface of Packer Avenue.[7]

Open doors became a matter of general concern only as in the course of time young women joined the instructional staff and, *a fortiori*, still later when young women became undergraduates. Some of both categories were very sightly indeed, and the department wondered whether a male instructor should not be enjoined to leave his office door somewhat open when conferring with a female student, and vice versa. Somebody then pointed out that the door should also be open if any instructor were conferring with an

[7]I could never see that the drilling *accomplished* anything. After it was over, the surface of Packer Avenue was about the same as usual.

undergraduate of the same gender suspected of homosexuality. As we explored the several possible combinations, it gradually became clear that the only comprehensive defence against turpitude, frame, and litigation would be to remove all the office doors entirely, and the problem was allowed to drop.

John Hertz, Ph.D. '58, now at Marywood, is remembered affectionately by all those who took his course in Business Letters. How and why he did it I no longer recall, but he must be the only staff member to get himself locked not only inside Christmas-Saucon Hall but inside the Mathematics department on a Sunday afternoon. It was an hour or two before he could get Professor Everett Pitcher to come across town and release him. The worst of it, he told my wife afterward, was that there wasn't a damn thing in the Math department that he wanted to read. On another occasion in Lamberton, where we ate for a couple of years, he was showing us the sophisticated way to open an individual bottle of so-called coffee cream; if it had been an imperial quart he could not have distributed it more prodigally over the light-gray suit he was wearing. When the cellar of his house in Durham flooded, as it did every spring, he used to keep a pet duck down there "to get some good out of it," as he said.[8]

But his finest hour came on the day when he set out to bring the beautiful, clean copy of his doctoral dissertation to the university and realized in Hellertown that he had left it in his briefcase on the roof of his car when he had returned to the house to pick up a fresh handkerchief, and that it wasn't there any more. His only copy, needless to say; all he had left were notes scribbled on the backs of envelopes that he had pilfered from the Steel Company years before. Words were inadequate he told me; nobody since Job could offer a comparison, and had he had an edged tool handy, it

[8]That house was always a lively place. It was infested with flying squirrels for one thing. And I wish you'd been there the night when Hertz and I tried to plaster over a stovepipe hole in the living room ceiling.

were touch and go but that he should end a profitless existence then and there. But the story has a happy ending, for some wandering peasant came upon the briefcase along Route 412, painfully spelled out the identification, and ultimately restored the manuscript to its scholarly progenitor.

Back in the forties one time when the university was considering a compulsory course in sex education, some of us wondered what would happen to a student that flunked it. "Give him a bachelor's degree," said Gellert Alleman '34 (last heard of at Rutgers). Alleman's supreme achievement, though, came when he generously presented me with a copy of his dissertation, done at Penn and published at his own expense. Within the volume a loose slip of paper bore the legend "Unautographed. Rare in this state."

Still more striking in a way was the extempore performance of a front-row student in English 2—I wish I remembered his name—one day when we were studying "The Garden Party," which deals with the growing up of an adolescent girl. "Her experience is just one of those many experiences that mark the development of a child into an adult," I was saying, "like your discovery that Santa Claus isn't for real." My student flung his hand to his head and fell back in his seat. "No!" he breathed brokenly. "No . . . oh no!"

St. Nicholas provided me with another happy day when my assignment of a seasonably appropriate theme-topic elicited from one freshman a straight copy of the famous "Yes, Virginia, there is a Santa Claus" editorial from the *New York Sun.*[9] He might as well have given me an original poem beginning, "In Xanadu did Kubla Khan/A stately pleasure-dome decree." But to do him justice he did not call me "Virginia"; he was just smart enough to modify the opening sentence.

The English department were an abstemious lot, on the whole, but one day Ernest Dilworth and I—and other faculty members whom I won't mention—attended a cheerful symposium of-

[9]He thought I was as illiterate as he was.

fered by Kappa Beta Phi[10] at the Hotel Bethlehem. It was the only appearance of this convivial group that I ever heard of around here, and they did it up fine, with food and drink as far as the eye could reach and as a centerpiece an almost lifesize swan sculpted out of ice. Afterward I was some way indisposed to spend the evening in the library, as I had planned, and instead went home, driving carefully. As for Dilworth, he was saying to me the next day, "It's a funny thing. I know I held my seminar last night, but I can't remember a thing we were talking about." At the next faculty meeting the late President Martin Whitaker alluded to this occasion in thinly veiled terms and severely deprecated faculty attendance at such a function. But I have been to many a cocktail party more raucous than that one.

Another source of happiness was the closet door in X-S 318. Identical with the door into the hall, it was frequently mistaken therefor by inexperienced freshmen who after a conference courteously bade me farewell and stepped into the closet among the overshoes and discarded textbooks. Best of all when the student whose grade I had refused to raise showed that he was angry with Teacher and charged into the closet in a passion.

Christmas-Saucon, the third floor anyway, was a decorator's challenge in those days, and most of us did what we could to overcome the depressing atmosphere of that ramshackle building. Catholicity of taste was emphasized in 318, which for years I shared with Dilworth; he featured the post-impressionists on his half of the wall, while I, who prefer representationalism, chose Jemima Puddle-Duck, a Pabst brewery wagon, Goldwater posters, and suchlike. Alleman had the picture of a young ass hanging just below that of S. T. Coleridge until Professor Smith made him take it down. Hartung displayed a collection of bricks, cinder blocks, and other building materials. Dudley Brown used to keep his laundry on his typewriter table. Jack Schug housed a previous year's apple core in

[10] I don't know why anyone needs a constitution and bylaws before having a drink.

a home aquarium labeled "Feed Me." Bill Digel '59 procured from the Food Fair, with the consent of the management, a 6' x 5' screamer proclaiming PORK LOINS. It covered one entire wall of his room.[11]

But the Quincunx of Heaven runs low, as Browne puts it, and 'tis time to close the five ports of knowledge.—Enough—if I have done a little to breathe life into those days of post-war disorganization, I have my reward.

[11]Digel some years ago bowed the knee to Mammon and is now with Du Pont. Al ways a good friend, he once instigated his brethren at Theta Xi to purloin a traffic cone for me. I had always wanted one but was too timid to exe cute the theft myself.

A Sea of Troubles

Spring '81

With this issue of the Lehigh *Alumni Bulletin* we reach a significant milestone, for it is the last to appear under the leadership of Harry B. Ramsey, B.A. '50, with a major in Journalism.

It has often been said that with the possible exception of checking *Pravda* for traces of revisionism, no editorial task in the whole range, scope, and gamut of journalism is so challenging, frustrating, and excruciating as that facing the editor of an alumni magazine. Small wonder, then, that after 12 years of such service Mr. Ramsey will, after the pages that you are now reading, let fall the helm from his far from nerveless hand.

But you cannot understand Ramsey the man until you have faced the nature of *Bulletin* the periodical.

Historical

Alumni magazines do not (apparently) go back very far into the history of formal higher education. What we know of the Big Two in classical Greece—the Academy and the Lyceum—shows no trace of them. Curiously, too, it shows no trace of the fraternity system, to which the Athenians should have been strongly drawn, thanks to their knowledge of the Greek alphabet and their mastery of the terse apothegm: "Love Conquers All," "Brotherhood Forever," "Beat Persia," and so on. In fact we don't find much trace of alumni at all, though of course there must have been some.

The Greeks at least tried, but the Romans show no sign of anything you could call higher education unless you include an outfit like the College of the Arval Brothers. I don't really have time to go into them here, but they were more a kind of agricultural association, like the National Grange. The Romans felt broadly that

Vol. 1, No. 1 October 10, 1898

The

Quarterly

of

Piscataqua

Polytechnic

College

"Floreat Piscatagua"

Portsmouth, N.H.

Yale bulldogs of '88: Yale 698, Opponents 0 (above). Cover of early Piscataqua alumni mag left something to be desired (left).

as soon as a youngster had licked the Dative with Compounds and the Jussive Subjunctive, he had all the education he could hold and it was time for him to start running for Quaestor.

Bologna (est. 1088) claims to be the prototype of the modern university, and indeed it has lent its name to the curricula of all subsequent institutions. But even so recently as the twelfth century the establishment cared little for its graduates, indifferent to their marital status, the number of their offspring, legitimate and illegitimate, and whether they were Guelphs or Ghibellines.[1] How Bologna ever got a new chemistry lab for Dr. Rappaccini to prepare his lethal vegetable pollutants in is hard to understand.[2]

Through the Middle Ages and Renaissance, alumni as such gradually became recognized. They often retained a pleasant association with Alma Mater and occasionally, unprompted, presented her with a chapel or a set of books or whatever. But as far as I can find—after one and a half hours of study—nothing you could call an alumni magazine appeared till the nineteenth century, in America, you might know, when it was discovered that a body of graduates could be *programmed* into a reliable source of financial support.[3] By 1900 every seminary that could afford it was publishing some pamphlet or other to remind its offspring where they got their education, how much fun it had been, and how Alma Mater had lost money on every one of them in spite of the generous endowment that no longer went so far today as it had gone a few years ago before the first Cleveland administration.

This pitch worked like a dream. At College X, for example, in the first year of the *Quarterly*, alumni giving soared from $2,315 to $7,865.40 before deduction for costs of publication and distribution: It was a plain brochure and contained no color plates. Furthermore, it was written free by members of the English department, always gullible, and it contained little more than a calendar of events. The great determining and identifying feature of the

[1]There was no annual fund drive.

[2]Professor C.F. Strauch tells me that "Rappaccini's Daughter" takes place in Padua, not Bologna. I hate people who raise petty quibbles like that.

[3]All Souls College (est. 1438) never had any undergraduates. Why have so few foundations emulated this sensible policy?

Class Notes was still to come.

Modern Times

Thanks to twentieth-century developments this simple picture is profoundly obscured, and you can begin to be thankful that you have nothing to do with such a production except maybe to put it under your coffee cup.

If the publication is quarterly, as it well may be, it is always behind the times. Long after the football season has dragged to its disastrous finale, coach "Stainless" Steele on page eighteen is anticipating it and says it's not too much to hope for the first winning season since 1937.[4] And no week-old gravy was ever less appetizing than reading in March about an economics conference last November. Some folks feel that a quarterly ought to be chiefly a journal of opinion and criticism, confining itself largely to subjects of long-range validity expounded by writers and scholars of major status: Milton Friedman on economics, Dr. Kissinger on diplomacy, Debora Kodish on folklore. But what board of publications can afford writers of that stature, quite apart from their irrelevancy to football and wrestling?

If that's a problem, the readership is another. Some foundation report estimates that if such a magazine were sent only to subscribers, the five percent of the alumni that *paid* for it would read it if only to justify the expense. Just as for some years I read *Mad* because I had subscribed to it to please my daughter, and I didn't want to throw my money away even though the content was too subtle for me.[5] A recent questionnaire sent out from a leading eastern university showed that on the basis of a 17.6 percent response readership coverage ran about as follows:

[4]Winning season! What I call a winning season was racked up by Yale in 1888: Yale 698 points; Opponents 0.

[5]Even so, I couldn't read her copies of *Seventeen.*

That's A Lot of Bulletin:

Category	Percent of responding readers
(a) Administrative Activity	.06
(b) Academic Activity	.03
(c) Athletic Activity	2.46
(d) Prominent Alumni	.002
(e) Class Notes	15.43

(a) The president gets an LL.D. from New Jersey School of Mines, the Trustees vote to cut faculty stipends during the emergency, five more deans are added to the establishment, and so on,

The administrators and the pedagogues too could help if they'd put their mind to it. Think of the recent homicidal publicity along the Madeira-Scarsdale Axis. I do not suggest encouraging guilty passions among deans and chairmen, but neither do I see why they shouldn't turn up more frequently. "A thoroughly good poisoning perpetrated by the professor of Christian Ethics in a respectable school of divinity . . . would be more precious to the discriminating amateur than all the vulgar atrocities which may be committed in Memphis in the next eighteen months," wrote Edmund Pearson.

(b) All courses are put on a P/F basis; the antiquated entrance requirement of a reading knowledge of English is dropped; X replaces Y as chairman of the Math department, just as Y replaced X three years ago; emeriti now must pay for paper clips and index cards, hitherto pilfered from departmental supply closets.

(c) Coach says that we have a tough schedule ahead of us, but you may be sure we'll give it everything, and that if Barhoot doesn't take too long getting used to his artificial foot, he'll be able to strengthen the left side of the line in the Rochambeau game. We have a good prospect for wide receiver from a high school in Camden.

(d) Returns indicate that such an article—"Bob O'Brien: A

Banker's Banker," "Whitten for Congress?," "W.A. Digel: The Romance of Teflon"—is read only by the subject himself, perhaps by his wife and progeny (who don't count in the stats), and by the proofreader.

(e) That is, the respondent has read the notes bearing on his class and on the classes immediately surrounding it. From the "Remarks," invited after the questions are completed, one infers that the reader's chief concern is to see whether he has survived contemporaries whom he particularly disliked.

Class Notes

The Class Notes are not only (as we have seen) the most (selectively) "popular" feature of the *Quarterly* but the most demanding; and the class correspondents are the most dedicated toilers in the whole vineyard of letters. They are unsung, frequently libeled, and almost always starved for material except on the rare occasions when they get a story too big for the space allotted to them. ("Write up the Tarnower Murder Case in 200 words or less.") Their reward is to see their names in print (big deal) and to attend their pregame party on the Upper Field once a year. They have to cudgel their classmates, a word at a time, to get any copy at all, and then it comes two days after their deadline. They go on, some of them, doing this for 10, 20, 30, 40 years; they will have their reward in a Better World, but not any sooner.

Class Notes are mainly of two kinds. They explain why the writer can't make Reunion this year—his wife is leaving him, his back seized up on him, he has to be in Washington—or they tell that he saw Butch in Boca Raton last winter and they had a great get-together, whose nature is not described. That is why in institutions so large that no one can remember all his classmates, some correspondents have come to rely on creative reporting, that is, they develop a figure or a circumstance as a clear improvement over reality. This nonesuch built the first split-level in Tierra del Fuego; in a men's room in the St. Louis airport he found himself at the next washbasin to the secretary of state's; his wife is a cousin of Bella Abzug's; he plans next summer to cross the Aegean on water skis, following in the footsteps of Agamemnon.[6] All honor here at Lehigh to William McAllister '66. See his columns in Reunion '75 and Winter '79, the latter a regrettable palinode. McAllister illuminated the earlier column with the fictitious giant clam that bit off the foot of Dr. Laurence Brickman and so created the liveliest column in my experience. Brickman is the kind of alumnus we need more of, and McAllister the kind of correspondent.

Forced to deal with the bleak sterility of his classmates' lives, if they bother to write to him, the normally unimaginative class correspondent cannot produce sprightly copy. For some years I read the Class Notes from end to end since only me could Mr. Ramsey coerce into making the annual awards: Best Column, Best Columnist, Best Column among the Odd-Numbered Classes, Best Columnist from New Jersey, and so on. Many a time I had to give a decisive nod to so-and-so merely because he spelled *accommodation* correctly or because he didn't spell *hopefully* at all.

A contemporary of mine who well and truly served his class at Osceola Textile and Secretarial told me that he almost welcomed the arthritis that crippled his hands and forced his retirement from alumni activity. He felt, he said, like the Prisoner getting out of Chillon.

The class correspondents may (and do) have their shortcomings: They forget to double-space, they misspell *accommodate* (as implied above), and they often put inadequate postage on their submissions.[7] A fig for these peccadilli! Bless you, honored friends!

At Last

As I look around, I am afraid that I have lost track of Mr. Ramsey, whom I originally intended as my subject in this valedicto-

[6]No, of course Agamemnon did not walk on the water. *Footsteps* is what we call a "metaphor."

[7]Or worse. What about referring to "the valetudinarian of our class"? Unless of course he really *wasn't* very healthy.

rily oriented tribute. What I think of as the Golden Age of the *Bulletin* is drawing to a close. Let us finally hasten to glimpse Mr. Ramsey in his present and honorable capacity.

A native of our nation's capital, Mr. Ramsey attended the Theodore Roosevelt High School when preparing to enter college, as he did during the winter of 1944. Here at Lehigh, thwarted by an insecure upper register from becoming a singer, he was directed to journalism as a *pis aller.* He did not graduate until 1950, but I have always felt that it would be tactless of me to ask him why. He is a member of Kappa Alpha. After graduation he toiled for a while on a daily paper in Rochester, New York. In 1963 he was recalled to Lehigh as a utility infielder for the Alumni Association. Six years later, having made good, he assumed the editorship of the *Bulletin.*[8] The rest is history.

Mr. Ramsey, who resides in Catasauqua, is married and has four children, two male and two female.

Some years of association with the *Bulletin*, though incoherent, have allowed me to become well acquainted with Mr. Ramsey and with his flair for both journalistic and alumni activity. He is a bluff, forthright man of full habit and flamboyant attire: bright tartan slacks are a common motif, and his necktie often flaunts his Lehigh affiliation. He wore a beard for a while but gave way to popular opinion and razed it. A democratic man in the best sense of the word—the word *democratic*, that is—Mr. Ramsey, running into me at a jayvee game over in the valley, will hail me just as if I were an equal and partakes of my peanuts just as if he had bought them himself: There is not a snobbish bone in his body.

If Mr. Ramsey has a *faiblesse*, he is often late for appointments: indeed, as I write these words, he should have met me three days ago. On the other hand, he has been generous to a fault in

[8]In those days the *Bulletin* was vaguely published by the university rather than by the Alumni Association. It now returns to something like the *status quo ante*, under the well-known aegis of George Beezer '57.

lending me his tape recorder in lieu of the *Bulletin's*, which doesn't work very well. I have ever found him even-tempered and understanding, and best of all, willing to put off any problem till next week, by which time, he feels, it may have solved itself.[9]

The chief headache at the *Bulletin* in the past decade, Mr. Ramsey says, is the relentless fiscal pressure, the unending necessity to find less expensive printers and paper as costs escalate. A mine of reminiscence, he recalls the unhappy behavior of the Brand X glue once frugally used on the labels of the overseas mailing. Loosening *en voyage* and falling off *en arrivée*, it left the postal authorities in Hong Kong and Bogotá, in Salonika and Capetown, with a lot of unaddressed *Bulletins*, and a lot of our far-flung alumni without news from Bethlehem.

Mr. Ramsey has no *learning* to speak of, but, surrounded as he is by persons who do, he manages finely without it. In fact I don't know that he spends much time *editing* anything.[10] Like Harold Ross at the *New Yorker*, he is most important as a driving force, a living symbol of the *Bulletin's* responsibility to the Alumni Association, and an inspiration to his contributors.

Mrs. Herbold and I, after some discussion, have decided not to give Mr. Ramsey a farewell party. We think he would have wanted it that way.[11]

[9]This is a perfectly wholesome practice, no matter what Benjamin Franklin said about it. Ennius, we remember, gave great praise to Q. Fabius because (as he [Ennius] put it) *"cunctando restituit rem,"* that is, "by stalling around he [Fabius] replaced the thing." It is not clear from these words what Fabius did that was so wonderful; but the point is that Ennius *thought* it was and that Fabius did it by procrastinating.

[10]The real *work* on the *Bulletin* has been carried on by Mrs. Herbold and by Bill Schellhaas '67.

[11]I forgot to give the good news that we are not losing Mr. Ramsey, who will soon be involved in (*inter alia*) producing the next Alumni Directory.

Six Bayer Sons And Their Sons, Too

Focus on Alumni

Throw a handful of buckshot at any group of Lehigh graduates, and the chances are that you'll hit a man named Bayer. Here we briefly inquire into this curious circumstance.

Curtis F. Bayer '35 is no stranger to the Alumni Association. In 1970 his many years of loyal service brought him an Alumni Award; and more informally he has won distinction by regularly attending Lehigh home football games even though he has to come from the Cleveland area to do it. Other details, however, may be less familiar.

Born in the Bronx, Bayer might not have come to Lehigh if he had not had grandparents living in White Haven, Pennsylvania, where on visits in early life he fell in love with railroads and with the Lehigh Valley in particular. And when he learned that the famous Asa Packer had not only built the LVRR but founded a university, it was clear to him where he must seek his higher education. (If his grandparents had lived in Newburgh, New York, would he have gone to Vanderbilt? Who can say?)

He entered Lehigh in 1931, proceeded with more than ordinary distinction through the Business College, and graduated just when you'd expect. His only real hardship, he says, was the Stats course with Professor Elmer Bratt, for he does not deny a certain weakness in mathematics and still can't see why a + b = c. (I'm the same way myself.) His spare time he spent down by the tracks watching railroad operations, chatting with personnel of all grades and specialties, and eventually coming to ride not only in the cars themselves but in engine cabs and cabooses—everywhere except on the rods.

It was natural, then, that upon graduation he sought the

Chatting with Curtis Bayer at the Penn half-time, '81.

Lehigh Valley offices in New York, where, however, he was brushed off with scant courtesy. Undaunted, he proceeded to the D&H, which referred him to Albany, and to the Erie, which referred him to Cleveland. Not wishing, though, to travel a couple of thousand miles for two more possible brush-offs, he now went to the Lackawanna—a bitter pill, since it implied rivalry with his still beloved Lehigh Valley: Bayer must have felt like an ardent and bellicose Southerner refused a commission by Jefferson Davis in 1861 and applying next to Abraham Lincoln so that he could fight *somebody*. To the DL&W Bayer offered himself on the basis of a six months' free trial, but the line had a softer heart than that; he was awarded $60 per month and was told to report on Monday morning.

He was first assigned to study the Lackawanna's unprofitable dining operation and wrought so well that when in no long time his superior was fired, Bayer was ready to become a superintendent in his place. In only a year he had effected a turnaround that converted a $150,000 loss to a $5,000 profit, and after that there was no stopping him. He remained with the Lackawanna till his retirement as vice president of purchases and stores.

Despite the heavy demands of his profession Bayer found time to marry, as we see by the following schedule:

Daniel K. Bayer, B.S. '59, president Rupp and Bayer, insurance, Harrisburg.

Peter C., B.S. '60, senior vice president Berwick Forge and Fabricating.

Thomas M., B.S. '63, president Pacific International Trust, Vila, New Hebrides. (An exciting post just now, I imagine.)

Stephen F., B.S. '72, assistant vice president Provident National Bank, Philadelphia.

Timothy C., B.A. '72, teacher, Friends Academy, South Dartmouth, Massachusetts.

Curtis F., Jr., B.A. '75, graduate student, Penn State.

(Thanks to convenient dating Peter, Curt, Jr., and their father were all here for Reunion.)

For the record there was also a daughter somewhere, but since she did not attend Lehigh nor even marry a Lehigh graduate, she doesn't really count. More important is that of the next generation. Daniel K., Jr., is even now in the Class of '83; his brother Mark and his cousin Peter C., Jr. are due to show up in August; and other grandchildren are waiting in the wings.

It is needless, Bayer says, to direct the academic orientation of one's progeny by twisting their arms. As his sons reached the age of five, he would take them to a home football game and spend the rest of the day around and about the campus. The direct pitch consisted of two motifs: (1) I'd love to have you go there too, but I wonder whether you'll ever be smart enough; (2) and if you are, I wonder whether I'll be able to afford it. This method worked like a charm, as you have seen. The boys sometimes had the unusual opportunity of coming to Bethlehem via private railway car to Stroudsburg and the rest of the way along the highways via thumb.

In other respects their careers were conventional.

Some years ago in these pages I had the pleasure of citing the language of a freshman treating the subject of Great Men. "Fathers are considered among my great men," he wrote. "They are propagating our race in an enviable manner." Discounting for ebullience and jingled diction, he might have been thinking of our subject. All honor to Curtis Bayer, an alumnus's alumnus. A few more graduates like him and we could close the Admissions office.

Togas For Everyone

Winter '79

Though not yet a major political influence on state and national levels, the university had many reasons to be gratified by the results of Election Day 1978 as its kith and kin, particularly the latter, both Democrat and Republican, were successfully distinguished by the electorate. We sent two congressmen to Washington, though Mr. Ramsey thinks — hopefully rather than knowledgeably — that we haven't sent even one in the past 35 years, if ever. And Richard Thornburgh, not exactly a member of the family but so close as to make no difference, substantially won the gubernatorial race in Pennsylvania.

Let's begin though, with Democrat Russell Kowalyshyn '40, who won reelection to his eighth term in the House of Representatives at Harrisburg for the 138th District. Kowalyshyn, a lawyer living in Northampton, trounced the Republican opposition by better than 2 to 1. This result was the more impressive because the 136th and 137th Districts went Republican, and the Democratic victory margin in the 135th was much narrower than expected.

In New England, Republican State Senator Mike Morano '39, of Greenwich, Connecticut, was reelected to represent the 36th District. He served as Minority Whip during his first term begun in 1977. Prior to that he had been a member of the Connecticut House of Representatives since 1960 and was elected Speaker.

Moving to the Sunshine State of Florida, Edward J. Stack '31 was elected U.S. Congressman, unseating the incumbent Republican, J. Herbert Burke. Stack, who holds the LL.B. from Penn and the M.A. from Columbia, was sheriff of Broward County. Regrettably, fuller details of this contest have not yet proved obtainable. But it appears that Stack was assisted by the colorful behavior of his opponent, who allegedly got into trouble through involvement in a brawl in a topless bar and then allegedly sought to corrupt one of the witnesses at his trial. In Florida such conduct is still felt to be prejudicial to a legislator.

Meanwhile, back in Pennsylvania, gubernatorial candidate Richard L. Thornburgh was turning the dope upside down as he defeated Democratic opponent Peter Flaherty despite the latter's 870,000 lead in voter registration. Thornburgh won 53 percent of the vote, with a margin of around 213,000.

Richard L. Thornburgh is not exactly a Lehigh alumnus, but he comes as close to it as he could get without actually making it. His grandfather, Charles Lewis Thornburg [*sic*], LL.D. 1925, came to Lehigh in 1895 as head of Math and Astronomy. The next generation contributed C. C. Thornburgh '11, Lewis Thornburgh '14, Richard B. Thornburgh '25, to say nothing of the governor's father, C. G. Thornburgh '09. His brother and a cousin ('42 and '48 respectively) are in there too, while other members of the family married Lehigh graduates and gave birth to yet further Lehigh graduates too numerous to mention. How Richard L. ever crushed out of this tradition to enter Yale instead is hard to imagine.

I don't know just when the Thornburgs became the Thornburghs or why. Thornburg House, named in honor of Charles Lewis, probably retains the older version.

Richard L. took an engineering degree at Yale, a law degree at Pitt. His subsequent career includes his service as United States attorney for western Pennsylvania (1969-75), assistant attorney general of the United States in the Ford administration, and deputy attorney general of the United States in the Carter administration until the appointment of Griffin Bell.

His victory seems largely attributable to profound discontent with the state government after eight years of the Shapp leadership and to his emphatically declared intention to clean up corruption.

Especially prominent by reason of proximity and dramatic

tension was the stunning upset—to use the mandatory phrase—and improbable success of Republican Don Ritter '61, in the campaign for the House of Representatives in the 15th Congressional District. A political newcomer, Ritter not merely won but won big by around 7,000 votes in Lehigh and Northampton counties. The seat, Democratic since 1932, had been occupied since 1963 by Fred B. Rooney, LL.D. '77, an old pro and in most eyes a shoo-in as usual.

The win was due no doubt to a variety of influences, but especially, in Ritter's opinion, to his relentless personal activity in the district during the campaign. His thumb calloused from pushing doorbells, he ceaselessly canvassed the area while his opponent was far less visible. It was a change, Ritter feels, for the electorate to realize that for the first time in modern memory an actual *contest* was taking place, that the Republicans had a candidate, not merely a *pro forma* sacrifice. Ritter worked Rooney's home ward extensively; and on a broader scale he woke up the apathetic Republicanism of Northampton County to the point of getting out 82 percent of its registered voters.

Not merely an alumnus, Ritter, who holds the degrees of S.M. and Sc.D. from MIT, has been working in the office of Vice President for Research Dr. Joseph Libsch, since 1969, as manager, research programs development, since 1976. This position has called for extensive contact with agencies of the federal government, a relation that, he says, "has provided me with a good mechanical view of the legislative process." From Dr. Libsch he has learned to be a manager, for instance, to run a "volunteer" organization; and "the faculty [at large] have provided me with years of learning at the forefront of many diverse areas: the humanities, the social sciences, and technology. My work at Lehigh has been to assist people to achieve their full research potential. And I would hope to call on many, including members of the Lehigh faculty, for special projects and research assistance."

Ritter expressed particular appreciation for undergraduate support, especially that of the College Republican Club with their enthusiasm and extensive footwork. "Who says that Lehigh students are politically unconscious?" he asks. The Republican Club, by the way, though long in existence, has burgeoned conspicuously in the past couple of years. With 40 or 50 active members, the largest political group on the campus, it worked arduously and well in every phase of the Ritter campaign.

It is now ancient history, but as of November 27 Ritter had his hands more than full of readjustment. He had to find a place to live in Washington, he had to find a staff, he had to worry about committee assignments: Ways and Means would be great, but unlikely for a freshman; Science and Technology was more probable, especially because there are only about three engineers in the entire House. He had to set up the offices he hopes to maintain in Allentown, Bethlehem, and Easton. He had to promise his family to come home as many weekends as possible; he had to give an hour of his overburdened time to the representative of the *Alumni Bulletin.*

Well before the appearance of this issue, we suppose, all these things shall have been accomplished, and more besides.

It is a sorrowful necessity to end this account on a note of sadness. Frank J. Meluskey '74, died of a heart attack only two weeks after he had won a second term in Harrisburg as representative of the 133d District, taking 70 percent of the vote from his Republican opponent. A Government major at Lehigh, Frank Meluskey was wholly committed to activity in public affairs and was named to "Outstanding Young Men of America." His death at the age of 26 is unbelievable but true.

A former honor student at Liberty High School in Bethlehem, Representative Meluskey was a freshman at Lehigh when he first ran for public office in the spring of 1971. Tirelessly concerned with civic responsibilities, he will be greatly missed.

Steckbeck's Progress

Spring '79

When my daughter was a good deal smaller than she is now, she used to go, accompanied by her mother, to the Lehigh gym for the swimming instruction open to faculty offspring. It was after one of these flounderings that my wife, who has picked up a smattering of culture through long association with me, told me that she had seen a myth come to life: Professor Steckbeck standing in the shallow end of the pool with a timid child under each arm; for all the world, she said, like Neptune gently indoctrinating two baby Nereids their first day out of the shell. At the same time, she added, he was observing through the back of his head the rambunctious shenanigans of some adolescents down at the other end and was straightening them out in a voice of thunder—which they hastened to obey. Since then I have never seen Steck unequipped with an imaginary trident.

I knew beforehand that there is no getting Steck into a few words, if into anything. For suppose that, like me, you can do just two things: plain knitting and reciting the first 134 lines of *Hyperion*.[1] You're easy to sum up. But Steck can do around 15,000 things and—as Lytton Strachey said of Francis Bacon—he is no striped frieze; he is shot silk. Yet when I realized in February that Steck was going to "retire" in June, I badgered him into busting up an afternoon for my benefit. I felt rather defeatist, I grant you, when I called at his office, for, as all his friends know, it generally takes wild horses to get Steck to talk about himself, and I didn't have any. But I found him in great courtesy not only willing to chat with me but to proffer a chocolate lollipop—my favorite flavor—of which he keeps a store in

[1]True 40 years ago. I still knit beautifully, but I can't do the recitation any more. There was never much demand for it.

Steckbeck leading students in worship; Steckbeck and Mrs. Steckbeck.

his desk.

Since Mr. Ramsey's parsimony requires me to compress into a few hundred words a life experience that calls for the spaciousness of a Pepys or a Boswell, the ensuing article can have no more coherence than a handful of buckshot thrown against a barn door.

Woman boxer — do it Steck!

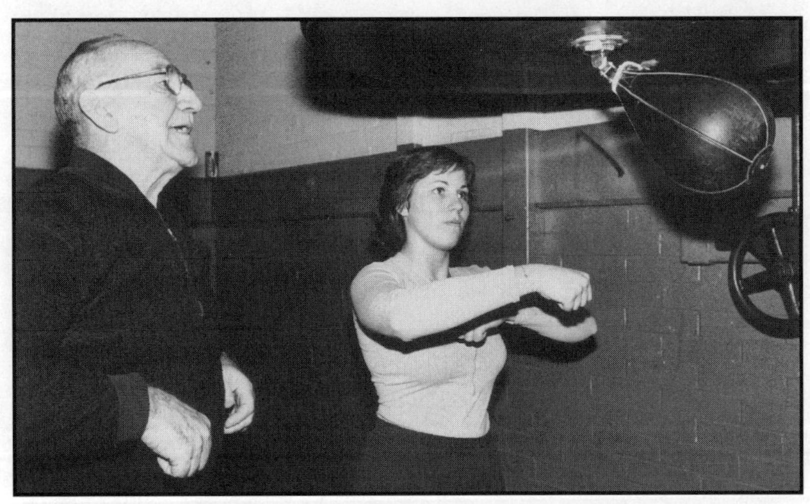

But it is well meant, and no one can say worse than that.[2]

John Steckbeck was born in Lebanon, Pennsylavnia, in 1914, one of a formidable generation of 11.

Though Steck's *enfances* are full of interest, we must deal with them summarily. He and his siblings were programmed to work shortly after they had learned to stand erect and were ceaselessly reminded that one had to work to live—a doctrine in this case as much metaphysical as economic. But the arts had their place as well: Steck began his musical career on the trumpet at the age of nine and a little later enjoyed voice lessons.[3] Thus two prominent strands of his life were spun early: physical activity and the love of music. So in later days, in Pittsburgh, Steck divided many a Sunday between Handel in the morning and football with the Americans in the afternoon.

The Steckbecks tended to abrupt formal education after the eighth grade; but our subject, rather against his parents' wishes, not only completed high school but—with a premedical gleam in his eye and his wardrobe wrapped in a paper bag—proceeded in 1932 to West Chester, having won a subvention of $90 for either a year or a semester, I forget which. It was a sum that went further in those days.[4]

West Chester took football seriously in those days too—the squad included 32 former high school captains. Steck himself was captain as a senior, though he tells me that musical athletes were then regarded as queers and athletic musicians as *Dummköpfe.* It was finally due to the influence of the future Mrs. Steckbeck, herself a pianist of distinction, that he turned to teaching and left professional sports behind.

In this story the play-by-play has to be less important than the

[2]Patient readers may recall my frustrating experiences with Mr. Ramsey's tape recorder on earlier occasions. This time Mr. Ramsey provided me with a toy instrument that he borrowed from his children, saying that he thought it simple enough to suit me (or vice versa; I didn't catch his exact words), and it worked fine. It was too bad that I forgot it till I was two miles from home and had to go back for it, that's all.

[3]If all the 11 little Steckbecks started trumpet at age 9, it must have been hell in the neighborhood for a few years.

[4]The young lady who kindly drove him down from Lebanon later married him.

picture. Steck could do *anything*. In his first teaching job, though he was primarily a musical supervisor, he also did Health and Physical Education and coached basketball, let alone in his spare time moonlighting as a tap-dancing instructor and a Bingo caller.

During the war he was frustrated in his efforts to enlist because he was regarded as more valuable for instructing the Air Force in survival procedures and physical fitness.

Nineteen forty-six found him assistant professor of Physical Education at Dickinson, where he coached everything in sight as usual. He remembers happily that as line coach he helped to spoil the first of the Leckonby years at Lehigh when Dickinson beat us 7-6.

Through the late Dave Dockham, out at Dickinson one day in 1955 with the lacrossers, Steck learned of the imminent retirement of Fay Bartlett, who had been directing the intramural program here, and was encouraged to apply for the vacancy. Having an appointment with General Sadler, then director of Athletics and All That, he drove to Bethlehem one day with his family.[5] The interview was rigorous and searching:

Sadler: Would you like the job?
Steckbeck: Yes.
Sadler: Think you can handle it?
Steckbeck: Yes.
Sadler: You have it.

New vistas now opened. For nine years at Dickinson Steck had been receiving an invariable stipend of $3,800. Without pampering him, Lehigh surpassed that figure and, no doubt, Steck could now enjoy many little luxuries to which he had long aspired. When in 1962 he returned here after an absence of three years, he felt it was like coming home. "I always felt I was created to be here," he told me.

Steck early and inevitably became a full-time member of the

[5] When Mrs. Steckbeck got her first look at the South Side, she like to fainted.

Lehigh community and liked it that way. See him, for example, assisting at a Christmas party at Sigma Nu, whereat he was to enact St. Nicholas, one of his favorite roles. See him fully costumed, fraught with two pillowcases stuffed with gifties, climbing an extramural iron ladder so as to make an appropriately dramatic appearance from upstairs. His full habit, however—for at the time he carried a robust 260 pounds—prevented him not only from squeezing through the designated window but from squeezing back out of it. "Where's Santa Claus?" cried the eager merrymakers below. Alas, Santa Claus was being unburdened and partially undressed by the helpful hands of the Entertainment Committee so that he could get into the house and take over the party.

He remembers the streaking nonsense of the sixties, when any possible show of hostility toward the Establishment was necessary to an undergraduate's self-respect. There was the time when Lehigh sought to outdo the fine performance of some southern outfit (North Carolina State?) that had fielded no fewer than 2,000 streakers. We wanted, as usual, to be Number One. Naughty young men, exiguously clad if clad at all, lurked behind bushes and between buildings awaiting their opportunity of exhibitionism. The campus filled with preadvised cars and cameras. The band paraded in yellow raincoats that flapped open in time with the stirring beat of "El Capitan." A Classics major fled up the hill with a Sabine girl over his shoulder. It was the biggest bash since the Saturnalia of A.D. 61. Though Steck had nothing whatever to do with organizing this event, his high profile got him a lot of the credit or discredit or whatever: It was rumored that the intramural program was giving quality points for participation in the foolishment, and the *Globe-Times* suggested that it had been officially sponsored as a contest in impropriety.

"Why do I take part in rallies? Because I like it. The bigger the crowd, the looser I get." Never looser, perhaps, than at one of the bonfires when the cook from Phi Kappa Theta, a woman of notable amplitude, did a strip so far as her thermal underwear, gathered Steck into her mighty bosom, and asked, "Can you breathe, dearie?"

Bright college days!

But it was not all fun and frolic. Came the time when—the handwriting too clearly on the wall—the intramural program was going to have to comprise girls in a year or two. "We began to create an atmosphere," says Steck, "as if the gym had always been intended for girls from the beginning." He introduced a couple of ice-breakers into the office—long-stemmed and goodly lasses wearing the meager skirts of that era, and through their agency converted the native ruggedness of the male undergraduates to the softer manners of civilized society.[6] By the time the undergraduate women landed on the campus a year later, they could feel right at home in the new climate. Their programs rapidly developed—they furnish 12 touch football teams, 200 swimmers, etc.—and will go on developing when there are more facilities for them to develop into.

Steck is pleased with such achievements as "co-recreation," as in mixed volleyball teams, and with such extramural extension as when our intramural winners face their counterparts at Muhlenberg or one of those other places.

There are around 100 girls in weight-training right now. "We don't put any weight on them or take it off. We just put it where it belongs."

Steck loves the whole far-flung program, founded on the principle that "if you excel, you'll be rewarded with some kind of recognition. The kids make it go; I don't. All we do, we offer the program and let them know it's there if they want it. Stay in bed if you want, but you'll be missing something. We announce a swimming meet: 500 kids show up. Same way with the Turkey Trot."

It's a superior program for a university of our size, he says, and he is full of praise for the reliable staff "who give of themselves and help keep me and the program going."

[6]"Gimme a ball," was the approach of the antediluvian Lehigh man. When the new generation had learned to say, "Could I have a basketball, please?" Steck felt that we were ready to admit women.

Then there was the children's swimming. One day when Fay Bartlett and Steck were sitting around and idly watching the mermen in the pool, the program for faculty issue occurred to them by spontaneous combustion. Almost from the beginning it was a success; the number went to 200, with peripheral activity among the progenitors, who unsatisfied with mere spectation, soon began to find themselves mixed up in cake and Coke parties, contests, challenges, and so on, including a swimerama, whose published program—still notorious among the in group—prompted a barrage of telephone calls to Steck's office. "Steck!" shouted Professor E.N. Dilworth (English). "Don't you ever read things before you put them out?"[7]

The pool offers a rich field for the study of human nature, like that of the young man who wanted to use it to test out a new, high-powered fuel in his toy motorboat. "You get that damn thing out of here."

Or the father of an 11-year-old girl, a child anxious to swim but perfectly and timidly resistant to all the efforts of her parents to teach her. "Now," says Steck slowly and emphatically, "do just what I ask you to do," as he shows her, step by step, precisely how to move first her arms and then her legs. And before the session is over, the child is swimming, while tears are streaming down her father's face. "You don't know what you have," he tells Steck.

And then suppose that you are a young man lying flat on the bottom of the pool, not snorkeling, it turns out, but drowning. You are extricated, compressed, and drained at the poolside, shipped off to St. Luke's for complete dehydration, and in less than three hours you are back in the gym, good as new but in a towering rage. "My towel!" you cry. "Where's the s.o.b. that took my towel? You can't leave anything around here anymore."

Finally we might look at Steck's long-time involvement with

[7]The trouble was an unprintable misprint, if you follow me. As for Dilworth, his conservatism in long refusing to wear trunks in the pool was a major obstacle to the advancement of Steck's policy.

the honored memory of the great athlete Jim Thorpe. It began at a time of Steck's life when he used to clean out attics, taking his pay in the memorabilia that he turned up in the process.[8] He found an early photograph that got him started on his collection of Thorpe-iana and reminded him of the day when he had seen Thorpe on the fifty-yard line at the Polo Grounds kicking a field goal, then turning around and kicking another to the opposite end. Steck is a mine of information on Thorpe's career. He resents as bitterly as anyone else the notorious repossession in 1913 of Thorpe's Olympic medals. And he remains disgusted with John McGraw for selling Thorpe down the river to the Braves in 1919 "because he couldn't hit a curve." "If you can't hit a curve," says Steck, "how do you wind up with a batting average of .327?"[9]

But most of all, Steck is indignant at the inappropriate sepulture of the century's greatest athlete at Mauch Chunk (a town that Thorpe never set foot in), where the monument is neglected and where no one but the elderly seems to care a hoot about having it there. "I told them," says Steck, "I'd be willing to pick up the body and walk with it all the way back to Oklahoma, where it ought to be." Steck is an honorary citizen of Jim Thorpe, Pennsylvania, but he says he doesn't hear from them anymore.

Everybody realizes that *retirement* is meaningless in Steck's vocabulary. A physical fitness center is opening in Allentown—a fine provision of racquetball courts and I don't know what-all—and around October 1, after (I trust) a restful summer, Steck will have an office there, and his work will continue.

"I've always been in competition," says Steck. "A kind of Vince Lombardi attitude.[10] Get it done, man, or get it. I guess I've

[8]As I understand it, Steck would leave you with a clean and tidy attic, taking as com pensation only such Stiegel ware, Shaker tables, and the like, as struck his fancy.

[9]See Steck's book *Fabulous Redmen* (the Carlisle Indians), 1951. If you can, that is; you won't find it in the Lehigh library.

[10]God forbid.

shown some abrasiveness I never intended, but I hope I've learned to control it by watching the people I work with. But mainly I've always believed in the paradox that you can't keep what you have unless you give it away."

When I was in his office, I saw on his desk a copy of Thomas à Kempis, beat-up and dog-eared like a book that's had a lot of use. Maybe we can take it from there:

He doth much who loveth much.
He doth much who doth well what he hath to do.
He doth well, who regardeth rather the common good than his own will.

The Pool of Bethesda

Fall '78

Now there is at Jerusalem by the sheep market a pool, which is called in the Hebrew tongue Bethesda, having five porches. In these lay a great multitude of impotent folk, of blind, halt, withered, waiting for the moving of the water. For an angel went down at a certain season into the pool, and troubled the water: whosoever then first after the troubling of the water stepped in was made whole of whatsoever disease he had.

—The Gospel according to St. John, chapter V

"Who makes the biggest contribution to this outfit?" asked a troublemaker late last winter. (He meant the university.) A good deal of aimless shilly-shally followed, and eventually I grew interested to the point of conducting a casual inquiry—almost a kind of poll—through the next three months. Though my basis was too narrow to carry authority, the result sounded plausible to me. Through the spring Dr. (Deming) Lewis showed consistently, leading John Whitehead by a quarter-length. But win and place varied week by week between Mrs. Janet Smith, then of the Personnel Office, and James Mathews, then our physiotherapist. The alternations apparently occurred as on a given day my respondents were more concerned with their fiscal or their corporal well-being, with their doctors' bills, or with their charley horses.

My scrutiny was timely, for since then both of the front runners have altered their vital relationships with the university: Mathews has retired, and—less unhappily—Mrs. Smith has moved from Personnel to Telephone Service.

Telephone Service, I find, is just a dressed-up name for the

Jim Mathews does bends and gardening.

university switchboard in Linderman Library, the system that makes it possible for a call to be routed accurately to any extension in the far-flung Lehigh grid. The hot news around Linderman, Mrs. Smith tells me, is that the present system, now deemed outdated, is in process of supersession and that next July the university will have a new one of unimaginably superior capacity. Anyway, I think that her transfer is a waste of Mrs. Smith, for no telephone hook-up can be half as tangled and involuted as the Blue Cross-Blue Shield-Medicare jungle, which she knows like the back of her hand. She can tell you in an instant whether you will get a nickel back on your nervous breakdown and whether extracting a wisdom tooth is dentistry or surgery. But I suppose she felt the need to shift to a less demanding responsibility.

Mrs. Smith, however, is still with us, at least. Jim Mathews was decommissioned as of June 30 and is now no longer even in the area. It is true that his departure was anticipated by Mr. Ramsey in the *Bulletin* of last spring, but most inadequately, in hardly more than a footnote—as if the assassination of Julius Caesar had been shoved back among the classified ads.

I got in touch with Jim last summer, and since he was frantically busy while I had nothing to do through the whole of August, I had him drive down all the way from his home in Easton to my Little House in the Woods so that I could chat with him without getting out of my TV easy chair. In view of his preoccupations, though, I let him off writing the article itself; and I didn't even ask him to type it up and put in the punctuation.

A few days beforehand I had borrowed the *Bulletin's* tape recorder, after a tedious briefing by Mr. Ramsey on how to operate it. Something must have slipped up somewhere, though, for afterward when I came to play back the tape, I heard Mr. Ramsey's voice from the previous Thursday saying, "Testing—one-two-three-four" and then nothing at all for an hour.[1] Fortunately I have a memory like a steel trap; I had fetched the recorder merely for window-dressing to impress Jim.

James P. Mathews was born at West Point, New York, his father being a master sergeant. In 1912, he says, but looking at him

[1]I don't think that Mr. Ramsey takes very good care of it.

you'd be more likely to guess 1932 at the earliest. Brought up in the nearby community of Highland Falls, he there enjoyed his formal education until he graduated from high school in 1930.

Then, in a sense, physiotherapy happened to him. Some of us older boys well remember the job market of 1930 and the way we grasped at straws, *any* straws, in the effort to keep off the streets.[2] In the desperate spirit of these times Jim found an opening in the Army Athletic Association and its program for trainees. With no clear idea of what he was getting into, he jumped at it with both feet and ultimately discovered that he was *liking* it and being provided with an excellent background: His vocation had found him.

In 1940 he married Miss Virginia Pascoe.

In the same year, after a decade with the Army, he wanted a change,[3] and joined the Naval Civil Service, being employed at an ammunition depot near Bear Mountain. Two years later he enlisted in the Navy itself and saw the world—specifically glamorous Guadalcanal—for two years more. Here he worked as a machinist's mate with the Seabees.

Though by this time the big party was over, Guadalcanal was still more of a cockpit than a winter resort. Jim tells me that he prudently suppressed his ten years with the Army since, had the facts been known, he would have been sent to a forward area where the chances of coming back in one piece were very small compared to those in the quietude of Henderson Field. Reading between the lines, I take this as an exercise in ironic modesty; I feel that Jim was just as ready to be slaughtered in a good cause as any of us. But all veterans can guess what really happened.

Jim, I feel certain, had no choice at all. An honored tradition in the Armed Forces—it goes back to the Battle of Monmouth, when Mrs. Pitcher wound up in the Field Artillery instead of in Special Services—dictates that no man or woman shall ever be

[2]We knew one chap so hard-pressed that he went with the IRS. It broke his mother's heart, and we never spoke of him again.

[3]Most Army people want a change after six weeks.

assigned according to his proper ability. To this end, on his enlistment he is interviewed, psychoanalyzed, fluoroscoped, and tested; and when his talents are identified beyond the shadow of a doubt, he is placed where he cannot conceivably use them; the system is well-nigh infallible. Eighth-grade dropouts rewrite Army Regulations for the Adjutant General, and sedentary accountants with shorthand and paralegal training are set to digging sanitation pits.[4] *Sic et Jacobo.*

Jim tells me, by the way, that Guadalcanal is 200 miles long. I was surprised: on the map it looks about the size of Plum Island off Newburyport.

He adds that he never in his life has seen anything so good as San Francisco rising from the sea in 1945.[5]

Now see the gay irony of Fate. Back in 1939 Jim had made the acquaintance of Hook Mylin, then, as the sportswriters say, Leopard mentor. During and after Lafayette's grid tilt with Army that year, Jim's skill in helping to repair and maintain some of the visitors' personnel had impressed their coach, who said so. In 1946, then, Jim wrote to Mylin, who was still mentoring at Lafayette, and then came to Easton as a trainer.

He soon grew tired, however, of traipsing all over the country with Lafayette teams; and when there was an opening for a physiotherapist at Lehigh, he came over to us after only one year at the other place.[6]

At that time the Health Service was bulging out of its exiguous quarters in Christmas-Saucon and was about to move into the wooden shack on Memorial Drive, across the street from the

[4]Take my case, for example. Fearless, a dead shot, and fluent in seven languages, I spent the war stateside as clerk in an AA battery that couldn't hit even the target plane.

[5]The Islands must have been beastly monotonous. A friend of mine who was with the Marines on Midway said that they seldom had more than three changes of movie per week, and there was only one squash court for the officers.

[6]No comment.

gym, a home that it occupied till Johnson Hall was ready in 1955. Though the building lacked charm, physiotherapy had all the room it needed and was not ill-equipped. There was no whirlpool, but a galvanic bath was provided, and ultraviolet treatment. Jim himself was chiefly responsible for the introduction of diathermy, which he prefers to ultrasound, if you follow me.

In 1950 his stay with us was interrupted when again Old Glory called and Jim returned to the Navy for two more years. This time he spent his hitch in the Mediterranean, which he compares favorably with Guadalcanal. Today there's not much to choose between them; but things were quieter then, and I see Jim enjoying the serene temples at Paestum, the figs of Smyrna, and the quaint naval base at Toulon.

Sprung in late 1952, he was consulted on the physiotherapeutic aspect of Johnson Hall and was afforded full cooperation. That is, the administration gave him all the room he needed, and all the equipment, including the hitherto lacking whirlpool.[7]

There he remained till the end of last June.

He worked a six-day week with one month of holiday each year. Though St. Luke's Hospital is always available as a back-up, people are generally supposed not to sprain anything on Sundays or during the hot weather; indeed he has spent many a summer day with little to do but sit around thinking long, long thoughts. Yet with the undergraduate body at its present size, the workload at other seasons is often formidable for a single practitioner. Many an evening Jim has been bushed flat out at seven-thirty.

You remember hearing of the man that used to bang his head against the wall because it felt so good when he stopped. Few go as far as that, but many of us have almost welcomed a pulled tendon or a dislocation just for the sake of getting Jim to put it right again and send us off with a rosy glow like a sunrise where the pain

[7]When the English department were similarly consulted with reference to their new quarters in Maginnes, all they could think of was a coffee-maker.

had been. Many a time—there was that day when something went off in my back with a report like a .22—many a time I have limped into Physiotherapy with my musculature in a Gordian knot. "Be my guest," Jim would say, and from him the cliché always sounded as if he meant it, probably because he did. After an hour I had no more inner tension than a cup of junket, and going home I would resolve to be kinder to my wife and family and to read a chapter of the Bible every morning.

Jim, in fact, was largely responsible for preserving (for better or worse) the viability of the instructional and administrative staffs. Seated next to Professor Joseph A. Maurer, M.A. '36 at a dinner one night, he said, "You know, I think you and Sam Missimer are the only ones I never got my hands on." It was hardly a week later that Professor Maurer came into Physiotherapy partly crawling, partly supported—virtually a terminal case—but when he left, he told me, he would have gone back down the hill on his skateboard if he had had it with him.[8] I don't know what the magic is, but it works.

Jim Mathews could raise the dead if doing so were not a federal offense.

I asked Jim, by the way, about the prevailing atmosphere—pungently medicinal—of the physiotherapy room. "What makes with the aura?" I said, "Wintergreen oil?"

"Dermassage," said Jim, referring no doubt to a proprietary unguent.[9]

The most popular trouble spots in the human frame, Jim

[8]Jim never did catch Missimer.

[9]Though obtrusive and clinging, it is not unpleasant. Compare earlier emollients. A Greek athlete after a work-out, for instance, would sensibly take a bath but then undo the good work by smearing himself all over with olive oil. (Who could afford it?) Then he would kind of scrape it off again with a strigil, whatever that is; it sounds painful. When he finally donned his chiton, he must have felt as greasy and itchy as an old—I mean he was very greasy and itchy, let alone smelling like a *Salade Niçoise* two days old. Give me Dermassage.

tells me, are just about what you'd think: the foot and ankle, the knee (a real bastard when it goes wrong), and the back, in that order. If everybody were careful to replace runover heels, it would be a better world.

Symptoms are often misleading. One scholarly case with chest pains rushes for an EKG but proves to be suffering from no more than cervical pressure, a lesser ailment, due to bending over his books for too long at a time. A bad back pain will panic someone else into diagnosing a ruptured disc, though the chances are 99-1 against it.

Really big days for Jim—Mr. Ramsey says that 85 patients is the record—were most commonly produced by intramural football and soccer.

Skiing without instruction is ill-advised. One enthusiast pulled the daylights out of an Achilles tendon; and then, as soon as he had been renovated, went back to the slopes and fractured the tibia of the same leg.

Jogging produces many a foot, knee, and back problem even among the faculty, who are supposed to know better. The Turkey Trot is a big contributor.

Jim himself keeps in shape with regular calisthenics and with hiking the Appalachian Trail. Where he finds the time and energy I cannot imagine.

A naturally romantic temperament made me hope for some colorful responses when I asked Jim how coeducation had affected his métier. Only in quantity, he disappointingly told me: There's a lot more work, girls being even more serious about athletics than boys are.[10] He thought that their appearance had "improved the whole atmosphere at Lehigh," but since I don't think so, I let that one go by. Maybe if I were a masseur I'd feel different. Maybe it depends on what you mean by *appearance.*

It is true that Physiotherapy now has two entrances, one M,

[10]One lass unparallel'd jumped off ATO onto a pile of snow, only she missed it. Jim says you wouldn't believe what she did to her left ankle . . . The Bed Race produces many a brush burn.

one F—until Equal Rights hears about them, I expect. Like the Air Mail, Out-of-Town, and Local slots in a postoffice, they lead to the same area, but they are so disposed as to prevent anyone's encountering the contrary gender *in puris naturalibus.*[11] Rather prosaically, Jim thinks of girls as merely people with distressed ligaments, and contretemps are rare. Occasionally a freshman will back away from the whirlpool, red as a peony, observing that there's a girl in there. "What of it?" says Jim, driving him in again, while the upperclass *flâneurs* lolling around on the tables say that *they* wouldn't mind being ordered in there.

There has been a further switch this fall, for Jim's successor, Mrs. Adrienne Hughes, is (obviously) a woman. At just about the time when she assumed her duties (September 5) Jim had his domestic and residential problems settled (September 8) in Yancey County, North Carolina, not far from the town of Burnsville.

"Why North Carolina?" I wanted to know.

Over the years, Jim said, he and Mrs. Mathews had pretty well covered the 48 states and parts of Mexico during his holidays. Idaho holds the number one spot in his heart, but he finds that real estate there costs like midtown Manhattan—a surprise to me, who thought that a homesteader could take up 100 acres anytime, practically for the postage. North Carolina, Jim's second choice, is not yet inflated out of range, and it has a less agonizing winter, even at 3,700 feet.

The Mathews' new home is secluded yet having a view, in wooded, mountainous country; and the neighboring amenities include golf, swimming, riding, hiking (of course), and half a dozen more that I didn't catch—a veritable *Tir nan Og.* The area is technically dry, but Jim's life is one of temperate sobriety, and he feels that he can manage.

I am sure that he will. And his innumerable friends will continue to remember him with grateful affection, and not merely when they feel a twinge of arthritis.

[11]i.e., bare-ass.

APPENDIX

Mr. Ramsey asked me to explain why I cited the Fourth Gospel in the headnote to this article. I had thought the reason obvious, but I don't mind explicating. Anagogically considered, the passage clearly prefigures my subject. The poolside porticoes of Bethesda are the alcoves of a physiotherapy room; the halt, the withered, and such are clearly older members of the faculty and staff. The troubled water is a whirlpool bath, and the angel is the physiotherapist, who turns it on. The necessity of getting into the water right away means that when you suffer from lumbago or some such, don't think that it will "go away" if you merely ignore it. Get it treated as soon as you can.

The Bible has an answer for everything.

Maurer Abiturus

Reunion '77

It was the last class before the Christmas Holidays. Our eyes dancing with anticipation, we sat waiting for Teacher to appear. As the door opened, we sprang to our feet as we had been taught to do, and, "*Ferias laetissimas, Magister!*" we chorused; "a very merry Christmas, Teacher!"

"Bah! Humbug!" responded Professor Maurer, snarling.

But we knew that it was all in fun. Soon we were relaxed in our seats, enjoying the festivities. The other members of the Classical Languages department joined us, and the hour was given over to merrymaking. Professor Maurer himself, supported by Professor Edna De Angeli, enacted farcical scenes loosely adapted from Plautus. "*Moechum calvum adducimus*" ("Deck the hall with boughs of holly") we sang. "*Dies irae,*" and other ditties appropriate to the season. Professor Feaver rendered sprightly songs in the Phrygian mode, accompanying himself on the kithara.

All too soon the bell rang, and we regretfully had to leave, the undergraduates to the Tally-Ho, I to my section of Freshman Composition.

I do not suggest that this Yuletide gala typifies the Latin classes of Professor Joseph A. Maurer. It may, however, anticipate the impoverishment of humane studies at Lehigh consequent upon Professor Maurer's July 1 retirement. But let us first consider his past.

Joseph A. Maurer was born not merely in Bethlehem but in Nisky Hill Cemetery—well, not exactly *in* the cemetery but in a house, since demolished, that stood within its precinct. Probably he attended elementary and secondary schools in Bethlehem or somewhere, though he would not have needed to do so. In 1928 he

Maurer at the organ.

entered Moravian College, graduating four years later. For almost a decade thereafter he remained at Moravian, teaching both English and Latin at first, then (getting the message) Latin alone, till early 1943, when international tensions deprived him of anyone to teach. After a short hitch as correspondence clerk at a local steel mill, he proceeded to the Country Day School in Princeton, where Latin began in the seventh grade and where he remained for four years. He was called to Lehigh in 1947, and he attained the rank of full professor in 1964.

In addition to his Moravian baccalaureate, he holds the M.A. from Lehigh (1936) and the Ph.D. from Penn (1948).

He was chairman of the Classics department from 1956 to 1975, at which time he was made chairman *pro tem* of Modern Foreign Languages—an area then in a state of dynamic paralysis, if I may trust the *Brown and White*, and where, like Timoleon to Syracuse (the one in Sicily), he brought peace and quiet. He has become professor emeritus as of July 1977.

Early days at Lehigh were not easy. In addition to Maurer, Classics consisted of Professors Wright and Crum, *ille*, as Maurer would say, volatile, and *hic* astringent. It proved necessary, for instance, that the Arts College should enter Maurer's marital or immarital status in its records. Miss Henry, the dean's secretary, first communicated with Professor Wright, who didn't know, but who thought that perhaps, and who wondered whether, yet supposed that there might be some way of finding out, while on the other hand . . . She then tried Professor Crum, who firmly said, "I approve." ("I can never get a simple answer out of that man.") In the end Miss Henry got in direct touch with Professor Maurer himself, called him to the dean's office, and asked him point-blank.

This question having been settled at last, things went more smoothly in the cozy little department, where Professor Wright devoted himself wholly to Latin, Professor Crum to Greek, and Maurer, with great versatility, was bisected: three-quarters Greek and one-quarter Latin in the fall, the reverse in the spring. Classics is larger today, but its development has been vegetable, as Marvell would put it, rather than flashy. There are still only three members, but now guest stars turn up from time to time for anthropological, artistic, and other ancillary services. And if the number of students is small beside that of the electrical engineers and mathematicians, every one of them is there because he wants to be.

It is a friendly, hospitable department. As I have already implied, I frequently took its Latin courses when my schedules allowed—not that I *needed* them, you understand, but because they were free—and I was always treated as courteously as if I had paid for them. Professor Frank Hook and I even studied Elementary Greek (in different years), though I believe that Hook didn't get much out of it.

Returning to Professor Maurer, his classes were a continual joy, partly because—aside from their substance—he was so effortlessly in command of his subject, and then because he was so cheerful about it, almost too cheerful in dealing with a tongue so solid as the Roman—Norman Douglas speaks of its "cold, lapidary construction." Is that a language to be treated lightheartedly? Sometimes I have felt almost like little Mary Augusta asking Matthew Arnold, "Why, Uncle Matthew, oh why, will you not be always wholly serious?" Yet somehow this gamesomeness did not prevent any of us from learning our lessons.[1]

But let us get a picture. It is appropriate, I think, to quote excerpts from a tribute to Professor Maurer delivered on May 5, 1977 at a Phi Beta Kappa chapter meeting. For the sake of alumni trained in the Engineering College I have taken the liberty of putting the rather difficult Latin of the original into colloquial English.[2]

"As Cicero said in speaking to the Senate of Catiline, my subject needs no introduction to this group, for I allude to Professor Joseph Abele Maurer, whose exoneration from the secretaryship of our chapter is no inconspicuous feature of today's agenda.

"I say little of Professor Maurer's classical attainments. Indeed, a teaching humanist has little to do. Once he has learned at school to read Caesar and Ovid and the rest of that crowd, he has it made for life. The texts do not change, and keeping a page ahead of his disciples is absurdly easy. What does he do with his time? Some decades ago a nosy Royal Commission were harassing Oxford in the customary way of governmental agencies toward their betters. And coming to R.M. Dawkins, then professor of Byzantine and Modern Greek, they asked him to describe his activities. 'I give an annual lecture,' said Dawkins, and added, 'but not every year, mark you.'

"All I can say is that Professor Maurer wrote his doctoral dissertation at Penn on Suetonius's life of Gaius Caligula. Since Caligula—with the possible exceptions of Domitian and Elagabalus[3]—was the nastiest Roman emperor in history, it says much for the native sweetness of the man—Professor Maurer, that is—that he was

[1]Humanistic jesting is often rather special. Well do I recall a day when a few of us were shooting the breeze at college long ago. Someone referred to Professor X as polymathic (very learned). "Are you sure," said Charley Travers, a Classics major, "that you didn't mean polymethic [very drunk]?" How we all laughed!

[2]The Lehigh chapter of Phi Beta Kappa tends to regard the university as one of its functions, not the other way around.

not permanently jaundiced by this potentially corruptive association.

"The heart of the matter, though, is the Phi Beta Kappa secretaryship, which does require constant attention, labor, accuracy, inconvenience, and forethought. To the onlooker it may seem a gut, to use Cardinal Newman's expression; but when once it was timidly offered to me—'Dr. Armstrong has nothing to do in his retirement, it will help to keep him off the streets'—I recoiled *tanquam colubra punctus*, as if stung by an adder. Yet Professor Maurer, in addition to his other duties, whatever they are, has carried this burden Atlas-like for seven years and even now lays it down with reluctance.

"In this organization the president has a little to do, the treasurer has a little more, and the secretary has the remaining 94 percent. He must correspond extensively, of course, generally on matters less urgent than frivolous. He calls meetings—no slight task in the light of the Lehigh calendar. He provides nominees to the council, which few wish passionately to become members of. He recalls and can cite the by-laws. Most of all, perhaps, he provides the materials on whose basis elections to membership are decided. No inconsiderable duty: The watchwords of this society are Friendship, Morality, and Literature; and while undergraduates today are probably as matey as ever, and while perhaps they are not much more immoral than they were 200 years ago, or at least not in the same ways, most of them have no more literature than they found in two years of nursery Spanish and one of freshman English if you

[3]The first of these has been immortalized by E.C. Bentley:

A man in the position
Of the Emperor Domitian
Ought to have thought twice
About being a Monster of Vice.

As for Elagabalus, he was a caution! To say nothing of his noticeable behavior in drag, he used to select four personable young women and . . . but it is a long story, and you can look it up in *Scriptores Historiae Augustae.*

can call it English.

"All these things Professor Maurer has done and done with distinction, mainly by himself. For earlier incumbents—I think of Professors Christensen and Yates—it was another affair, for Miss Henry in the dean's office did all the real work. Not so with Professor Maurer, who in addition has innumerably entertained the chapter and its guests—an activity unmentioned in the by-laws—in his own home with five or six choices of ardent spirits, to say nothing of malt brewage, cold cuts, rye bread, spreads, dry-roasted peanuts, and three sorts of pickles—occasions supported by the unfailing kindness of Mrs. Maurer, who must often have wished her husband an illiterate.

"*Quid superest?* What remains to be said? Professor Maurer, in addition to his Latin and his Greek, is fluently at home in Pennsylvania Dutch. He is a musician of distinction. Most admirably he agrees with me in believing that the Christian Church is not served in being converted to a left-wing agency of the United Nations—if I am not being redundant—nor by its liturgy's being rewritten in less-than-basic English.

"Were there present a devil's advocate—as there is not—it is true that Professor Maurer could be shown something less than the well-rounded man he seems to be. Though as an undergraduate at Moravian College he earned no grade less than A on the academic side, his record in Physical Education was not even undistinguished; and I have gathered that, an indifferent baseball player, he was still less effective upon the basketball court. But Charity should look with a blind eye on the delinquencies of half a century ago, all the more, no doubt, in that they do but humanize the man, whose clay, I must remind you, is even as yours and mine.

"*Quid futurus?* What lies ahead? It is not in the aggressive nature to retire. We remember Tennyson's Ulysses, who felt how dull it is to rust unburnished, not to shine in use. Yet it may not be too much to hope for him that, relieved of his chief burden, only flightingly preoccupied with such nugatory academic formalities as must remain to him, he may spend the best hours of his golden days in the wholesome meditative practice of omphaloscopy—or, if you will, of umbilicospection—or, if you must have it, of contemplating his navel; that is, if he can still see it."[4]

Truly no inventory can sum up a polytropic personality. Yet I should add that for three years Professor Maurer edited *Classical World,* a learned journal of worldwide distinction. He still has both his tonsils. He has set Latin papers in the Advanced Placement program. He has emceed the Faculty Dinner. He has given up cigars. He knows everything about historic Bethlehem. Having mastered the organ in his spare time, he was for seven years organist at the Fritz Memorial Church and is ever ready to make with a prelude and fugue in an emergency. For 20 years he has been advisor to Alpha Chi Rho and has no doubt discouraged them from some of their more imaginative enterprises. He has received the Lindback and (on May 10 of this year) the Hillman Award, the latter being the Lehigh equivalent of a crown of parsley. Altogether I see July 1, 1977, as Black Friday.

Housed in Coppee Hall when he first came to Lehigh, Professor Maurer was later translated to Lamberton, which he compares unfavorably with the Tower of Babel; then to Price, which I compare unfavorably with the Tower of London; next to Maginnes, where he first felt himself in civilized surroundings; and at the last back to Coppee. As the circle symbolizes perfection, this *periplus* may stand as a final statement upon the accomplishment of an invaluable preceptor and admired colleague.

[4]Anachronistic if not libellous. Rational diet and regular exercise have made all the difference.

Has Anybody Here Seen Corelli?

Fall '80

As everyone knows, the profession of a college teacher with tenure is one of cushioned sloth. He works nine hours a week, if you call that work, he fools around all summer, and in these days he may not even have to attend Commencement. But the handsomest amenity of them all is the sabbatical year: at the end of each sexennium in the classroom he is encouraged to go away for 52 weeks, the farther the better, and recharge his batteries. In such year his stipend is doubled as a matter of course, for sipping Kirsch in Wengen or liqueur chocolates in Cap d'Antibes is naturally far more costly than Pepsi-Cola in Hellertown.[1] When he returns, he is supposed to have been born again or at least put on 25 pounds.

So when in September 1978 Professor David M. Greene (English) was miss'd on the custom'd hill, it was supposed that he was living it up on the Costa Brava. Not at all, as it turned out: Professor Greene was staying at home and putting a book together. Indeed, even now when he has long been returned to the banks of the Ilissus,[2] he is still putting it together. And if I seem to make undue fuss about it—for professors are always putting books together—I do so because I think that it's going to be far more useful than most of the books that get put together. Not parochially confined to the English field, it is addressed to the world of semi-pro music lovers. In fact *Greene's Compilation*, as I call it in default of its

[1]When people ask me where I went on my sabbaticals, I have to confess that I never accepted one. Warmly attached to my colleagues, my work, and the Lehigh Valley, I couldn't imagine leaving them for so long.

[2]In plain English, "a year after returning to Lehigh." I have recently been reading Carlyle and find it almost impossible to state anything intelligibly.

forthcoming title, is a biographical dictionary of composers, beginning with the inevitable Greeks and coming down to the day before yesterday.

It seems that Professor Greene, who for some years had been writing distinguished criticism for *Musical Heritage*, came to the attention of two editors at Doubleday engaged in promoting a series of "popular"[3] biographical dictionaries and already disappointed by the scapegrace behavior of their original choice for the music volume. Recognizing in Greene a person of stainless integrity, they turned to him for help in their project.

The planning of the dictionary has been left in Greene's hands, the format and all that, and he confines it to composers who have appeared on recordings that are more or less readily available in this country: around 3500 thumbnail sketches ranging from a couple of lines to six or seven pages. "The articles are as nontechnical as I can make them without being insulting," says their author, and he has not burdened his pages with bibliographies, discographies, and the like, matters of less concern to the common music lover and already handy to the elbow of any pro. When Greene says "composer," by the way, he means composer. Considering, then, Godowsky and Paderewski, both noted as pianists, the first probably won't make it, but the second just might since he spent a good deal of his spare time in minor-league creation.

Such biographical information is already around, of course, in a variety of forms from Grove's *Dictionary*, which comprises *everything* and at present costs about $1,000, to a short short with a hundred big names in it as offered at your friendly naborhood drugstore. "I am hoping that what this will do is fill the need for something in between, for people who are past the beginner's stage but are not really interested in the scholarly side of it," says Professor Greene. He reasonably hopes too that his work will not reduce its owner to pauperism. If inflation doesn't run completely

[3]Isaac Asimov did the "Scientists and Technicians" volume, if you see what I mean.

wild, it ought to appear somewhere in the $35 area, far less than you'd pay for a pair of good pewter candlesticks.

Greene's Compilation will be chronologically arranged and so will serve as a kind of history of music, too. An ingenious device in the shape of an alphabetical index is included. Thus if you think you've heard of someone named Palestrina but can't remember in which millennium, you don't have to riffle through 2,000 years to nail him down; the index will do it for you in a trice.

I asked Professor Greene whether in addition to the strictly biographical he touched on critical matters, at least in connection with the more prominent entries—Brahms, let's say, as opposed to Hoagy Carmichael.[4] "Oh yes," he said, "I have tried to encapsulate, as they say these days, as much information as I can to say why this composer is important, what it was he contributed, and who it was he imitated."

Then I was especially interested in the Greek side of it because, thanks to Professor Douglas Feaver (Classics), Lehigh has been a hotbed of Argive tunefulness for a quarter-century and more. Even I, tone-deaf as I am, have contributed to this study. From the depths of our pond here[5] I once dredged up a monstrous turtle about the size of the ones that Darwin used to ride around on in the Galapagos Islands. I then summoned the late Professor Basil Parker (Biology), another music lover, who came over with a formidable handgun and blew the turtle's head off, not in any spirit of anti-amphibianism but in the service of the Muses. He took the corpus home and buried it till the microorganisms and things in the soil should have consumed the palatable parts; then dug it up and presented the carapace to Dr. Feaver, who (following in the footsteps of Hermes) constructed a lyre in the classical tradition. I am proud to say that after many years this instrument is still a prominent

[4]My sister-in-law thinks that "Star Dust" is worth more than the collected works of Mahler. She may have a point.

[5]This body of water, being full of extravagant fauna, is not really so much a pond as a mere. I expect to catch a coelacanth there sooner or later.

feature of Dr. Feaver's collection and is heard whenever its owner presents one of his lectures with musical illustration.

Anyway, getting back to Greene, only a handful of Greek composers are known by name, and most of their output has inevitably vanished. Greene has recently acquired a recording by a Spanish group operating in France—all very Mediterranean—of every surviving scrap and tatter of Greek music. As to the authenticity of the renditions he has no opinion.

Greene is rather disappointed to conclude from his exhaustive spadework that just about all the picturesque and memorable anecdotes are lies: Handel did not really disturb his family by practicing the harpsichord in the garret at night, Schubert did not die heartbroken over a *Backfisch* called (of course) Mitzi, and Arion was not really saved from drowning by a friendly dolphin.[6] It's the same everywhere. King Canute never sat enthroned by the seashore, Richard III could not have been saved by any number of horses, and nobody ever preserved the Netherlands by sticking his finger into a hole in the dike. There is no romance in the world of scholarship.

Greene was also disappointed in that his labors involved no travel. He tried to find legitimate reasons for going to Norway, Salzburg, or Rome, for example, but there weren't any: Nothing that he needed was farther away than New York. So much for the sabbatical leave spent on golden beaches or in mountain wonderlands.

Dr. Greene's background is extensive and miscellaneous.

[6]I'm particularly fond of the dialogue between Mozart and a young aspirant to musical distinction:

Asp: I wonder, Wolfgang, if you'd show me how to compose a symphony.
Moz: Aren't you rushing it, Putzi? Why don't you start with something simpler, like maybe a song?
Asp: *Aber* Wolfgang, you wrote your first symphony when you were eight.
Moz: Yes, but I didn't ask anybody how.

He has from an early age been a devotee of Euterpe, Erato, and Polyhymnia.[7] Long ago he embarked on voice study, only to discover (no doubt too modestly) that he had no voice. Again he wondered whether he might not become a high school band director till he concluded that he was a better writer than conductor and that high school students were intolerable anyway. Inadequate technique disillusioned him with the pianoforte: he needed almost four minutes for the "Minute Waltz." Nodding acquaintance with the trumpet and the fiddle never ripened into true love. Only the clarinet—that ideal instrument, portable, welcome in any combo, and gentle enough to be practiced in the home—was genuinely sympathetic, and he wishes sometimes that he had not given it up under the pressure of circumstances.

One of the circumstances must have been formal study in the field of English, which we have rather lost sight of in this exigent context.

Out of all this richness Greene drew his qualifications for his long affiliation with *Musical Heritage,* which he began by testily abusing the quality of their then writers, an approach that naturally soon developed into warm affinity. Beginning with translations for record jackets, he became *Musical Heritage's* chief writer for some years and still produces several one-page articles every three weeks for this frequent periodical and its concern with new and old recordings.

Long before that, however, Greene had been ingathering records for himself at a frightening rate, partly because he liked hearing the music better than reading the scores, partly because if he wanted to hear *Acis and Galatea,* he didn't want to wait for a production at Palisades High School. His collection, methodically assembled, now dominates the living room, the upper story, and the basement of his home: over 12,000 records according to the most recent tabulation.

[7]Sorry. Should read, "He has always loved music." Carlyle again.

This hoard has proved of very great significance to the university library, for Greene has not merely brooded over it, Fafnir-like. A dozen years ago when his students in Opera as Drama, unhappy because the library had no record collection, asked whether, granted the funding, Greene's plenty might be taped for university purposes, Greene was delighted to agree. The project was enthusiastically received, and as a reward Greene was permitted to do all the taping himself, a task now almost three-quarters completed. The results constitute the nucleus of the so-called Media Library, a precious addition to the university's cultural opportunities. At present borrowing is impermissible, but through a program of retaping it may be opened up in the not-too-distant future.

And now we must leave Professor Greene as he sits on the porch of his house, which clings to a steep hillside falling away to Wydnor and the Saucon Valley. It is late afternoon, and the sinking sun gilds the broad panorama to the southeast. Professor Greene would like to sit still and immerse himself in the loveliness for half an hour. But there are still 3,000 records to put on tape. Wearily he picks up another cassette. . . .

Solemn Musick . . . Heav'nly Harmony[1]

Reunion '80

After the relentless *longueurs* of a winter in the Lehigh Valley, even a grudging spring such as we usually get around here is welcomed by all except, perhaps, those who are going to retire from formal service to the University on June 30. What are they to do with their time? Will their once-deferential colleagues speak to them any more? Would it be better to move to Florida and learn Spanish?

Thoughts like these must have run through the mind of Professor Robert Cutler of the Music department as on April 20 he sat in Packer Church listening to a rendition of the St. John Passion by the Lehigh Choir. Let us try to understand him.[2]

Musicians are different from normal people. I, for example, supremely normal, took piano lessons for six years to no end except that I can offer a lively attack on "The Wreck of Old 97" in F with very few mistakes. Professor Cutler, on the other hand, though never discovered playing the spinet in the attic in the middle of the night, mastered the piano before bothering to take lessons and at the age of 10 was known to a small but discriminating following in southern Westchester for his interpretation of Chopin. (Is it too much to hope that he wore a black velvet suit and Windsor tie? Probably.)

Though mainly a keyboard and vocal specialist, by the way, Cutler was at one time a clarinetist too. His 50-year-old instrument, long abandoned in a broom closet up at University Heights in the Bronx, was repossessed a while ago and brought to Lehigh, where

[1]Milton . . . Dryden

[2]In speaking with Professor Cutler, I had my usual trouble with Mr. Ramsey's children's tape recorder, but Professor Cutler kindly got it going for me.

Bob Cutler conducting, looking at sheet music.

it now supplies the Music department with spare parts as required. Clearly Cutler was a young man of unusual promise.

Playing the organ.

Robert B. Cutler was born in New York, by which he means Manhattan, and he is rather proud of it, though it is hard to see why when you consider how many others have done it. At an early age he moved (or was moved) to the purer air and bucolic surroundings of Yonkers, then virtually a country town. The Yonkers *Statesman*, however, used to insist in a heading that "The Subway Must Come to Yonkers," and though it never did, Yonkers now enjoys all the other disadvantages of the big city.

He received his early education in local schools and at 16 was ready for an undergraduate career at Bucknell, partly because, already an ardent golfer, he dug the 18-hole course blazoned in Bucknell's promotional literature.[3] He enrolled as an engineer because, he told me modestly, in those days that's what you did if you showed no aptitude for anything else, and with tuition at $150 per semester, how could you lose? But after changing his curriculum for several semesters, he wound up as an English major—it gave him more time for golf—an influence that still shows in his wide vocabulary and in his *ex tempore* employment of sentences containing subordinate clauses.

A master's degree in music at Columbia completed Cutler's formal education in 1935, and he proceeded to the Trinity School on West 91st Street, to remain there for 12 years, off and on in the sense that for over three of those years he was pursuing hostile submarines for the Navy. This wartime service was largely uneventful, he says—which seems hard to accept; it sounds hair-raising to me—but not wholly unrewarding. On watch one night and advised by a subordinate that ominous vibrations were being recorded, Cutler satisfied a long-entertained desire by firing a flare pistol and woke everyone up by calling the ship to General Quarters. As he took after the enemy, he was also standing on the steps of the Capitol receiving the Navy Cross from the President, when his captain, aroused from a sound sleep, appeared to direct operations. "Our job isn't to play tag with a submarine; it's to protect that ship," he pointed out, indicating the escort, which was receding full speed

[3]There was some other reason too, but I couldn't pin him down on it. Let it go.

ahead after a 90-degree change of course. As it turned out, no blood was shed; but for an unforgettable minute or two Cutler had been standing on the quarter deck with John Paul Jones.

The war over, Cutler was in the late forties invited to join the NYU music department through the agency of a parishioner in the church where he was sustaining his second occupation as organist. At NYU he remained for five years.

Now, at last, in 1954 his meaningful life was about to begin, for he had a phone call from William Schempf at Lehigh, offering him employment. Schempf, who toiled here in the period 1947-1957, was at the time just about all the music department we had; and because his heart was largely given to the band, he was anxious to get the Glee Club off his back.[4]

The Department of Music, then, became Schempf and Cutler. (At present it is swollen to four and a half members, the one-half being Cutler himself, held over for administrative purposes during the current year.) The physical provision for departmental operations was fairly simple too: a cosy 9 x 12 cubicle in the sub-basement of Grace Hall. Choral work was hard enough in gracious circumstances, Cutler found; instrumental was just short of lethal, and Schempf regularly went home deaf after a rehearsal, requiring over two hours to get his ears back.[5] Furthermore, the men's room was unattainable during wrestling matches, when the upstairs gate would be locked. Eventual translation to the broader expanses of Lamberton Hall was a blessing upon the quality of Lehigh music and the sanity of its instructional staff.

In 1957 Schempf left Lehigh to go to some military school

[4]Not that Schempf wasn't conscientious in the vocal field. Listening to my editor, Mr. Ramsey, then an undergraduate aspiring to the Glee Club, Schempf broke off the audition after a phrase or two and switched Ramsey to Journalism.

[5]Surely they went upstairs to practice? I cannot see the band rehearsing in 108 sq. ft. Schempf would not have been temporarily deafened; he would have been killed.

up the Hudson and was replaced with and by Jonathan Elkus, who remained for 17 years. Cutler thinks himself most fortunate to have been associated with two such musicians, regretting only that the advent of one hinged on the departure of the other. Like Joselito and Belmonte considered as bullfighters,[6] both men were brilliant, one traditionally, the other off-beat. In addition Elkus was dynamically intrepid in the fiscal area: concluding that the Glee Club was inadequately subsidized at the rate of $433 per annum, he demanded more and cowed the administration into providing it. When he left, it took two replacements to fill his shoes. "Bob," he told Cutler, "I think I'm doing more for the department by leaving than I could do by staying around."

Even the two newcomers eventually proved insufficient thanks to continually swelling demand: a fourth member was added in 1976, and yet another in 1979 when Cutler himself was diminished to 50% and the marching band was transferred into the possession of Dean William Quay, who, I believe, exercises his authority by deputy. As I write, furthermore, there are three Music majors, and Cutler is happy to observe that these are not mere eccentric aesthetes with attenuated sensibilities; one of them, for example, is distinguished for achievement in chemistry and has made Phi Beta Kappa.

Cutler was named acting chairman of the department in 1957 and chairman a year later. He was somewhat surprised by his promotions—Dean Glenn Christensen used to call him up and promote him without any of the normal shadowboxing. But since at the time Cutler was 50% of the department and had seniority as well, it doesn't surprise me at all. With the congenial Elkus his sole associate, furthermore, Music was free of the factionalism that so often vitiates administrative effort.

As he looks back, Cutler rightly feels some temperate glow of accomplishment during his tenure. He has raised the sights of

[6]This striking simile is mine, not Cutler's.

the choristers at Lehigh, sophisticating their judgment and extending their territory. When he first came, the Glee Club's repertoire was characteristic: spirituals, shanties, and suchlike.[7] Well aware of fairer, more challenging vistas, Cutler began to open windows for them. Stravinsky's *Oedipus Rex*, for one, an opera-oratorio rare in being a major work designed for male voices only. Cutler's Machiavellian process was to discuss *Oedipus* with his cohort, to play recordings, once even to travel some of them to New York to hear it—regretting all the while that such a fine *oeuvre* lay outside the Glee Club's capacity. He continued this needling until some of the more aggressive types began to *want* to do it, then to insist on doing it, and finally Cutler allowed himself to be persuaded. In the end *Oedipus* was presented with 45 voices and proved a complete triumph, as well as a change from "The Bells of St. Mary's" and "MacNamara's Band."

Oedipus, by the way, finely illustrates the great gulf fixed between musicians and the rest of us. Professor Cutler tells me that Stravinsky had its words translated from Greek into Latin; *Everyman's Dictionary of Music* says from French into Latin. Anyway, they were translated from *some* language into Latin "in order," says Everyman's *Dictionary*, "not to distract the ordinary listener by verbal association." The simple truth is that no ordinary listener can tell what language a choral group is singing in without consulting the program, let alone catch any of the words. And, especially if Cutler is right, translation into a dead language from an even deader one is a mad way to *obscure* the words you're singing. Language apart, why have words at all if you must hire a philologist to render them unintelligible? Surely this is to misconceive the purpose of language?[8]

Professor Cutler's mastery of his art was beyond praise, and I am sorry that I can afford only one illustration of it, keeping my terminology as colloquial as I can for the convenience of the lay

[7]If you saw the Asa Packer film, you saw Cutler rehearsing "Vive la Compagnie" in his shirtsleeves.

reader.

First of all, you must understand that it's comparatively unremarkable for a well-indoctrinated performer or group to function efficiently when everything's going well. The test of mastery is how it withstands the unexpected, the contradictory, or the demoralizing. "I once suffered the agony of watching an inferior Harvard eight row to victory, stroked by a Yale spy!" wrote Dr. Walter Traprock once. "He had been put in at the last moment when the Crimson regular developed a sudden rose-cold. His Yale training had been so good that, try as he would, he simply couldn't row badly."[9]

Once, then, Cutler and the Glee Club found themselves out in Pittsburgh to rehearse a version of *Carmen*—a strongly choral work—with the Chatham College Choir. Now here is the rather subtle problem: the well-known Seguidilla[10] employs the key of E; and right after it the men in the chorus begin to burst out in C: "Here come the bulls" or "Hurrah for Escamillo" or something of that sort. On this occasion the police, wishing to censure an improperly parked car, broke up the music at the worst possible moment: who after a five-minute interruption could remember the pitch? "Play C for the men," whispered Cutler hoarsely to the bassooniste, who was day-dreaming with her reed in her mouth and who panicked by his instancy, blew C#. Cutler's heart sank as disaster loomed, but he need not have worried. The Glee Club, so flawless was their hardwon selfcommand, hailed the bulls in C—bless their hearts—and the rehearsal was saved.

Of course Cutler welcomed the girls in 1970 or whenever it was. Most of the world's great music was composed for mixed

[8]For choral passages anyway, why subsidize a top-flight poet like von Hofmannsthal or Auden? You might as well sing it in Gullah.

[9]*Dr. Traprock's Memory Book* (New York, 1931) ch. V.

[10]I looked up *seguidilla* in my Spanish dictionary just to be sure of the spelling, and I really was surprised at what I found.

choruses, he says,[11] and the difficulties of effecting integration with lassies from other institutions was not inconsiderable. Suppose you have a Saturday night concert and the girls turn up Friday night or (worse) around noon on Saturday. How would you like to rehearse them first with the men and then put the lot together with an orchestra in time for appearance at 8:30? "A traumatic experience," says Cutler with believable feeling in his voice. He much prefers having his sopranos handy by.

The Lehigh Glee Club, in case you're wondering, was commendably well behaved on its visits elsewhere. Once a drunk ran amok with a firehose at Wells; once eyebrows were raised at Hood when many of the Lehigh contingent were discovered sleeping untidily in the living room of a girls' dormitory, for in those more sophisticated days such frowsiness was known to be in dubious taste. Otherwise their behavior would withstand the closest inspection.

The men themselves were not unaffected by the gentle influence of coeducation. A hardy lot in the old days, they became more sensitive, says Cutler, declining to say just what he means by that.

The success of the Music Department is the more admirable in that Lehigh is not the most fertile field for the cultivation of the arts; it takes a great deal of repastination if it is to remain productive. Cutler estimates that he spent only about 10% of his time on music; the rest was claimed by people, who had to be urged, exhorted, cajoled, and inspired. Yet many of his personal[12] relationships have been the most satisfactory part of his life here.

The Department, just for the record, is interested in instruments as well as in voices, and in the oboe as well as in the

[11]Indeed? What about the Goldberg Variations? What about "Till Eulenspiegel"? What about "Tiger Rag"?

[12]"Of course," said J. D. Leith, sometime Dean of Students, "*you* see them at their best. If you meet them mainly as plagiarists and shoplifters and . . ."

sousaphone. The band of course inevitably has a high profile, as everyone knows who has ever attended a football game in Taylor Stadium and seen the XCVII form their famous marching LEHIGH and later shout witless vulgarities across the field at the opposing stands. As for indoor instruments Professor Cutler says that a wide range of programming is possible, though it depends somewhat on the fortuitous presence of the right expert: that is, no sense in trying a horn concerto unless you have a horn virtuoso on hand; after he graduates, it's too late. Other productions call for unreasonable technological aids. Our one cannon would be inadequate to the demand of the 1812 Overture, and the Metallurgy Department itself could not supply props enough for the Anvil Chorus.

Yet despite many discouragements—on the old houseparty weekends hardly 50% of Cutler's personnel would show up, and he thought repeatedly of bookselling or of a hardware store as an alternative to music—Cutler has found it a good life.

Now he is neither looking forward to next fall nor fearing it. It will work out, he feels. He has never applied for anything in his life, and so again something pleasant may happen to him without. So far as he knows, he will continue in the area, in his house with its five and one-half acres on the far side of the mountain. He will go on filling in as organist at the Eighth Church of Christ Scientist in New York. His life has always been saturated with whatever he's doing at the time so that in other ways he has fallen far behind in its demands; now he wants to round out his work at Lehigh and then try to catch up—with his letters, for example.[13]

To be sure, if a high-powered organ appointment should fall into his lap (the Mormon Tabernacle) or a sabbatical fill-in with a fine choir (King's College, Cambridge, or the Wiener Sängerknaben) he would give it a good, hard mull before saying no. But he is not counting on it.

Last April, as I said, the choir gave a first-rate performance

[13]He was so eager and happy about this that I didn't discourage him by telling him that it can't be done.

of the St. John Passion. As he heard it proceed under the baton of Professor Sametz, Cutler hoped that the audience might irrationally suppose this excellence to have been characteristic of the group while it was under his direction. I don't think he needed to worry. Everybody knew it.

Mack Bibliophylax[1]

Winter, '77

For how can it be possible that a man can act as Warder of the accumulated record of the world's wisdom, piety, learning, and experience, and hold the same in necessary reverence, if he be not a person of sober and Godly life, learn'd, virtuous, chaste, moral, frugal and temperate?[2]

That of James D. Mack is a name well known to all readers of this publication as belonging to the erstwhile class correspondent (now regrettably retired) of 1938 who in that capacity gave accurate and distinguished service for eight years. What few are aware of, however, is that he has for an even longer time served as a not unimportant member of the Lehigh administration, having been assistant to the university librarian (1946-48), acting librarian (1948-50), and librarian (1950-76). During this time, Mr. Mack also served as chairman of the *Council of National Library Associations*, and president of the International Association of Technological University Libraries. He is a member of the Grolier Club, the Bibliographical Society of America, and the American Library Association. His recent translation to the post of curator of rare books, only modestly publicized here and there, has called some attention to this side of his career but deserves greater emphasis.

[1]I prefer the demotic term to the somewhat precious and affected *librarian*, which latter I have been editorially compelled to use within my text.

[2]Epigraph and subsequent citations from "Philobiblos," *The Old Librarian's Almanack*, 1774.

James Mack

Some background is necessary.

When I had my first library card and took out *Tom Sawyer* as my initial choice, I saw librarians as young women with funny pencils (on account of the date stamp attached) who let you take your book after they had processed it. If I thought about it at all, I must have thought then that in addition they put the books back on the shelves on return, glued them together when they needed it, and maybe dusted them now and then. It was some years later that one of those young women—a neighbor of ours; her name was Edith Book, it really was—told me that she had gone to *school* to learn her trade before she was trusted with her funny pencil. So I began to understand what in graduate school I understood much better, that there is more to librarianship than changing the date on the rubber stamp.

For in addition librarians are supposed to know the difference between quartos and octavos (one is larger), how to get the books back on the shelves not just anywhere but where they belong, and how to expunge rude inscriptions from the blank surfaces in open stacks. As they proceed to higher and higher echelons, their responsibilities increase in proportion. With a relentless flood of new publications every day, they must decide what to buy out of a limited budget (and according to their borrowers they always guess wrong), and where to put it with limited shelf space.

> *Any mere Trifler, a Person that would Dally with Books, or seek in them shallow Amusement, may be Dismiss'd without delay.*

At a certain level librarians must learn to regard the borrower as a nuisance if not as an enemy. My wife, once seeking such-and-such a title at 42d Street, was fixed by a gimlet eye and asked why she wanted to take it out. "I want to read it," she said, and then, collecting herself, added that she needed it for a paper that she was writing at Columbia, which, I am sorry to say, was not true. More recently my daughter was grilled at NCACC when she sought to learn about methane gas, which the librarian supposed to be a cheap, homemade substitute for mescaline. Folklore, which in this case I easily believe, tells that when Charles I was in Oxford during the Civil War, Bodley's Librarian refused to let him take a book out overnight. The regulations were perfectly clear: they mentioned no exceptions for royalty or anyone else, and a library of prestige cannot illegitimately cater to every insomniac monarch who merely wishes to read himself to sleep.

Higher still, a real librarian, as opposed to a check-out clerk, is expected to write and publish now and then something of a scholarly nature, and that cuts into his free time. Thus, Mr. Mack has made a complete collection of first editions of the extensive works of John (*Thirty-nine Steps*) Buchan and produced, for his master's degree, the first bibliography of Buchan to be compiled. He has written (1966) a biography of Matthew Flinders, the explorer who first circumnavigated Australia, and effected (1957) a then complete bibliography of the work of the late Professor Gipson. Such production is comparatively easy for a librarian, of course, since he is always in the library anyway, but even so it calls for a certain amount of effort and deserves its word of praise.

> *But the Librarian lives and dies unknown to Fame. . . . He lives protected, avaricious neither of Money nor of Worldly Fame, and happy in the goodliest of all Occupations—the pursuit of Wisdom.*

I should add that bibliography is no joke, calling for rather more than simply describing a book as published by Ticknor in 1868. It is a profound mystery with a jargon and symbolism as farfetched as the Vedas or Boolean algebra. This is not the place to dilate upon it; I say only that if you rise so far through its levels as, for example, William B. Todd, Ph.D. '49, you approach the vertiginous height of being intelligible to only the handful of your peers on earth.

> *Your Books obtain'd, behold the Problem rise*
> *How best secure them from unworthy eyes;*

Though it is no longer the issue that it once was, librarians sometimes still must exercise vigilance over what they purchase and what they lend, as we see from parental protests over the availability of *Naked Lunch* to fourth graders. Some are still alive—though they are a prey to riper years—who were around when *Huckleberry Finn* was deemed a pernicious work, unfit for the perusal of any reader. On the whole, though, the modern librarian lets his readers' morals take their own chances. When *Memoirs of Hecate County* enjoyed a mild *succès de scandale* a few decades ago and was kept from our freshmen, Mr. Mack let me read it after only brief hesitation; and later, when I sought the first Kinsey Report, for purely sociological reasons, he released it to me after learning that I was in my forties.

But I was intending to touch on the rare books, the care of which is Mr. Mack's present concern. Lehigh has 7,000 of them—a small assemblage by some standards, but if you had to move them by hand you would think you were transferring the Bibliothèque Nationale. Our collection goes back to the establishment of the library a hundred years ago; in the last two decades of the nineteenth century we had (somehow) a goodish amount of money available for purchases, and a fortunate thing, too, considering what book prices have been up to since then. Thus we have all four of the Shakespeare folios, which reminds me that the Bodleian, when the Third Folio appeared in 1663 sold off its copy of the First as obviously superseded; many years later, coming to its senses, it had to replace the discarded volume to the tune of $15,000—which today would be a yard sale figure. We have the Audubon *Birds of America,* that series of double-elephant folios (39" x 26") so massive that only a man in the fullness of his strength can lift one of them, the reason being that Audubon's birds are pictured lifesize and you need a lot of room for the turkey. Miss Lucy Osborne of the Chapin Library used to give thanks, she once told me, that the ostrich was not an American bird.

Must you have a look at Gilbert's *De Magnete* (1600), and are your hands clean? Mr. Mack can help you to it. Or Holinshed's *Chronicles* (1577), a compilation that made Shakespeare's career possible? Or Hakluyt's *Voyages* (1589), to which William B. White, Ph.D. '55, owes his doctorate? These are not books to be found at your neighborhood drugstore, nor yet in paperback at the Lehigh bookstore.

The Lehigh collection was strikingly enhanced in 1955 by the acquisition of the valuable Honeyman Collection, gift of Robert B. Honeyman (B.S. '20, L.H.D. '59) and Mrs. Honeyman, and it is among its treasures that Mr. Mack spends his days.

So what makes a book rare? Not simply rarity. My copy of *Uncle Wiggily and Baby Bunty,* inscribed particularly to me by Howard

R. Garis himself at Wanamaker's in 1918, is not merely rare but unique. Yet Mr. Mack would have no place for it. On the other hand, T.L. Peacock's *Letters to Edward Hookham* for example (1910), which I bought at an auction in Hecktown for 75 cents, would presumably be acceptable if the collection did not already have its own copy.[3] I don't know what makes a book rare except that a bibliophile will pay a lot of money for it and is jealous if someone else beats him to it. It doesn't have to be readable, nor even legible, though it may be both. Mere age may be unimportant, as many folks with "old Bibles" have discovered. But do you remember Art Buchwald's story of the poor man who, though he had a Gutenberg Bible in the family, didn't want to sell it? "You wouldn't want it," he said. "It's in lousy shape. Some guy named Martin Luther scribbled all over it." Mr. Mack would take that copy if it turned up, scribbled or not. But I think that in the end a rare book is one that you find in a rare book collection.

Why does Lehigh want 7,000 rare books anyway, to the point of commissioning Mr. Mack to curate them? The real reason is seldom admitted: a respectable university library is *supposed* to have a treasure room, just because. Next, it makes you feel good to know you have them even if you never read them, like knowing that you own the Orloff ruby even if you never dare take it out of the bank. And just possibly you are offering a priceless service to scholarship, for there are students, especially burgeoning textual critics, who *need* to see, for example, the 1623 Shakespeare folio; the Penguin editions, handy as they are, simply will not do if you are developing a theory of Shakespeare's punctuation. That is why the University of Texas, in spite of being in Texas, is a Holy Land for scholars: Its oil wells have ruthlessly combed the collections of Europe to a fare-thee-well, if I may mix a metaphor. Finally it may be now and then that someone wants to *read* Jamblichus's *De Mysteriis*, not just look at

[3]Well, it *did* have its own copy but some time since 1950 thrust it out onto the open shelves. Pure spite, probably.

the watermarks, and if he lives in Bethlehem he will not have to go to New York or Washington to do it.

> *I am so be-pestered and bothered by persons insinuating themselves into the Library to get Books that frequently I am near to my Wit's end. There have been days when I was scarce able to read for two Hours consecutive without some Donkey breaking in upon my Peace.*

The rare books are located at the east end of the library on the second floor and may be reached by elevator if you have a respiratory problem. Most are austerely housed in a large room with protective cases, a vault, and all that; the Honeyman Collection, more *gemuetlich,* in its own apartments with "Honeyman Collection" on the door and comfortable chairs within. Hours are nine to four on the five important days of the week; Saturday by prearrangement. Undergraduates should note this schedule with possible reference to the fall of 1977, when their visiting parents might find the collection as stimulating to visit as the snack bar or the heating plant. Mr. Mack was prepared on October 30 to extend hospitality to our visitors, but as it turned out spent the entire morning in undisturbed meditation.

> *Keep your Books behind stout Gratings, and in no wise let any Person come at them to take them from the Shelf except yourself.*

Not that Mr. Mack functions merely as a presence. His charge is "to maintain, preserve, improve, and promote the use and growth of the Rare Book Collections of Lehigh University." Its specifications enjoin him to house and preserve,[4] to promote interest, to correspond, to purchase, and to sell, to arrange exhibits and to budget, and—it isn't stated, but I can safely assume it—to write reports for the provost's office. In his redundant hours he may work upon, nay, *is* working upon, a centennial brochure describing the

[4]For years the preservation has been instrumentally in the hands of junior members of Professor Tom Haynes's family.

collection and its history.

Since the collection is not a closed-end operation, Mr. Mack would be happy to see it grow not merely better known but larger. How he plans to go about this augmentation I do not know. But if you have an unquestionable treasure at home—yes, Martin Luther's copy of the Gutenberg Bible, an Ovid stained with Marlowe's blood, *Love's Labour's Won* (in any condition), or a Malory with King Arthur's annotations—Mr. Mack will be very much pleased to hear from you.

> *I have not found Wives to be altogether a too heavy Encumbrance. They can dust Books, and at times, they may be trusted to arrange the volumes properly in their places. Beyond this, it would perchance, be rash to go with them.*

Mr. Mack, by the way, lives a quiet life in a charming, secluded home by the Lehigh and New England Railroad right of way in the Santee Mill area. He is married, and I have never seen Mrs. Mack in the library.

I hope that these scattered notes may help to make the Rare Book Collection a variable mecca both for visitors to the Lehigh campus and for its denizens. On the next parents' weekend I expect to hear of such pushing and shoving as the augmented staff will be hard put to cope with.

Pedagogical Payment

Reunion '79

The stipend arising hence would hardly have indulged the schoolmaster in the luxuries of life, had he not added to this office, those of clerk and barber, and had not Mr. Allworthy added to the whole an annuity of ten pound.

—*Tom Jones, II, 3*

Something over a year ago the FCC, or Faculty Compensation Committee, held its first meeting, a prelude to continual and ongoing activity whose concern is, as the name suggests, faculty compensation. It is impossible at this date to issue more than an interim report, if that, for the situation is, in the fine word of Chairman Joseph A. Dowling (History), fluid; and that solidity of accomplishment that the faculty eagerly anticipates lies somewhere in the womb of time. What is possible, however, is to acknowledge the existence and labor of the committee and to pinpoint a couple of its problems; but especially to give the background of the question a quick scan while hoping not to neglect any essential consideration.

Virtually detached and disinterested in my retirement, I am not holding a towel for anyone. I want everyone to win and be happy.

* * *

First, the historical tradition, and I ask you to forget Lehigh for a while and to take a world view. The paradigmatic pedagogue[1] has always been seen as idealistic (or simple), impractical, absent-

Dwelling which may typify faculty homes of the future (top). Maddened by debt, Prof. Webster is driven to crime (above).

[1]*Pedagogue* originally meant one who leads children. It still does.

minded, and broke. Like so many other stereotypes, this one is sometimes true and sometimes not, but also, like most of them in this, it has a factual basis. The immemorial neurosis of the teaching profession derives from the dichotomous belief that education is fearfully important but that it isn't worth paying much for.

I don't know when it all started, but a long time ago. At least as far back as Lascaux (101,979 B.C., more or less). No one can prove it, but I feel perfectly safe in saying that the teachers of those days were the high-minded and frequently disparaged ne'er-do-wells who encouraged the brighter children to waste their time lousing up the caves with painted reindeer, saber-toothed tigers, and the like, while the jocks were learning to do things that mattered: chipping ax heads, exterminating the wisents in the neighborhood, concussing each other.

Piling up 104 millennia of evidence, like *The Golden Bough*, would be superfluous in this concise publication; a spot check is good enough. In Greece "schoolmasters held a humble situation," says the *Oxford Companion*, and things were no better in Rome where "the teachers were often slaves or freedmen." It's true that Vespasian tried to do something about it and endowed a handful of state professorships with stipends of 100,000 sesterces. That sounds like a cornucopia, but who knows what a sesterce would buy you in the First Century? My own estimate is that 100,000 s. today would fetch you about $65 a week. And mind you, that was for the top of the profession.

The situation in the Middle Ages is pretty well summed up by Chaucer in his portrait of the Clerk, of whom we remember chiefly that he was undernourished, shabbily attired, and penniless. And like an idiot, if he succeeded now and then in cadging some money from his friends, he went out and bought books with it.[2]

In almost modern times it was the same old story. Some of us think of Harvard as of Eldorado. Not so in 1849, when Professor

[2]If you think books are expensive now, be glad you didn't live in the fourteenth century.

John W. Webster (Chemistry), unable to maintain his family—a wife and three children—on $1,200 a year,[3] fell into debt to Dr. Parkman, was badgered again and again for repayment, and eventually sought to disembarrass himself by mortally bludgeoning his creditor in the chem lab and subsequently taking him apart for convenience in disposal.

A mere 84 years later when I myself first undertook to instruct the young, the preparatory school that employed me paid me $500.[4] I got room and board and laundry too, to be sure, but the laundry shrunk the hell out of all my good wool socks. When the headmaster let me go at the end of the year, he told me that if he had been able to re-engage me he would have substantially augmented my stipend.[5] So I suppose that I made good in a sense; and indeed the next school I went to paid $900. Laundry was not included, but I had a washbasin with hot and cold running water right in my own room.

These casual references will support the contention that the teaching profession through the ages has not been cosseted and that if its members sometimes wish that they too could be traded to the Phillies, their restiveness is intelligible.

Anyone that thinks the answer is easy should ponder carefully the following in-depth analysis.

1. Any teacher and the authority that employs him are by definition in an adversary situation, like parents and children, man and wife, or a pet lover and his destructive cat. This may be lived out quite amiably and often is; but it often is not, as any TV news program out of Philadelphia will show. Human nature and the price of food being what they are, every teacher wants to be in the 50 percent tax bracket, and every frugal administration wants to

[3]In 1938-41 E.N. Dilworth and I were getting $1,800 at Carnegie. You just can't stop inflation.

[4]Two round-trips from New York to this anonymous institution cost me about $190 that year.

[5]Big deal!

pay him in clamshells.

2. Plain, ordinary jealousy.[6] If it is known that the Folk Dancing department averages $300 per year more than the Division of Ceramics, there will be muttering and dissatisfaction among the potters. Or listen to an indignant correspondent in *The Pennsylvania Professor* (March 1979): "The faculty members at the state colleges are paid more than the faculty at the state universities as well as at the private universities in the Commonwealth. Furthermore, these state college faculty are not so well qualified as their counterparts at other schools." And so on.

3. From both faculties and administrations the verbiage of idealistic commitment rises continually to heaven like the smoke of morning sacrifice. But whatever may have been true in Chaucer's time, today they both—and quite rightly—have as lively an awareness of money as Harpagon. One of the sharpest bargainers I ever knew was a sociologist whose classes were ruthlessly inoculated against the materialistic values that had made this country into, as he put it, a spiritual wasteland.

4. We teachers are all nice people, and probably some deans are too,[7] but not one of us is as precious as he thinks he is. And when the time comes for us to look into St. Paul's mirror, we are all going to be embarrassed. This enhanced self-regard of ours is necessary to our mental stability. Perhaps no one in, for example, the Lehigh English department thinks he is the equal of Aristotle or even of George Lyman Kittredge, but he knows perfectly well that he has greater stature than his salary says he does.

5. Though almost any little tantrum results in litigation today, the profession is still immune, so far as I know, from malpractice suits. Should it be? If my hopeful son, in anticipation

[6]Formal education, no matter how long continued, does not seem to immunize the average human being against Anger, Sloth, Gluttony, Lechery, Envy, Covetousness, or Pride. And see I Cor., xiii, 2.

[7]I once heard Dr. Harvey Neville define an assistant dean as a mouse learning how to become a rat. Just in fun, I imagine.

the prop and comfort of my sunset years, a clean, conscientious youngster, loving his country and honoring the Church, an Eagle Scout—if he goes away to college and then $25,000 later comes home a Social-Democrat, a lycanthrope, and a guitar player—fit for nothing but HEW—perhaps his preceptors are as liable as the surgeon that a few years ago grafted a right thumb onto a left hand. Maybe there's as much slag in academic freedom as there is in the First Amendment.

6. Nobody ever has enough money. In the days when I housed my books in orange crates and furnished my little home with pieces that Grandfather had put out in the barn in 1905, I used to feel that I'd have it made if I could afford real bookcases some day and chairs that at least wouldn't disgrace a yard sale. I now enjoy these luxuries, but I see that I absolutely must have a Sheraton sideboard to make the place livable, and maybe a small Kirman for the living room. Everybody I know has had the same experience. To make it worse, whatever we can't afford today will cost twice as much next month. Now retired, I console my still active colleagues by reminding them that the Social Security bite they suffer from helps to keep me in cold comfort.[8] Anyway, the point is that no adjustment to pacify the pangs of this morning is going to assuage the lusts of tomorrow.

7. Faculty folklore assumes that trustees can generate money thaumaturgically, like the Federal Reserve, and that any fiscal bind a college finds itself in is in some way the fault of the board—hidebound reactionaries to a man, seeing their faculty not as a nest of singing birds to be cherished but as a labor pool to be kept submissive through malnutrition. I doubt it. I was a trustee once, one of three that ran a battery beer fund in the 797th AW Battalion, and that experience showed me that neither magic nor miserliness

[8]Food doesn't cost *me* much. Give me my wooden bowl full of dried peas, and a flask of homogenized yak's milk, and I can meditate for a full day. It's really the other fellow I'm thinking of.

is implied in the position nor much gratitude returned to it. We were not infrequently charged with sequestering monies to support revels of our own on the lee side of the dunes, though in these allegations was no word of truth;[9] we were simply husbanding the fund's far from limitless assets so that our comrades-in-arms could enjoy a real screamer on the last Saturday night of each month. *Mutatis mutandis*, I feel sure that most governing boards behave with similar integrity, doing the best they can with what they have.

8. A speculation. If through a series of unbelievable developments any given university achieved a state of equilibrium, it would stagnate as surely as it would if the instructional staff finally discovered the answers to everything and no longer had to teach, just to communicate. Plato might like it, and maybe St. Thomas More. Fortunately there is no danger of such stasis, and the presently competitive tension keeps the ruddy glow of health on every countenance, whether pedagogical or administrative.

Such considerations—and they by no means tell the whole story—show why a compensation policy is nothing that can be hammered out in a couple of rainy afternoons, no matter how much good will there is among the ivy. It is almost a comfort to be retired and on the sidelines with nothing to hope for nor fear. Though every *suranné* as a matter of course finds that shortly after his departure his sometime associates are enjoying largesse from which he himself is forever debarred.

* * *

Well, the FCC, as I was saying, was born early in 1978, and as I was also saying, it is still far too young to have achieved anything final. It's possible, though, to look at a few of the simpler specifications of its task.

[9]The trouble we got into in April 1944 was a tempest in a teacup. As the judge advocate himself said afterward, a firm reprimand would have been sufficient.

Most important, probably, FCC thinks it would be a good idea if the Lehigh faculty, according to rank and discipline, were supported on something like the level attained by 14 more or less "peer" outfits, including BU, Carnegie, Princeton, MIT, and Penn. It finds, though, that in 1977-78 we didn't shape up so good:

Average Compensation[10]

	Prof.	*Assoc. Prof.*	*Asst. Prof.*
Our Peers	34.5	24.5	19.0
Ourself	32.4	23.0	18.5

Now hear the FCC's objectives in the uninspired language of the original:

"A. To raise the average compensation of Lehigh faculty by field and by rank to the corresponding average compensation by field and by rank of an agreed-upon list of other reference universities;

"B. To[11] then, by periodic comparisons with the average compensation by field and by rank of those other reference universities and by necessary salary adjustments,[12] maintain the equality of Lehigh faculty average compensation by field and by rank with those other reference universities; and

"C. To maintain the principle of merit in salary administration."

Right on!

You will note that A and B are perfectly simple: All you have to do is find a lot of money somewhere. The present requirement is a mere $820,000 spread over three years. The FCC thinks that a

[10]Compensation means salary plus frills like rubber bands, departmental stationery, Social Security taxes, and suchlike.

[11-12]Look, to routinely split an infinitive now and then is harmless and may even be fun; but when the interrupter is 23 words long, it may be malignant.

good whack of it can be squoze out of the endowment and a lot more from a hike in tuition. The Trustees already think they know where they can find half a million.

But C is a real stinker. Perfectly justified, no doubt, but as touchy as Three Mile Island. A committee report alludes to "average" merit and "high" merit. Now it is pretty harrowing to be a department chairman anyway, but just wait till a new injunction requires you to tell some of your non-coms that their merit is only average. Incidentally, the committee makes no allowance for three other categories: less than average merit, no merit whatsoever, and less than no merit.[13] Perhaps the least meritorious member of the Lehigh faculty is of average merit, though in that case I don't know where the average comes from. If FCC and the administration, having opened this Pandora's box, can deal with the fallout, they can go right ahead and achieve a permanent settlement of ethnic hostilities in the Middle East.

Other dilemmas include summer school salaries, readjustments in retirement contributions and medical coverage, and I don't know what-all. A good deal of the relevant literature I have read is as unintelligible as form 1040, yet I am sure that its heart is in the right place and that an Arcadian future is in the works. Just what its shape will be remains a question.

Watch this space for news of developments.

[13]Like there was this here-unidentified scholar—*de mortuis*—at Nameless A&M. He used to inveigle female undergraduates into a janitor's closet to share with him the pint of Overholt without which he never was, while patting their fanny. How would you rate him?

Anyone For Tenure?

Fall '75

Commencement at Illinois Central College this year was not just another ceremony for Charles A. Wright, 37-year-old associate professor of German. Aware that his contract was not to be renewed, he came to the end of his employment even as he received an engraved plaque honoring him as teacher of the year. Professor Wright's feelings were—not unreasonably—ambivalent. "If [the plaque] had not come from my students, I might have been inclined to leave it on the podium," he is quoted as saying.

Why was this teacher—valuable in at least the eyes of the undergraduates—let out? Because fewer and fewer students were choosing to study German, a language that is soon to disappear from the curriculum of Illinois Central.

Professor Wright's dilemma dramatizes something of the problem of academic tenure—nothing could dramatize all of it. Was a rule at Illinois Central contravened or was Wright's dismissal on the level? Was Wright a less valuable member of the academic community than he was deemed by his students—to whom much of his career was necessarily a closed book? Should Illinois Central continue to employ a professor of German after it ceases to offer any course in his field? Why is German falling off at Illinois Central? Is it partly because of undergraduate sentiment protesting the stringency of a language requirement? Did his own admirers contribute to Professor Wright's dismissal?

Eight hundred miles to the east we may be interested in Professor Wright if only because the tenure issue is alive at Lehigh as at most places. In *Lehigh Horizons* for November 1974 Dr. Albert C. Zettlemoyer, provost and vice president, discussed the tenure situation at some length. The *Brown and White* gets excited about it from time to time. The Forum's proper committee produced in

Armstrong lectures on dieting.

August 1974 over the signature of Professor Frank S. Hook of the English department a report that is required reading for anyone concerned with tenure at Lehigh. And it seems clear that the pressures of the future will keep this issue in a lively state, here as elsewhere, for some time to come.

The essence of the problem is fairly simple and would remain so if people would only let it alone, being the mutually comfortable adjustment between employer and employed. The chief specifications are that a university is supposed to operate in a purer, more idealistic air than, say, a steel mill; its faculty, though salaried, think of themselves as professional men, not as wage slaves; and the volume of production from year to year is more stable than at General Motors. A college wants a faculty—though Stephen Leacock thought a smoking room and a library far more important—the best faculty that it can catch and hold on to. Faculty-oriented persons want to be employed by a college. Stability is preferable to anxiety. Both college and teacher prefer a stable relationship to an unstable one. When a college has determined that Professor Sturdley is as desirable as it had always hoped, it is pleased to offer him "permanent employment," that is, a job till retirement age unless he disqualifies himself through losing his mind, exhibiting dangerous criminal tendencies, coming drunk to class, etc. Sturdley is now tenured and enjoys the additional advantage that although the college can only with the greatest difficulty get rid of him (should it wish to do), he can leave it at reasonable notice if he wishes to when that offer at last comes through from Hopkins or Michigan.

The angles on this simple matter, however, are so numerous that books could be and indeed have been written on them. If the files of the American Association of University Professors (AAUP) are stiff with hair-raising accounts of academic disharmony on the tenure level, the fault generally lies in human nature, so largely unamenable to the civilizing influence of even a liberal education and the bracing air of Academe. For if the ground rules at College X are plainly stated, understood, and adhered to by both Professor Y and the administration, there need be no particular difficulty for years at a time.

Yet tenure has had its ups and downs probably ever since education was institutionalized. I heard the other day that the first two presidents of Harvard were fired—presidents taught in those days—one for moral, the other for doctrinal reasons. Could either have been axed today? It is possible that Aristotle had personnel problems at the Lyceum. The important thing here, though, is that Lehigh today has a rational tenure policy, executes it equitably, and in recent years has suffered little worse than occasional sound and moderate fury. Sanctified by the approval of the AAUP, it works something like this: an assistant professor shall be promoted to associate professor and granted tenure after seven years in grade unless he is notified by the end of the sixth year that his next one-year appointment is terminal. Decision to terminate or to continue lies primarily with the tenured members of his own department, who send upstairs a recommendation that is normally accepted and confirmed there. The pattern varies somewhat from department to department—Music with three members and Religion Studies with four are in a different boat from Mathematics with members as far as the eye can reach. But it makes a demand in terms reasonably proportional to the length of a staff member's professional life, and any trouble it gets into is through human muddling, which no system is proof against.

In considering a junior colleague's fitness for tenure, his department is expected to take a hearty look at three areas, in two of which he should have performed creditably: teaching ability, scholarly production, and "service to Lehigh." The first is self-explanatory (in a sense); the second means publication of suitable, i.e., intellectually oriented, material produced *con amore*, for no compensation, and generally appearing three years late in a non-profit periodical; the third, any activity that calls this Lehigh-affiliated individual to public attention in a favorable or at least harmless way, as well as committee work—often a Herculean demand—and all other contributions to the intramural bloodstream.

It may sound easier than it is. The best judges of one's teaching ability are apt to be alumni at least ten years graduated, by which time they have learned, *inter alia*, the difference between instruction and entertainment, but when it is impossible to get them together for a vote and too late anyway. An unsolicited testimonial once informed a friend of mine that a course of his had been the writer's happiest and most valuable academic experience at Lehigh; another (unsigned) described the same course as a pure waste of time, a bore from beginning to end. So even those in the best position to know may not have a very useful opinion. "The selection and promotion of faculty," wrote J. K. Galbraith, no hidebound establishmentarian, "is a matter for careful, mature professional judgment. This is not for students. And it is vital that those making the judgment be required to live with their mistakes. . . . As Churchill said of democracy, selection of faculty members by their peers is the worst of all systems except for the alternatives."

Production seems as though it should be easier to judge, but it often isn't. The amount of bibliographical room it takes up is inconclusive: *Principia Mathematica* looms no larger in a listing than a letter to the Bethlehem *Globe-Times* protesting the textbooks adopted at Liberty High School. Worse, you will have to read your colleague's article to see what it's worth. But then? He has written, let us say, on the role of the Salvation Army in the French religious wars of the sixteenth century. But you, though an historian too, are a nineteenth-century American specialist, and all you know of the Salvation Army you learned from *Major Barbara*. What's your opinion worth?

Service to Lehigh is rather easier to evaluate, but it is also the least weighty of the three criteria. So it may seem almost a miracle that the worthy ever achieve tenure, or would so seem if it were not that continual contact with a candidate for five or six years allows a departmental opinion that proves at least as reliable as any other will do. And it may be added that we are not speaking of a popularity contest, for anyone who has been caught in the process remembers promotions that were supported in the face of personal antipathy.

Apart from the disturbance wrought by those who dislike anything that's already in existence, only two hostile charges today attract much attention against the tenure system. The first is not worth much; the second is more troublesome.

It is suggested—commonly by persons outside the profession—that once a man has achieved tenure he feels free to go to sleep for the next 25 or 30 years while his yellowing lecture notes grow brittle and disintegrate. Various proposals seek to counter this accusation, but at a good college it has little weight because *that* kind of man does not achieve tenure at all. If the members of his department in recommending his advancement after years of association do not know whether he is a person of integrity and dedication, they may themselves as well give up trying to form an opinion on any subject under the sun. Scrub that one out.

The other contention takes us back to the Midwest and to Professor Wright, who, you may recall, was being let out because there wasn't going to be anyone for him to teach German to. Put oversimply: the shifting tides of undergraduate demand—justified in this case—may very easily subject tenure to uncomfortable stresses. In an extravagant flight we may fancy a once vigorous department with four tenured members—three of them youngsters in their forties and thus far from retirement—to supervise one M.A. candidate, six majors, and altogether only 27 students of any kind at all. For, for some reason, the tidal shift has rolled down upon Accounting, where the congestion is so great that the cleaning ladies in Drown Hall have to proctor the quizzes.

The answer is to modify, reemphasize, and manipulate, so as to make any necessary readjustment as painless as possible. At Lehigh last spring the tenured faculty were something like 225 out of around 400; a high proportion, for in private universities 50 percent or a bit less is common. In a discrepancy of 14 to 20 percent there is room for maneuver without gratuitous injustice to any individual. The university presumably does not wish to multiply grievance by increased turnover in the lower (and less expensive) echelons, but even more presumably the last thing it wishes to do is to break faith. And though, like its peers, it is suffering from the frolicsome expansiveness of the sixties, at least it is in a better condition to pay for the party than some of them are.

The Lehigh administration does not wish to establish anything like a fixed ratio of tenured to nontenured staff and has said or done nothing to suggest that it ever will. At present, however, tenure is granted more slowly and deliberately, and this deceleration will continue for some time. It would be a valiant prophet who could say for how long.

If we wish to worry about anything, we can look out the window and worry about governmental intromission and about unionization.

It is hard to believe that our legislators, ever ready to exact compliance in areas—hiring, for instance—in which they have no particular knowledge and should have no authority, will keep their hands off tenure forever. If the present methods of awarding it appear unsatisfactory, just wait. Roughly, what external authority can do is to insist on and sometimes disastrously enforce statistical compliance with a chart symmetrically exhibiting sex, race, geographical origin, color of eyes, and so on. Pretty, but not the way to run a university.

Obvious adjustments having been made, the same can be said of union organization. This exists at present beneficently in the civilized behavior of the Lehigh chapter of AAUP, membership in which is voluntary. But there is no legal or historical reason why the AAUP—or some other—might not become bargaining agent for the Lehigh faculty. And there is no reason to suppose that the ultimate effect would not be degenerative—our own little contribution to the decay of American education.

We haven't reached that corner yet, though plenty of our contemporaries have. The longer we pursue our present course with common sense, the longer we can maintain the semblance of an academic community. When we have been converted into a light industry, it will be time to drop the term *university*.

Tenure is the decent right of teachers to live their lives and follow their calling with a reasonable degree of security, stability, and independence, they being the kind of men whom these conditions will not deteriorate. It is based on mutual respect and collaboration. It is in goodish working order at Lehigh, and we should take satisfaction that it is.

L-in-Life Kisses

Reunion, '78

The three most overused phrases of our time, said Harold Mohler '48, are as follows:

1. I just can't understand it; I know I mailed that check five days ago.
2. Of course I'll still have respect for you in the morning.
3. I'm from the federal government, and I'm here to help you.

Mohler, however, was not primarily concerned with social satire nor with hackneyed phrases as such; rather he was engaged in passing the L-in-Life cup to the newly chosen 1978 holder, Walter S. Holmes, Jr., '41.

The date was April 20, the location the Sky Club in New York, and the sponsorship that of the New York Lehigh Club. As for Holmes, chairman of the board and chief executive officer of C.I.T. Financial Corporation, he has been distinguished among Lehigh alumni almost from the day he joined them as a bachelor of science. Most recently he became an alumnus trustee in 1974 and a life trustee in 1977. He is chairman of the trustees' audit committee and a member of the finance and development committees.

He headed the Greater New York campaign of the first phase of Lehigh's New Century Fund development drive. He also is active in the Annual Giving Fund in the New York area, is a member of the university's Asa Packer Society, and was an alumni trustee and member of the board of the Alumni Association from 1973 to 1977.

From 1974 to 1977 Holmes was a member of the College of Business and Economics visiting committee; he is an honorary member of the Lehigh chapter of Beta Gamma Sigma, national business and economics honorary; the university has conferred

Eugene Grace '99

upon him the honorary degree of LL.D. It is perhaps unnecessary to add that in his spare time he has enjoyed an admirable business career since he began by joining Haskins & Sells after his graduation.

The L-in-Life award, established in 1939 and first presented to the late Eugene Grace 1899, annually honors an alumnus especially for outstanding service to the university.

Mohler's strictures on contemporary platitudes, then, were not so much diatribes against the inanities of our day as aspects of the eulogy that he addressed to his successor.

But the Mohler phase of the meeting was not the first. For one thing the emcee was Martin H. Pearl '54 of Brooklyn, president of the Lehigh Club of New York. Besides introducing the speakers, Pearl produced a splendid anecdote—new to me, anyway—unfortunately too long for retelling here. If you run into Pearl, though, ask him about the A&P's vice president in charge of prunes.

Samuel W. Croll, Jr., '48, president of the Lehigh Alumni

Association, spoke first. It was a pleasure, he said, to be here, and he added laudatory observations on the '77 football season, on Lehigh fund drives, and on associated matters. Lehigh people are wonderful, he concluded.

President Deming Lewis said that it was always a privilege to speak on this occasion. He touched warmly on his pleasure in a long association with Holmes in many various activities in support of the university's development. Holmes, the president pointed out, had sent two sons, Stephen '68 and Richard '71, to Lehigh despite the cost these days of a college education. If that isn't loyalty, Dr. Lewis implied, what is?

Now Mohler took over in a vein perhaps a trifle lighthearted for this generally austere ceremony. After praising the Lehigh Club for the excellence of its appointments and spreading more gold leaf on Holmes's career, he went to work on those undergraduate days when Holmes was in Business, not in Engineering, ignoring the antique assumption that Lehigh is an engineering school pure and simple. Let us remedy that old solecism, he suggested, and proceeded to endow Holmes with a bandanna and Casey Jones cap as symbols of his belatedly achieved status, an engineer indeed. Later, in presenting the L-in-Life bowl itself, he had not, he said, wished to pass it on empty; silver dollars and fruit and other things had been rejected as unsuitable for various reasons before the solution of a handy 25-pound bag of chocolate kisses. A magnificent gift, but Mohler works for some candy company, I believe, and was probably able to get it at a substantial discount.

Holmes in response said that it was a great night for the Holmes family. He summoned up various of the primitive conditions of college life in the prewar era—chapel attendance and other hardships—and noted that in the world of commerce, too, things have changed. Firms used to grant interviews to aspirants to employment, for instance; now it's the other way around. He himself went to Lehigh because his father told him to; but in today's more permissive climate his two sons had been given all the colleges in the country to choose from, he said, adding that if they happened to choose Lehigh he would pay their tuition. He reflected that despite Mohler's acid remarks, he himself had been an Engineer at the inception of things but that he had smartened up later and switched to Business. But no matter how widely things might change through the years, certain principles remained permanently fixed, most notably the need for a fund drive.

What might be called the meeting in its public aspect was provided by Dr. Harvey Picker, professor of international affairs at Columbia. As he surveyed the state of higher education in several other countries he concluded that it was continuing healthy in the United States but noted that it would stay that way only so long as a considerable segment of the educational community saw higher education as a privilege to be deserved: if the automatic diploma ever becomes universal, nothing but cultural disaster can follow.

Back then at the last to Holmes, he rose to a solemn finale: "Walt, may I end this evening with a word of caution? After hearing what has been said of you this evening, I offer it in the interest of Jean and your sons. It is: 'The surgeon general has found that praise is not injurious—if you don't inhale.'"

When the dust had settled, everyone felt that the cup was in good hands for the next year.

Reverend Signiors

Fall '76

Late almost any Thursday morning during the academic year, interested observers on the third floor of the University Center may note a dozen or more persons of riper years gathering in the salon at the west end of the faculty lounge. All of them wearing shoes, many neckties as well, they offer a striking contrast to the younger element pressing forward to the dining room. Quiet and deliberate, they finger the magazines on the center table and address each other in gentle, well-bred voices as they ask where Professor [Ralph] Van Arnam is, who the speaker is going to be—"I forgot to look at the list"—whether it's time to go in and sit down (for the grandfather's clock is generally fast) and say that every week it's harder to find a parking place. They are the Retired University Faculty club collecting for their weekly meeting.

* * *

During the first year of my retirement I was braced by various former students who remembered me without rancor and asked me either (a) how I liked retirement or (b) what I did with myself these days.

Such questions I answer in equivalent clichés, which are as true as most clichés are—that is, true. (a) I love it, and I wish I had reached it years ago; (b) the only problem is trying to remember how I ever found the room for full-time employment.

This is not an autobiography, and I mention these things because apparently they are standard practice among the emeritos, whom I am centrally concerned with. The unsurprising truth is that retirement has both its bad side and its good one; but granted

RUF members l. to r., seated: John Tremper, Ray Armstrong, Harvey Neville, Ralph Van Arnam, Cassius Curtis, Bob Billinger. Standing: Ernest Dilworth, Edward Cutler, Voris Latshaw, Albert De Neufville, Wilbur Spatz, J. Douglas Leith.

reasonable health, it's worth waiting for.

What's bad about it is, for one thing, its symbolism, too obvious to be dwelt upon. In addition a feeling like that of having irrevocably graduated from a beloved college; a reduction to a kind of second-class status, of not much understanding, perhaps of not even much caring, what's going on any more; of not being depended on for anything. And, at the end of the month, of not being paid.

Yet the rewards are great, especially for him who still haunts Academe. To see on the departmental bulletin board the notices of staff briefings that he will not attend; to learn that the last faculty meeting ran two and a half hours without concluding its business; to see the shining faces of innumerable undergraduates to whom he will never have to try to teach punctuation or accounts receivable or whatever it is that the engineers study, is like a blast of Benzedrine. Yet better still is the knowledge that if the weather report is sinister, he can stay home, for no eight o'clock class awaits him: the world's greatest happiness is lying in bed in the consciousness that sometime associates of his are writing assignments on a blackboard.

The university, moreover, is happy to enhance these amenities, nay, generous in enhancing them. Our bumper stickers still allow us to park if we can find the space. Our ID cards continue to admit us to the library and to the stands on the occasion of athletic contests, barring the *partie de futbol* vs. Lafayette. We may still enjoy without charge the cold roast beef sandwiches at the parents' luncheons and the hot filet at the faculty dinners.

Some of us, too, deeply appreciate the extension of office space. At present, for example, in the English department a spacious double room is occupied in a sense by Professors Severs, Strauch, Dilworth, and myself—though it may sound congested, no two of us are ever in there at the same time. To our advantage we can pick up mail and purchase $.10 coffee—for how much longer?[1]—and at the same time we are making a contribution in keeping the History department from expanding onto the fifth floor of Maginnes. It is heartwarming to retain a key to the old surroundings, even

[1]Not much, I find. Coffee advanced to $.15 on September 8.

though the teaching assistants no longer genuflect before speaking to us.

But I rove, as Burton says.

Among the several felicities of the retired state the RUF club, dramatized at the beginning of these notes, is outstandingly pleasant. As its name suggests, it is composed of retired university faculty members, as many as live within reasonable distance, are ambulatory, and are not fiercely individualistic. Since its founding in 1962 by the late Dean Wray Congdon it has provided a firm, yet almost invisible structure within which one may enjoy the continuity of the Lehigh association without the least feeling of pressure.

Nobody clearly remembers how Dean Congdon came to start it; he may not have been its onlie begetter, but no matter. From the beginning it was open to every retired faculty member, no matter what his departmental and political affiliations, and it took pains to extend each one a personal invitation, as it still does. Though under masculine domination at present, it is free of *geschlechtlich* chauvinism, and its gatherings will doubtless provide a more even mix in the near future. Its common pattern is to eat lunch at a long table in the Asa Packer Room each Thursday, and later to listen to an invited speaker who has something to say in the informal setting of the *east* end of the faculty lounge. The whole operation requires two hours.

The RUF is a model of rational structure: it has no by-laws nor even a constitution; it gets along without officers, committees, subcommittees, and *ad hoc* committees; it has no bank account or annual audit; it has not yet passed a resolution advising Congress on anything, nor has it ever sent a delegate to a convention. Still, it manages somehow.

What it does have are dues and a responsible official. The former are three dollars per year. As for the latter: in earlier days the management changed annually, but in the spring of 1970 RUF was fortunate enough to enlist Professor Van Arnam (Astronomy), one of those unusual individuals who, because they are efficient, hard-working, and eternally patient, may be sure of unremunerated employment as long as they can endure it. Van Arnam, whose original notion of retirement was assuming work at Moravian and Muhlenberg, issues the invitations, he provides the speakers—no inconsiderable task—he takes the attendance, he keeps the books, and he collects the dues, which he faithfully stashes in a bureau drawer, often showing at the end of the fiscal year a surplus of three, four, or even five dollars.

The speakers are presumed to be willing and able to talk unoppressively on subjects of general interest. They may come from within the organization, from within the university, or from anywhere else. Since they receive no more honorarium than lunch, their variety and competence illustrate either the prestige of RUF or Professor Van Arnam's powers of persuasion. It is sometimes not too difficult to nail members of the faculty and the administration, but mayors, editors, Pennsylvania legislators, and college presidents from one end of the valley to the other are not at everyone's beck and call. And the pattern of events is not seamless; now and then we may enjoy a special treat with color slides displaying contemporary China or the Trenton and Princeton battlefields. Occasionally we do without a speaker at all, as when this year we traveled to both Muhlenberg and St. Francis de Sales to see what our colleagues are doing and to compare luncheon facilities.

Now it is time for a few statistics, to lend weight and respectability. Professor Van Arnam checks the roll at each meeting, as I was saying. He does not do this for any vital reason—no one is awarded a gold star for perfect attendance—but because decades of classroom experience are not lightly discarded. The complete figures since 1962 would be supererogatory even if recoverable, but the 1975-76 record may be briefly stated. Of the 21 on the roster, Professor Van Arnam himself, appropriately, was champion, having met 33 of the 35 dates. At the other extreme Miss Edith Seifert (sometime bursar), though paying her $3, attended no meeting at all. The average member came to 13.5 meetings, including that of January 8, 1976, one of those days so foul and icily perilous that merely opening the front door is to risk suicide; the speaker didn't make it, but nine dedicated members did.

Further interesting analysis shows that the 1975-76 group represent something like 623 years of service to Lehigh—a creative estimate, for some of the dates in the university catalog are simply ridiculous, and I preferred guessing at the right ones to bothering my friends by telephone.

It is not clear that RUF particularly appeals to persons of any particular academic background. Engineers on this campus are supposed to be more clubbable than others, but the 1975-76 group reveals four administrators—that is, considering Dr. Harvey Neville as a president rather than as a chemist—three physicists, two mathematicians, and two mechanics; while Accounting, English, Chemistry, Metallurgy, International Relations, History, Biology, German, Astronomy, and Geology contribute only one each. I see no significance whatever in this distribution.

* * *

My mother-in-law one time was planning to go to a 1900 class reunion at Bryn Mawr and sharing with me her amusement at some of the contingent scheduling. “On Friday we'll have lunch at Adela's in Paoli,” wrote the class secretary, “and I hope she won't have one of her spells. Louise wants us all to come to tea at her place in Ardmore on Saturday if she is on her feet again by the end of May.” Well, I have a spell every now and then, and *my* feet aren't all they used to be. What lies ahead for RUF, or, as I prefer to call it, the Golden Age Association? Who else will join our ranks? Are there any untouched speakers left in the valley? Can Professor Van Arnam hold the line at $3? Only time will tell.

My title in this issue, as most of you are aware, comes from *Othello*, I, iii, 76. When you're checking on it, why not read the rest of the play, too? It's not bad.

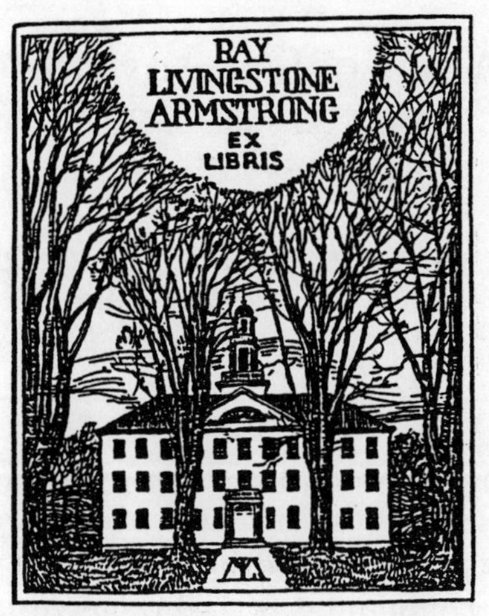

Little Victims

Why English Anyway?

Musings on a life of letters

Winter, '85

> *I have been in the scholastic profession long enough to know that nobody enters it unless he has some very good reason which he is anxious to conceal. — Evelyn Waugh*

"And what do you want to be when you grow up?" I asked the fifth-former, who was an inch and a half taller than I was. His name was Frederick "Ted" Lanyon, we had just finished a tutorial, and we were both in the community of Uxbridge Academy. "I don't know," said Ted. "How did *you find out*?" For all my 23-year-old maturity, this was a new question, and when I fretted it out later in the day I found it unanswerable. You go along quietly minding your own business, and the next thing you know, you're teaching English in a boarding school and eating hash three times a week. In the end I had to conclude that English had some way *happened* to me. If I had ever entertained any intelligible future for myself, I had wanted to be a banker so that I would have a cutaway to wear at my daughter's wedding. But I did not at the time have a daughter, nor even a wife. A classmate wrote me that there was an opening at Uxbridge that fall, and he knew that I could read and write.[1]

Years later I started putting Ted's question to my elders and my contemporaries. Some would not be pinned down. They told me in effect to shut up and mind my own business.

Others were motivated by mathematical incompetence. I

[1]In this way major decisions are generally made. You meet your future wife because she is behind you in the line at the A&P, and you find that her dog likes Alpo just as yours does.

guess that was part of my reason, after all. My mother saved all the report cards ever issued to me in grade school; every one of them read "deficient in Arithmetic." But I was a formidable competitor in a spelling bee.

Yet other colleagues said that it was because they had always liked to read and sought a milieu in which they could read all the time. This was rationally valid, but they had not realized that much of their reading would be written by undergraduates.

Nobody I can remember spoke of a spiritual commitment; not one of them bore a banner with a strange device up into the Alps till he froze to death or even contracted a head cold. Any friends of mine would have been indoors down at the Gasthaus, drinking kirsch and playing Scrabble.

If Ted and I were still at Uxbridge, he might urge me more urgently.

Q. What *is* English anyway, Mr. Armstrong, sir?

A. It is a wide-ranging vineyard wherein we find many mansions, including mixed metaphors, spelling, elementary grammar, authors' names, book titles, psychical development, business letters, the history of the motion picture, world classics in a dozen non-English languages, drama and stagecraft, the use of the dictionary, ballad singing, the Old English language, the Middle English language, Gothic (generally an elective), folk-dancing, and the family tree of the Plantagenets.

Spelling. This is the essential element, the beginning of wisdom. Anyone that can spell can generally get by. But woe to him that, applying for a Lehigh appointment, opens his pitch by addressing Dear Profesor Hook; better that a millstone were hanged about his neck. And what are we to say of a continuing education program—it's out in the Midwest somewhere—reported recently by the *New Yorker:*

Engl. 102 Spelling Imporvement
T 6:30-8:30 P.M.
Engl. 102 Spelling Imporvement
Th 6:30-8:30 P.M.
Engl. 103 English Grammer
TTh 6:30-8:30 P.M.

Authors and titles. A long-ago and brief contemporary of mine, Ellison, could never keep these straight. You probably know the kind of thing: *Tess of the Baskervilles, The Hound of the D'Urbervilles, The Native's Return, The Return of the Native.* Who "authored" "Young Goodman Brown," John Greenleaf Whitman or Walt Whittier? Or am I thinking of "Young Widder Brown"? *Caesar and Cleopatra* and *Antony and Cleopatra* were far too much for Ellison because both playwrights began to spell their surnames SHA-. The end came for him when he found that *Henry IV* was by both Shakespeare and

Pirandello. He quit teaching and went into real estate, where I believe he has been very successful.

Psychical Development. Goethe used to "fall in love" with girls on purpose: He wanted to enhance his own ennoblement, which is all that most of us need to know about Goethe. Some people want to read *Paradise Lost, Prometheus Unbound, Tristram Shandy,* and *The Rape of the Lock* so that they may become better people and more beautiful souls. They do not succeed in this. But they might succeed if they read with a better motive, looking for pleasure or even joy.

Use of the dictionary. A dictionary is a work not thrown together to catch the Christmas market. The Oxford took fifty years to produce, and it will never be finished. The dictionary that your parents gave you when you graduated from Secaucus High, the one you put your coffee cup on, didn't take that long, but it took long enough, and it has lots of useful words in it, most of which you don't know. Undergraduates seldom open their dictionaries.[2] It is easier for them to feel offended because a writer has employed diction that strays outside the 800 words that they came to college with and will die with.

Old English is a real heller of a mess. For one thing there were too many kinds of Angles, Saxons, and Jutes, Magesaetas, Hwiccas, and Meonwaras, and the Lord knows whatall, all speaking it differently. Worse, it represents a repulsive transition between a more orderly antiquity and a more orderly posterity, like a little boy whose voice is breaking. Just to show you, it not only declines its adjectives—a piece of damfoolishness in the first place—but it declines them in two different ways, if that gives you an idea. The study of Old English goes a long way to explain the Norman Conquest. As for the Plantagenets, English wouldn't be the same without them.

[2]"Yeah, but I don't want to write all this flowery language." Nor should you nor does anyone want you to. "I fell down the stairs last night." That is braw, masculine English unimprovable; nothing flowery about it at all.

They account for 25 percent of Shakespeare's dramatic work alone. So much for the content of "English."

Q. Has your profession, Mr. Armstrong, brought you into contact with many interesting instructors and colleagues?

A. Oh, I don't know. There was this colleague at Nameless Tech who was rather a gay blade or wanted to be thought so. He used to meet an 8:00 A.M. class clad in white tie after a night of upper-class revelry. Or at least that's the impression he wanted to give. It was disillusioning to learn that in fact he had arisen at 6:30 as usual and donned formal clothing in an effort to seem the man about town that he was not. He even tugged his tie a little to one side and smudged it with a grubby finger.

More to the point was A. J. Carlyle at Oxford, who briefly tutored me in 1930: a white-haired, ruddy-faced elderly gentleman. I once read him a paper conscientiously lauding some prose work of Milton's, during which exercise a lovely smile rose and spread over his face. "Oh, my dear fellow, bosh!" he said, and showed me that Milton was generally no great shakes as a prose writer. This did me a world of good, and since that day I have always tried to clear my mind of cant, to use Johnson's phrase.

W.W. Lawrence (*Beowulf*) seldom looked his class in the face but turned 90 degrees and stared out the window. F. B. Granville, still meeting classes in his mid-70s, could seldom get through a 50-minute period without stepping to the lavatory. R. G. Buehler, who frequently wore plus-fours as folks did in those days, seldom got them tightly fastened: Often one leg would slip down during the hour, and on a gala day, both legs did.

It is noteworthy that in the 20 years or so of my formal schooling, I never had to suffer under more than two real stinkers: a sullen, peroxided slob in 5B and a dyspeptic in the French department at college. Both long dead, and nothing in their life became them like the leaving it. My preceptors in English, at whatever level, were ladies and gentlemen whom I remember with nothing but affection and gratitude.

Q. Do you care to say anything about students?

A. Yes, indeed. The trouble with our work is not colleagues; it's disciples, who are capable of anything and capable of nothing. Powell McBain at Carnegie, the very first class he ever faced in his life, this girl fainted, and Mac had never even been a Boy Scout. Two students of mine have disturbed classes by suffering fits or seizures, but I was more troubled by another girl at Carnegie who had this pet praying mantis that rode around on her shoulder. I am not fond of the Insecta as a group, and to have this man-eater grating its teeth right in the front row—for Winnie's surname began with a B—was unnerving; whenever I looked at it, it was staring straight at me. Or take William W., alphabetically located at the back of the classroom, who confessed to me after two and a half months that he wasn't getting much out of the class because he was too far away, considering how deaf he was.

With one cheerful featherweight I spent a half hour or so disemboweling his last three papers. "A sentence must have a subject somewhere, Roulston. . . . Look up the spelling of unfamiliar, difficult words . . . this is a dangling modifier; look how it turns the whole sentence into an absurdity," and so on. He was very agreeable and receptive. "Well, now, Mr. Armstrong," he said finally, "what can I do to improve my writing?"

Sometimes students plagiarize. It is easy enough if the practitioner is dishonest and painstaking. But there was this lackwit who on one day of fearful joy presented me with the famous "Yes, Virginia, there is a Santa Claus" editorial from New York's old *Sun*, a composition almost as well known as the Gettysburg Address. He was just smart enough to rewrite the opener, knowing that Virginia was not my name, but otherwise he was perfectly faithful to his text.

Where do such people come from? Someone once addressed the Q and A column in the *Herald-Tribune* book section to ask whether any reader could help locate a poem that began

In Zanadu *[sic]* did Kubla Kahn *[sic]*
A stately pleasure dome decree.

Or the college aspirant of whose style I give a more than adequate specimen:

> The belief of Shakespeare's was that these evils which lay beneath the very culture of the Renaissance Period, where about to be taken to the surface in the following years and introduced in true realism to the people of the future, ethopian world. Whether Shakespeare had gained his ultimacy in this tragic realism or evil is a question which is still unanswerable even to our present day of wonder ideas.

Maybe nothing can be done for people like that, but in human charity (I suppose) someone ought to try.

Q. Is there any hope for the future of English studies?

A. Probably not. Yet English departments illustrate the virtue of Hope as few other enterprises do, except perhaps the publishers that peddle collections of freshman readings.[3] The basis of their activity is the belief that somewhere lies the Philosopher's Stone to make writers not only competent but ardent of an entire freshman class. Assistant professors also lust after greater achievement on higher levels, but they still feel that if they could lick the freshman

[3]Yet I wonder even about the publishers. You remember the way Roman dermatologists spoke of their patients? *Numquam moriuntur neque convalescunt. Absolutum'st.* "They never die and they never get well; it's perfect." Does a publisher of freshman texts ever think that way?

problem, the rest would follow.

I doubt it, because the freshman problem cannot be licked.

But some people never stop trying. There was this man Pauley—Joe Pauley—at Anonymous A&M. He had once read that Schartz-Metterklume story in Saki and had high hopes for learning by doing. Even when you fry an egg, he felt, you are not merely preparing for yourself a nourishing meal; more important than the mere *experience* is your *imaginative grasp* of the concept *"fried egg."* Extending the principle into the study of letters, Pauley reasoned that a student after some instruction from a blacksmith would not merely fashion a horseshoe; he would appreciate—*feel*—the poem of "Felix Randal" as he could not do without such experience, and if he suffered four terminal diseases at the same time, so much the (aesthetically) better.

Pauley was no bland visionary. He knew that many experiences could not be orchestrated—the Garden of Eden for a student of Milton, let's say, especially during the winter term at Michigan State. But he could produce Hell in conjunction with Dante, for the experience of human beings in afflicting each other is almost as long as Satan's: Force a student to listen to eight unbroken hours of TV broadcast, including "Another World," "Remington Steele," and "Happy Days," with selections of country-and-western music in between.

Well, then, Pauley would provide watery peril for readers of "The Wreck of the Hesperus," *In Hazard,* &c.[4] Members of a Poe seminar would be sent to Mauch Chunk for whitewater boating ("A Descent into the Maelstrom") or could listen to a talk on elementary cardiology ("The Tell-Tale Heart"). You see how it would work out. Clearly valuable but difficult to schedule in a normal academic week and inadmissible in certain contexts.

Pauley said there was no need to dramatize certain aspects

[4]Not too difficult. Professor Hartung, who paddles a coble on Lake Nockamixon, tells me that if you're caught in a squall off Stover Mill Road, you might as well be on the Grand Bank.

of Housman:

Oh I have been to Ludlow fair
And left my necktie God knows where,
And carried half way home or near,
Pints and quarts of Ludlow beer . . .
And down in lovely muck I've lain,
Happy till I woke again.

or certain other aspects of Shelley:

What are kisses whose fire clasps
The failing heart in languishment, or limb
Twined within limb? or the quick dying gasps
Of the life meeting, when the faint eyes swim
Thro' tears of a wide mist boundless and dim,
In one caress?

To any student seeking such goals as these, academic credit was felt to be irrelevant.

Then there was an innovator—I forget his name—that not only encouraged the appreciation of literature by telling his students to produce it—anyone can try that—but demanded that they should work *inside* the performance they were studying. Let us suppose that the lovers in "The Eve of St. Agnes" did not elope that awful January night; suppose that Madeline said, "Look, Porphyro, we won't get five miles in this weather; maybe we ought to wait and try it in April." Problem: Replace Keats's stanzas 37-41 with five stanzas of your own in which this switch in the scenario is harmonized with its context.

Q. What's the greatest difficulty for a student of English?

A. I can't answer for anyone but myself. For me English was a second language. At home we always spoke Latin—I heard hardly any English at all till I entered first grade. To this day I sometimes find that the words in their proper order to put difficult is, and if surprised or frightened I am more likely to cry "*Mehercule!*" than "Holy Moses!"

"But stay! [I speak the words of S. J. Perelman.] The orchestra is playing 'Good Night, Ladies' and already the police wagons are backing up to the rear entrance." Tomorrow will be another day.

Sometime neighbors in exclusive Bucks County, Armstrong and Perelman encountered each other at one of the Sundance concerts. Failing to distinguish between Rows D and E, Armstrong took Perelman's seat, from which he had to be courteously extruded. The two never met again.

Cletus

English Gives Him a Hard Time

Winter, '75

The antihero of this article is Cletus. He has no face and no surname. He entered Lehigh last September, and he writes even worse than his father did in 1946. His situation is distressing, for sending Cletus to college costs as much as building Buckingham Palace would have done 40 years ago, and his father figures that he's paying for as good an education as President Garfield got on the other end of the log; but he isn't getting it. Cletus isn't any stupider than his father; and except for being human, he is not perverse. Furthermore, his English class probably meets in a fine new building with wall-to-wall carpeting and a working elevator, and he cannot move about it without tripping over works of art. But he doesn't write any better than he would if the floors were bare and not a symbolic bedspring in sight.

The reasons are numerous and subtle, and books can be written on them; in fact books always are being written on them. Let us glance scantly at a few of them, remembering that not much of the trouble is truly Cletus's fault except for his healthy, normal aversion to work.

Nobody wants Cletus to become a fine writer; or rather the unavoidable composition courses he encounters at school or at Lehigh aren't and shouldn't be interested in trying to make him one. They can't. If anyone is to become a fine writer, he will become one, no matter what you do to discourage him: you might as well try to suppress Mozart's interest in music. You can encourage him and then get out of his way before he runs you over. But Cletus isn't going to write anything more elevated, perhaps, than a business letter. He will need to say what he means in language that his reader can understand and to say it without any such barbarism as his reader will find offensive. "Dear Profesor Harting," began a letter of application to the chairman of the English department. There are worse misdemeanors than misspelling, but that letter wasn't read. The discouraging thing is that Cletus is less and less able (or willing) to reach even this modest goal. "He has good ability," his father told me once, "only he finds it hard to do the flowery kind of writing they want in college." Flowery not at all. Something rather harder, economical, and astringent.

Cletus is not much interested in language for its own sake. Perhaps there is no great harm in that; not everyone can be interested in everything. But we all use language, while few of us play the French horn. And anyone can learn himself partway into a subject without following his heart there. This lack is too bad for Cletus, for if he had at least held hands with sound and structure, he would be a better writer. He has a good ear; born at the right time he would have had no trouble in distinguishing Teagarden on trombone. But he is at a loss with language: the sweet falling of the clauses makes no impression on him. He will sometimes repeat a darling phrase four times in seven lines till his reader would gladly escape into the artless reiterations of Dick and Jane. And challenged to improve such a passage, he sets to work in the worst way—against which he has been specifically warned—supplying what he hopes are synonyms. If some brief though effective exposure to poetry had ever touched him, he would have to attend to some of the possibilities in verbal rhythm. But he could never understand poetry, he says. For the predictable reasons: reading is work, and he didn't work at it; and he wouldn't look up the unfamiliar words.

Everybody has heard that easy writing makes hard reading, a statement as true as most apothegms are. For a normal human being, to write his best will be hard work as long as he lives and can hold a pen. Did he once think that when he grew up he'd know all the words in the dictionary and wouldn't ever have to open it again? Did he think that some day the knack would descend on him from

Professor Armstrong among his things.

Armstrong in meditation.

heaven and all he would have to do would be to let his pen run along by itself? Better he should learn to ride a unicycle on a tightrope.

Cletus writes better, he says, on a subject that interests him. He doesn't, actually, but he takes less time on his essay, which is just about as good (or poor) as his work usually is. Next week, however, he feels that elapsed time and quality must go together: "I spent four hours on that theme, and all I get is a lousy D." If he had spent 40 hours on it he would still have got a lousy D. Or should have, for, as we shall see, he may have the wrong instructor.

Grammatical ignorance. Cletus has profited from no instruction in grammar. It is needless for a linguistic analyst to spring up and point out that English is not Latin and that the day of the schoolmarm is over. Yes, yes, we know all that. The truth is that the structure of English is usefully demonstrable in grammatical terms: English has parts of speech and singular and plural and subjects and predicates, just like lots of other languages; and Cletus is at a disadvantage when his pedagogues discover that he doesn't know the jargon. He does not distinguish ACTIVE from PASSIVE: told to activate a passive verb, he changes its tense. Asked to subordinate, he reacts as if asked to hang by his thumbs; and a dangling modifier might be the riddle of the Sphinx. It isn't his fault. He has been cheated all along the way, and if Teacher wants to discourage, for example, REASON IS BECAUSE, Teacher must go as far back as Hengest and Horsa to show why and how.

Reading maketh a full man. Cletus has apparently read nothing, or at least nothing under such auspices as might have helped him to profit from doing so. Pressed, he will admit that yeah, they had to read some stuff at school; and pressed further, he may yield up a title or two. But since he cannot even recall the subject matter (nor sometimes the author), he has clearly not been influenced by the style and vocabulary. One of the three prerequisites to writing well, Ben Jonson said, is that one should "reade the best Authors," not because he is going to copy them but because they enter him into a region where using language effectively is a way of life, the climate of the neighborhood. Television, by the way, is probably not at fault. True, Cletus has wasted a great deal of time watching it—once a fan of "Sesame Street", he now prefers "The Avengers"—but any red-blooded American boy would have wasted that time anyway. Look at Tom Sawyer. Look at Studs Lonigan.

Pedagogical sentimentality. Aware that once upon a time

comparatively venial faults like the split infinitive were visited with great wrath, today's instructor wants to turn himself into a mother-figure for Cletus. Instead of chiding, he is likely to console, or try to. Aware that editing must include fault-finding, yet unwilling to break Cletus's spirit, he pats each solecism indulgently on the head while praising Cletus for having chosen a good subject—which anyone can do. Why should Cletus bother? Just as everyone in the Army used to be awarded the Good Conduct Medal as a matter of course, every freshman at Lehigh will be awarded a C merely for having been around. A partisan of progress can conclude nothing cheerful from the rise in the grade averages, for we approach a stage where C will acknowledge only minimum writing ability, D and F being reserved for imprisonment and death respectively. We hear that according to present indications almost every senior at Yale will graduate *cum laude* in another year or two.

Art is long. When the language requirement in the Arts College was under fire a couple of years ago, one objection seriously advanced against it was that many students found the study of language DIFFICULT. A cultural milestone as significant as the invention of movable type. The climate that Cletus has been living in has that kind of malaria floating around in it. "I always had a hard time with English," he tells his preceptor, who has been explaining the use of the apostrophe. Well, Cletus got through school and into Lehigh, while knowing how to use the apostrophe isn't much harder than telling left from right. Cletus could have mastered the apostrophe but nobody cared much whether he did or not, and assuredly he didn't. We see a compeer of his proclaimed on a barn down Route 412: "Birenbaum Farm's," clearly a building belonging to a man named Birenbaum Farm. Or (more alarmingly) in Connecticut: "Beware of the Dog's." (Or Watch Your Step.) What will such a one do when faced by an Absolute Expression?

"What can I do to improve?" asks Cletus in a rarely conscientious frame of mind. The simple answer is to stop doing all the things that you have been doing wrong for the past three months and that you have been told of again and again. But Cletus goes away sorrowing, because the price is high. Perhaps he will never reach the height of that administrator who brought joy into the Lehigh community once by announcing that the Flagpole ceremony would take place in Packard Auditorium IN LIEU OF RAIN. But he sometimes takes things for granite; the betrayed may find themselves in lurches; and he has no idea why the yearbook is called EPITOME, or rather he has an idea, but it is wrong—he would die sooner than look up a word. He could care less, he says, meaning that he could not care less and in a mood of high seriousness he may write, "This would be an investment in the purpose of knowing what the future holds to come." As "People's Democratic Republic" means vicious tyranny, so Cletus's language, more mildly, means something else. God is impassable, he says in another lofty flight; and called on the spelling, he revises to "God is impossible." Peace, peace, perturbed spirit.

There is no more constant activity in a college English department than the never-ending endeavor to find a magic formula for freshman composition. A radically different approach, a new book with pictures in it, the thumbscrew and the rack, longer periods, shorter periods, visual aids, hypnosis—whatever it is, someone has tried it without reversing the course of history.

But rather than develop further this depressing thesis let us be happy that there is a barn in Gilead, as Cletus would say if there were any Scripture in his background. The principal of a New York school, in commenting upon the plan book of one of his teachers, has expressed himself as follows: "Are all your childring receiving practice for MAT regardless of Math program in which the mig be involved." It will take Lehigh and Cletus several years to catch up with that.

The Warp of Language[1]

Spring, '80

Of the Armstrong Legend at Lehigh the aspect I am proudest of is that a surprisingly large number of my freshman students learned to write an English style muscular, yet flexible, reminiscent of Hazlitt's. Even today, in the fifth year of my retirement, folks come to call on me at Grendlesmere[2]—discouraged colleagues, grateful alumni, and so on—all with the same question. "How is it," they ask, "that a surprisingly large number of your freshman students learned to write an English style muscular, yet flexible, reminiscent of Hazlitt's?" This article is an attempt to provide a partial answer.

The whole story, of course, would fill 350 pages of the book that I am now[3] engaged in writing. And inevitably much of my success was due to charisma. But much more arose from certain sensitivity exercises of which I here describe two. In doing so—for my exposition is based principally upon live illustration—I have concealed the identity of the contributors and have now and then corrected their spelling and punctuation.

As far back as the first Roosevelt administration I was

[1]In the beginning this was a perfectly superb, tightly articulated essay of some 9,000 words and was intended for the previous issue of the *Bulletin.* Thanks to the parsimony of my editor, Mr. Ramsey, who fed me a lot of claptrap about the cost of paper, printing, postage, and so on, it was held up for three months and gutted into what you see here: a few whitening bones picked over by vultures.

[2]This, in case you have forgotten, is our country place in exclusive Bucks County. We gave it the name. Before we purchased it, it had been known as Sucker Pond for some reason.

[3]Erratum. It should read *not.* I am *not* engaged in writing a book about anything.

meeting things like this:

> . . . men have died from time to time, and worms have eaten them, but not for love.
>
> —*As You Like It,* IV, i, 110-112

"What does Rosalind mean when she says that?" I asked the Fourth Form at Asheville. "What it means," wrote one of them, "is people die and get buried and then worms come and eat their body not because the worms like to eat it but because the worms have to live."

Two features of that explication—with which I personally do not agree—struck me: the painful prolixity of the pauperized diction and, more forcefully, the enrichment it brought to my awareness of Shakespeare. That passage has never been the same to me since. And so I *felt* what previously I had only suspected, the prolific, multilevel depths of the English language.

Thanks to getting married, the war, and all that, for some years I had little time to develop a stylistic philosophy. But in the bracing atmosphere of postbellum Lehigh it came back to me through the vectorship of a freshman to whom English was a second language—second by about 15 lengths—and who told me that political economy was when a government ran the country as cheap as it could.[4]

This definition kept nagging at me all the more because I

have always welcomed anything that would distract me from what I am supposed to be doing. I rummaged around for a while and came up with "civil engineer," like that courteous engine-driver who once let me up into his cab while he was idling on the wye at North Bennington and told me what all the handles were for. And there was "standing committee," that fine flower of comitology that has no chairs in its meeting room and so gets through its work in no time at all instead of wasting three or four hours in the usual way.[5] And "bumper crop," a wheatsheaf on the front end of a car.

Worn out by these efforts, I turned over the study to my disciples, a few selections from whose (unidentified) work appear below. In the spirit of academic scholarship I take credit for their labor and ingenuity just as if they were my own. I should add that some of the items are rather sophisticated and will perhaps be merely puzzling to the alumnus who has forgotten his learning.

Cardinal Sin: Unrighteous behavior on the part of a prominent churchman. See *The Duchess of Malfi*, Burckhardt's *Renaissance in Italy passim,* and so forth.

Carnal Knowledge: Necessary to a butcher and useful to the alert housewife, who must understand what *brisket, plate, tenderloin,* and so on, mean.

Corporal Punishment: Retributive disciplinary measure imposed by the humblest grade of NCO. It doesn't technically amount to much, his authority being virtually negligible. But often effective when devious, as when Corporal X, finding himself alone in the orderly room, fiddles with the duty roster and the transfers. In this way many a refractory duty soldier has found himself Latrine Orderly for a whole week together or on his way to the Aleutians.

Ethical Drugs: These are placebos that you may purchase without offense at your friendly neighborhood pharmacy until some time next week when FDA will discover that they may or may

[4]No such government is known to history.

[5]"Standing Ovation" is when a hen lays an egg without sitting down first.

not cause nettlerash in gerbils. Opium, battery acid, and so forth, are *un*ethical drugs.

Familiar Spirit: While the average ghost merely stands at the foot of your bed and makes like an owl, this one gets right in with you between the sheets.

Mare Nostrum: Any medication employed by equine gynecologists. Maybe "gynecological hippiatrists" would be the preferable term.

Natural Child: Any child permissively reared; i.e., he (or she) is lazy, dirty, raucous, and ignorant. Most children are natural children to begin with, but fortunately some are compelled to wash, and shut up. In these last rests the hope, if any, for the future of civility.

Offensive Team: Broadly speaking, any team that opposes Lehigh. Specifically a squad that came here one time in the early fifties, still smarting because we had busted a winning season for them the year before. They bit, scratched, and spit in the pile-up, and many a Brown and White operative had his hair pulled after his helmet had been knocked off. And their language!

Pedestrian Literature: The *Pilgrim's Progress* is a good specimen. Or *In His Steps, The Six Proud Walkers,* and so forth.

Petty Officer: A naval term, but the Army is full of them, too. Captain E.G. Haney for one, vulgarly known as "Chicken Head." He once gave me a severe wigging because I had neglected to dust his souvenir paperweight from the Grand Canyon. He kept this thing on his desk and thought it was perfectly beautiful.

Public Relations: An X-rated phrase. If you have a Bible in the house, see II Samuel, xvi, 22.

Refractory Cement: Who needs it? Lay your sidewalk today, and in the morning it has surged up till it looks like a relief model of the Alps. It was used on Pawnee Street. What was wrong with the old-fashioned kind that stayed where you put it?

Servile Rebellion: I never understood this until I read that the chief purpose of Wat Tyler's revolt (1380) was to obtain a free pardon for having revolted. Risings conducted in a spirit of whining apology have small chance of success. Hence the failure of Tyler, of Spartacus, of the German peasants in the 16th century, and so on.

Social War: It is even more ceremonious than a civil war. In the latter, hostile sentries fraternize and compare photographs of their children. In a social war there is a daily armistice, and tea is served between the lines around 4:30.

Spoiled Priest: (A) St. Alphege, for example, martyred by the Danes in 1012, tediously bludgeoned to death with ox bones. (B) Any clergyman overwhelmingly pampered by his parish. See the Act I solo of Dr. Daly in *The Sorcerer.*

Terminal Disease: An infection picked up in Grand Central or 30th Street. I once caught impetigo from a pay phone in Long Island Station.

By this time it is obvious that such analysis deepens one's semantic experience of formerly bald, hackneyed phrasing.

Further enrichment was suggested to me when I read how S.J. Perelman punished an undersized pickpocket by dousing him in the water of Narragansett Bay, or, as he explained to his father, "taking a little dip in the ocean." Again I turned my volunteers loose on a linguistic project, and from the wealth of their production, I am selecting, as before, a few typical exercises.

1. In 1807 Zebulon M. Pike, the explorer, dissatisfied with his failure to achieve advancement in the Army, refused to explore anything at all for six months or so. This episode is familiar to historians as Pike's Pique.

8.[6] A man-at-arms, looking out from the battlements of Dunsinane, saw Birnam Wood advancing cross country and panicked. "Cheese it," he cried, "the copse!"

17. When the longtime and faithful caretaker at Niagara died at the age of 79, his funeral was attended by very few mourners. Moved by this circumstance, one of those present went home and composed the touching ballad "Just a Cortege Small by

[6]This nonconsecutive numbering is left over from the Ur-version of my essay. It shows you how much is lost.

a Waterfall."[7]

31. At the close of the day's interminable hearing, the defendant's lawyer hastily retired to his office, for he had little time to get into costume and makeup if he were to be punctually on hand for the dress rehearsal of the minstrel show at the Century Club. A bailiff glancing in did not recognize the helper who was applying burnt cork to the jurist's countenance. "Who is this," he mused, "that darkeneth counsel?"

38. Two staff members from the American consulate in Algiers were leaving the elaborate obsequies of a monarch who had ruled his country well and truly for over three decades. "They're going to miss him badly," said one. "Yes," rejoined his friend, "certainly a Dey to remember."

52. There was this musicologist engaged in writing the life of a well-known continental composer, and greatly painstaking, he was seeking out the scenes among which his subject, born a country boy, had spent his early days. But finding himself astray, he stopped a passing peasant to get directions. "You might as well go back up the hill," said the rustic, "there's no Haydn place down there."

54. An attractive girl employed by a physical culture institute died untimely and was buried on a bleak, windswept January afternoon. It was the pathos of the event that prompted Stephen Foster to compose "Masseuse in the Cold, Cold Ground."

60. After a long and brilliant diamond career, this outfielder retired and took a job with a picture magazine. Leaving the office one day during the rush hour, he was tripped up in the crowd and was unintentionally stepped on by the man behind him, who thus found himself treading *Life's* dark Mays.[8]

To the average freshman entering Lehigh in those days a

[7]Contributed by a student who after graduation became a mortician. You will recognize other offerings of his later on.

[8]A particularly subtle entry. See (if necessary) any hymnbook that includes "My Faith Looks up to Thee." Stanza 3.

word meant practically nothing. But if he took advantage of the opportunities that I made available to him, he came to know that a word could mean practically anything. My task, which I was trying to achieve, was by the power of the written word to make him hear, to make him feel—it was above all, to make him *see.* That—and no more, and it is everything.

Cymini Sectio

Reunion, '75

So long ago that many have forgotten it by now, there was the story of an American guest in a prosperous English country house way back in the days when English country houses were allowed to be prosperous.

"Will you have coffee, tea, or chocolate, sir?" asked the maid, as she courteously roused him on his first morning.

"Tea, please," said he, wanting coffee but determined to observe Anglican folkways.

"India, China, or Ceylon?" said the maid.

"India, please," he responded, still taking on local color.

"Do you prefer lemon, cream, or milk, sir?"

"Milk, please."

"Thank you, sir. Jersey, Alderney, or Guernsey?"

The moral of this story is that it is hard to tell how far to carry the intrinsically laudable wish for nice discrimination.

Accordingly the academic world since time beyond memory has struggled unsuccessfully in its attempts to evaluate the performance of its clientele. In other fields, like Applied Theology, decision has been easier: If a suspected witch floated on being thrown into a duck pond, she was guilty and could be burned; if she drowned, she was innocent. No problem. But Lehigh, like every other institution with a heart and a conscience, is still responsibly pursuing the *ignem fatuum* in several directions at the same time. The question, in plain, unvarnished words, is this: is the viable praxis of didascalic mensuration precisely attainable?

The university is at present convulsed—or *lulled* might be a closer word—as it ponders the alleged crudity of the hallowed ABCDF of the grading system and the alleged precision achievable if one adds pluses and minuses: a total of 12 grades in the place of five. (A+ does not exist, and F is absolute.)

The immediate question goes back at least as far as a blast on the ram's horn by Professor Robert Folk, B.S. in E.E. '53; B.S. in Phys. '54; M.S., '55 and Ph.D. '58, of the Physics department on February 19, 1974. Professor Folk was losing sleep, he said, because he must award the same grade (A) to two students whose numerical achievements were 99 and 77 percent; and well he might be. His restrained, gentle, and sedative proposal did not seek to impose the need for fastidious judgment upon the entire faculty; it sought only to allow it to those insomniacs who chose it.

It is hard to see why this temperate project has implied many persons in protracted meditation. On the face of it, it would seem to menace from only two quarters of the horizon. A student with an Old World preceptor might feel aggrieved at the award of only three points for a B when—had he only been assigned to a section across the hall—he might have reveled in 3.3 from some liberal. And it is bound to cause more trouble for the registrar, who has enough as it is. Yet since *registrar* is merely a synonym for *scapegoat*, this objection is negligible.

At all events, though little has so far happened supraliminally to Professor Folk's project during the last year, it has stimulated great activity in the shadows. Permitted speculatively during the current academic year by a faculty vote, it is said to be under study by a subcommittee of Educational Policy—which is to proclaim an open meeting in the near future. The Forum also has a committee pondering it; the registrar's office plans to generate some hard figures on it one of these days. The *Brown and White* has assumed a hostile stance toward it, bracketing it with Saturday classes as a work of darkness. And no doubt various underground groups and individuals are fretting over it.

Clearly, as Professor Folk handsomely recognized, some "disciplines" differ from other disciplines. To oversimplify, we consider a class in sixth-grade arithmetic: It offers an examination comprising 20 questions worth five points apiece; the instructor checks each paper against the answers in the back of his book, grades with confidence, and has a good night's sleep while Professor Folk is tossing on his pillow. On the other hand, take such a course as one recently proposed by Professor Frakes in the English department, "Anglo-Saxon as a Second Language." Run that one through your abacus. What shall it profit or unprofit a man if his idiom is chronically debased by Kenticisms?

For traditionally the humanities have employed different, nonmathematical evaluations, the forked hazel-twig rather than the minedetector. Many of our older instructors are familiar with

1. The "gradual." Leaning over the balustrade, the instructor determines standings as the blue books, class cards, and the like, that he drops come to rest on this or that step of the staircase below.

2. The "aleatory." The instructor rolls a pair of dice against each student's name as he goes through his book, snake-eyes being worth a straight A, and so on.

3. The "historical." Instructor X notes that Instructor Y gave the student a B last fall. Clearly, then, the student is worth another B if X and Y are on good terms; a C if they are not.

And so on. There are also advanced devices for finer tuning. Via the Lehigh Family convention, the student who has sent his instructor a Christmas or Easter card costing at least $.25 exclusive of postage will, if a borderline case, receive the higher grade. Some conservatives still rely for advice at least on "vatic" methods, observing the flight of birds and the condition of entrails. I myself closely scrutinize the windbreakers and T-shirts of my disciples: if they reveal affiliation with my own fraternal organization, they are worth one-half to a full grade to their wearers. Professor Glenn J. Christensen and I once collaborated in smoothing the way for Walter Trillhaase '53, whose skilled foot at that stage of the football season had not once failed to add P.A.T.

A stubborn faction holds that even five grades are too many and that four are enough. Certainly the Educational Testing Service demonstrated for years that persons of goodwill correlate satisfactorily in a four-way discrimination. Any instructor should be able to identify Class I: Superior; likely to graduate with honors and to spend much of his life at international congresses. Class II: A solid admirable student. Lacking the unstable brilliance of Class I, he would make an acceptable husband for your daughter. (Or, in the spirit of the times, spouse for your issue.) Class III: Only grudgingly acceptable, like the garage that you built of cinderblock because you were damned if you paid for porphyry at today's prices. If your daughter marries him, she will have run away from home first. Class IV: He should pay extra for being allowed to make use of the classroom.

But to continue, a 12-point scale might well, it is said, keep some pedagogues sleepless even though Professor Folk finds mandragora in it. What of the aspiring History major who confuses Charles the Fat, Charles the Bald, and Charles the Simple? How much credit does he deserve for placing them—correctly—in France? How much demerit for associating them—incorrectly—with Charles the Bold? No, no, it is urged. Such a one is an obvious C on the five-point scale and is II or III on the four-point, depending on whether or not he is overcut.

The Pass-Fail crowd are fast losing ground as their intellectual position grows more and more plainly untenable. As we know, Academe, like the bright lexington of Youth, will soon include no such word as *fail*; so *pass* becomes meaningless, a testimony to nothing.

In sum, then, the world of higher education has in the grading system a perennial, insoluble, fascinating challenge that will be imperfectly muddled in different ways by different practitioners. Let Professor Folk have his swink to him reserved, as Chaucer puts it; so long as he is willing to allow for the greater crudity of perception among his colleagues, we shall all remain friends.

Note: Mr. Ramsey has asked for an explanation of my title because he does not understand it. A cliché to Macaulay's schoolboy, it is perhaps obscure to the lewd reader—lewd does not mean what you think it does; it means uneducated— and so I render it as "the process of cutting cumin seeds in half." If it still is not clear, get a cumin seed and try to bisect it. . . . RLA.

Per Aspera

Spring, '77

I was reading Barbara Raub's article on financial aid to college students (Winter Issue), at the same time beset by college entrance problems in my own home. This conjunction summons up the entire complex issue of the exasperating, mind-boggling process whereby a sub-freshman anywhere becomes a freshman somewhere even though his parents are—not paupers; that would be easy—shabby-genteel. It seems clear that perverse orientation, irrelevance, and fruitless endeavor are the hallmarks of the total procedure. If some of these historical and exemplary reflections derive preponderantly from my own kith and kin, it is not because they are at all remarkable; rather they are typical, and they save me the trouble of doing any work.

I. Choosing a College. This was easy in 1700, when your choice lay between Harvard and William & Mary. Today it is no joke, at least if you take it as seriously as you are supposed to do. I have not counted the institutions listed in Cass & Birnbaum, *American Colleges*, from Abilene Christian to Youngstown State,[1] but they occupy 725 pages, so I suppose there are at least 1,500 if I conservatively reckon 2.07 per page. Some, no doubt, are easy to eliminate. The Jewish Theological Seminary is out of the question for many youngsters, and Webb Institute of Naval Architecture (87 men, 1 woman; Webb should be paradise to a girl who has a hard time getting dates)—I was starting to say that Webb, though free, is unsuitable unless you want to build tankers, battleships, and the like,

[1]It is curious that in a country this size nobody begins with Z. Why is there no Zangwill Secretarial? No Zion Evangelical? And by the way what happened to Bob Jones University, long my favorite? It used to be down in Nashville or thereabouts.

Wadham College.

as so few do. Still and all, there are a lot of places left, and Cass & Birnbaum make them all sound pretty attractive.

The conscientious candidate should no doubt make rational choices among the, let's say, 1,000 colleges left over after exclusion as above. He will weigh such considerations as instructional excellence, strength in his chosen field, topographical and architectural beauty, the library, athletic eminence, and so on, and he will arrange in order of preference the 25 academies that suit him best—an interminable chore.

Actually this seldom happens. It appears, rather, that human nature—in one case not even that—is in the ascendant over patient logic. There have been other procedures.

A. Mere Inadvertence.

1. A certain New Yorker headed for Lehigh, who never having been far west before and supposing Pennsylvania a

small place, carelessly got off the train in Easton, asked for "the college," and was deep in forms in the Lafayette Admissions office before he discovered his error. Embarrassment and natural shyness forbade him to extricate himself.[2]

2. (Name suppressed) Haverford '30, who during the summer was informally viewing various campuses to get the "feel" of them and reached the Merion Cricket Club by mistake. He selected his Alma Mater on that basis.

3. My father. Having attended a Methodist boarding school, he was headed for Wesleyan. Being downtown in Bennington one day he ill-advisedly used for a vital piece of correspondence the stationery of the Stark House—a now long-defunct hotel—because it was free and handy, I suppose. Wesleyan responded all right, but the answer came (naturally) to the Stark House and waited there for almost two years before Father got it. In the meantime, disillusioned with Methodists, he had gone to Hoosick Falls on some errand or other in September 1889 and there encountered an acquaintance named Sherwood, who, it appeared, was thinking of college, too. "I'm going to try Williams," said Sherwood, "Why don't we go together?" Two days later they took the Boston and Maine to Williamstown, and Wesleyan's loss was Father's gain.

B. Horse sense, literally. John Henry Newman's father was undetermined as to Oxford or Cambridge for his son till the very day of driving him to the university. At a crucial turning en route Mr. Newman gave the horse its head; the horse turned west rather than east. As Strachey points out, if the horse had turned otherwise there would have been no Oxford Movement.

C. Sibling (or other) hostility. My wife went to Wellesley

[2]Page 1 of the business section of the Sunday *Call-Chronicle* for February 6 publicized the careers of Scott Armstrong, Lehigh '60, and Larry Johnson, Lafayette '74. Armstrong, at the Wharton School in Philadelphia, is a distinguished moralist specializing in commercial casuistry. Johnson is in Arizona processing kitty litter.

because both of her sisters had gone to Bryn Mawr. Another contemporary of mine had wished to go to Smith, which accepted her, but wound up at Skidmore because of a classmate whom Smith had accepted as well. "I spent the last three years at school promising myself that after I graduated I'd never get within 100 miles of Celia again."[3]

D. Propinquity. Look at the trouble you save if your college is right across the street. Columbia is a splendid university, but I daresay I chose it for graduate work because though it was 12 miles from home, the subway ride cost only a nickel each way.

E. Imprinting. I was not so cloistered in my youth as to be unaware that there were in the United States other colleges than Williams. Indeed, thanks to Frank Merriwell and Dink Stover, I had a kind of romantic awareness of Yale, though, knowing I was no athlete, I realized that it was no more practical than my wish to drive a locomotive. I did not seriously suppose that there was anywhere actually to *enter* except Williams. I have heard similar accounts from graduates of other institutions.

F. Desperation. My daughter is attracted to almost every seminary in Cass & Birnbaum but cannot find one that satisfies all her aspirations and foibles. If it isn't too far south for skiing, it is too far north for camellias. At Maine Maritime she could not major in Harp, or prepare for the merchant marine at Carnegie-Mellon. It seems hopeless; and in the end (for at this writing the question is unsettled) she may have to open Cass & Birnbaum at random and take what she gets.

II. Entrance. Having blundered into a choice, a candidate is faced with application for admission. This once-simple affair becomes more intricate every year.

A. In 1889 Sherwood and my father arrived in Williamstown three days after the opening of the semester. Bearing documents to show that they had enjoyed secondary education, they went

[3]Saratoga to Northampton is about 135 miles if they haven't changed it.

directly to the president's house to offer themselves as freshmen to Dr. Franklin Carter. "I think there's an empty room somewhere," he said and personally conducted them to a dormitory where indeed there was a study full of broken and discarded furniture. "We'll have that taken out," said Dr. Carter, and two days later they were full-time members of '93.[4]

B. By the 1920s college entrance had become far more troublesome, though nothing like what it is today. I had to fill out one or two forms, explaining why I wanted a college education (a hard question) and how many cigars I smoked during an average day (an easy one), but I was never subjected to an aptitude test or to a College Board paper of any kind. I was certified. Is that possible any more? My preceptors, aware that I was remarkably able for a lad of 13, issued me with a four-year guarantee. I applied to only one college; I didn't want to go anywhere else. There was some confusion as to whether I had to supply my own mattress and if so in what size, but everything else went like a breeze.

C. Most ways the contemporary situation is no doubt too familiar to require description: with its limitless ambiguities and documents it dominates two years (per offspring) of a parent's life. But the most depressing feature of it—seldom openly recognized—is the brilliance of everyone else's children.

I have a goddaughter, on a full scholarship at Westminster, so tiresomely able that if she ever gets less than A+ in anything including field hockey she is reluctant to come home to dinner for

[4]The dignity of a college presidency has risen spectacularly since then. Some time ago at a nameless institution one found oneself in August the acting chairman of the English department, which at that season comprised oneself and one instructor. Faced with a policy decision of no mean order, one was so ingenuous as to cut the red tape and to address a memorandum to the president himself, bypassing heaven knows how many deans, feeling justified by one's significant (though temporary) status. For this impudent violation of protocol one received a very severe wigging; one might as well have asked the Pope to play the melodeon at a Salvation Army shelter.

very shame. Her mail (her mother tells me) is already crammed with solicitations from Vassar, Radcliffe, &c, though she will not be ready till the fall of 1978. And there is the son of a friend. In various nationwide ratings he had never scored out of the 1st or the 99th percentile—I forget which is the high one—and his big problem is whether to take a two-year whirl at Harvard first—just for a taste of the collegiate experience—or to go directly to the Institute for Advanced Studies. My daughter, I have been forced to conclude, is the only normal student I know—except in English, where she is subnormal—and what chance she has against this throng of Hypatias and Leonardos must be almost too small to take seriously. I need my long and happy acquaintance with generations of Lehigh freshmen to remind me that every now and then a mere incompetent slips through the net.

III. Securing Financial Aid. So you can get into college, but you can't afford it. Mrs. Raub made it clear in her article that oceans of scholarship money surge around the candidates whose families—or 98 percent of the parents in the country—cannot afford a college education at today's prices or think they can't or would just like to find out. She less emphatically observed that even getting your feet wet is a labor more Herculean than achieving admission. Every source that you investigate calls for time and trouble, the process being so cumbered with demands, caveats, exceptions, percentages, pure intrusiveness, and references to your last 10 IRS returns that it is a full-time job for whichever parent is not already ruining his eyesight over the admission forms.

A typical challenge is presented by PCS (Parents' Confidential Statement), one of the most popular traps and a form that must make the Internal Revenue itself blush for pure jealousy. All that can be said in its favor is that (unless you are a farmer) it does not send you into metaphysics. It does, however, require your tax figures for 1975, which are somewhere in the attic in a folder labeled "Press Clippings." If you own your own home you look like a Morgan partner, for your little $8,500 shanty is now valued for insurance purposes at $100,000. Do you have annuity income (as

I do)? Some of it is taxable, some of it isn't, and Leibnitz himself could not say which is which, especially because the liability varies every year till it all becomes taxable on the principle that as you become less affluent you should be taxed more heavily.

Broadly PCS encourages prodigality and other forms of fiscal irresponsibility. If you are not in debt now, hurry and borrow something before it's too late. The frugal and prudent are (as usual) the patsies. If that's what you are like, you will discover after hours of myopic research in the attic that you can easily afford unaided to educate your issue and to give him his own Thunderbird as well. If you have to spend the next four years on pasta (cheap, yet filling) PCS could not care less. And over all hangs a cloud of atavistic guilt. Like the upright citizen who quails, he knows not why, at the approach of a state trooper, the applicant, though his figures had been certified by Peat Marwick Mitchell & Co. is sure that some way, he knows not how, he has been dishonest.

Many colleges supplement PCS with nosy inquisitions of their own, some of them suitable for the Delphic oracle. How much money will the candidate earn next summer? How much do you allow for "extras," whatever they are? Who knows? I project a stage in which they will want to know the number of bathrooms in your house, and another when, like an adoption agency, they will visit you and poke about inspecting your sheets for tattle-tale gray and your glassware for Crystal Fatigue.

Such scholarship assistance as I enjoyed in the good old days when I was an undergraduate was based firmly on the knowledge that my father was a clergyman and, *ipso facto*, indigent.

That millions of adolescents enter college every fall is a splendid tribute to the American belief in education or to a parental resolution to get them out of the house *à tout prix*.[5] I have a long feeling, though, that the whole thing is going to collapse some day; and hearing recently of a new educational breakthrough insuring

[5]Cf. "Happy Days," ABC-TV. Once.

illiteracy in two languages instead of the traditional one, I am almost certain of it.

The World According to the Brown and White

According to Keats, autumn is a season of mists and mellow fruitfulness. Whether he would have put it that way if he had known Lehigh is matter for conjecture. Probably not, if I am any judge as I ponder the four months just past.

Here in Kintnersville where the world is quiet, I am often compared by my neighbors to the Lady of Shalott as I watch the westward-passing pageant of university life not directly but as reflected in the *Brown and White*, which, like her mirror, may soften the realities to the point where they don't too badly upset the viewer. It is that romantic and delicately tinted prospect of Lehigh in the fall of 1983 that I hope to share with you.

For a long time now the *Brown and White* has been my favorite newspaper, partly because it is the only one that I get free, partly because it is fraught with familiar names, but most of all because it keeps me in touch with an exciting wonderland twelve miles away from my safe-house, something like viewing a rerun of *The Wizard of Oz* in a sociology course. But unfortunately I see not a meiny of Sir Lancelots but something more like a detachment of the Dead Rabbits. A fraternity is alleged to have booted a decade of its membership from their chapter house: with brethren like that, who needs enemies? Representatives of Domino's Pizza, which delivers to the campus, have been picturesquely harassed: one spirited yahoo, for example, sought to relieve himself upon a Domino driver from a dormitory window. "University Holds Rape Lecture," I read (somewhat ambiguously) on page 4.

It makes me think of the *Police Gazette*, an unlamented periodical that some of us older boys remember. Printed on paper a horrid shade of pink, it devoted itself extensively to disreputable trivia of the same kind and was not admitted to well-conducted homes. I used to read it when I was getting a haircut. The *Gazette*

entered my home only once, not because I wanted to study the girls photographed at Palm Beach in the then-stimulating one-piece bathing suits, but because I wanted to cut out a fine picture of Wilbert Robinson, longtime manager of the Dodgers, who was quoted as making an unjustifiably sanguine prediction for the 1923 season, when, as it turned out, the Dodgers finished sixth. My mother let me cut out Robby's portrait, but she destroyed the rest of the *Gazette* with her own hands.

The *Brown and White* has its softer side, of course. Like Robinson it forecasts athletic achievement, and like Robinson's, the encouraging prophecy is often more fun to read than the follow-up on Sunday morning. It is the nature of the Fourth Estate to distort facts just as (more skillfully) poetry, fresco painting, and the IRS instruction book do. For under the picture of two junior misses disposed on the October grass, I read that they are enjoying "a few minutes of solitude in the sun on the University Center front lawn." Solitude? In front of the University Center? With a news photographer hovering ten feet away? Still more engaging is the treatment accorded Dr. Ruth Westheimer—hitherto unknown to me, she is hailed as a sexologist of note among folks that make a hobby of that sort of thing. Anyway, Dr. Westheimer is said to have "trained the best lovers in the tri-state area."[1]

But the big news when I opened this meditation appears under the head that reads, "Hotel Parties Receive Blame for Irresponsible Drinking." For 48 hours I was too busy to get beyond the headlines, and I pursued a perfectly irrelevant line of thought on the ingenuous supposition that a hotel party was a party given in a

[1]A tremendous statement that makes me wonder who evaluated Dr. Westheimer's accomplishment and how he arrived at his judgment. To say nothing of the geographical stricture: Did Dr. Westheimer come in a bad third in Connecticut, for example, or did she not proselytize so far afield? I read also that she "delighted the crowd with her explicit references to sex." Surely references to sex even more explicit than Dr. Westheimer's can be heard without one's taking the trouble to go to Grace Hall and sit around for an hour waiting for a speaker?

hotel. Like any other party it might be well behaved or it might not. I have alluded elsewhere in my memoirs to a Kappa Beta Phi symposium at the Hotel Bethlehem many years ago, an occasion dignified by a lifesize swan carven from ice. There was no shouting or horseplay, despite the raffish reputation of the host organization. In one corner I overheard a three-way discussion of the symbolism in *Pélleas and Mélisande* and later I myself was involved in upholding John Stuart Mill as a precursor of Pragmatism, a subject of which I knew nothing.

Parties at the Hendrick Hudson in Troy were somewhat livelier in days when I had an informal connection with Delta Phi at Rensselaer because of a cousin who actually belonged to it. The Eighteenth Amendment being in force then, most prudent social groups anticipating some gala would go to Grafton for the applejack made there by a skilled resident who used nothing but pure ingredients and time-honored methods and who let it go for twelve dollars a gallon. Mixed about half and half with unsweetened grapefruit juice, it made a soothing, just slightly astringent, potation that crept up quietly behind the celebrant: his impulses grew generous and his dialogue wittier; sometimes he found that he could speak Latin or German without ever having studied it. The point is that he was good for hours at this rate, and not till about 3:00 A.M. was he likely to pull the telephone out of the wall, drop a water bag from the mezzanine, or any of that.

Elsewhere than in Troy, though, a hotel party could mean real trouble, as those familiar with the life and times of Roscoe C. ("Fatty") Arbuckle are aware. Or look at *The Young Manhood of Studs Lonigan* (chap. xxiv) for a real blockbuster, the kind that even in Sodom would have excited deprecatory comment. Good-for-nothings like that, to be sure, would never have been admitted to Lehigh. Take, for example, the girl that—but the book is in print and you can look it up yourself.

You have anticipated me, dear Reader, in understanding that all these reminiscences are based on a fallacy—*Ignorantia Pura* is the technical term in Logic—namely, I did not know what "hotel party" means in the jargon of our day. According to the *Brown and White*, it is a get-together whereat "a different alcoholic drink is served in each room of living quarters." There have been, says Dean of Students William L. Quay, "a lot of reports of irresponsible drinking at these parties . . . creating some very bad situations."

So what else is new? Most parties offer a choice of refreshment; it generally turns out that if bourbon makes you break out all over, your host goes down cellar and fetches up some gin. (If you need Campari to be happy, you shouldn't be allowed out at night.)

Wherever there are drinks, there may be "irresponsible drinking," is it not? Anyone that mixes them up because they occur in different rooms is even more of an ass than most people and will get himself into trouble wherever he is. Too bad that he fractured his spleen, and lost most of his teeth, but some rain must fall into each life, as they say.

The university is far from indifferent to this menace; indeed it has been long awake to it, as a consultation of the current *Lehigh Handbook* will show. If committees and legislation can do it, the atmosphere here will soon be as sedate as that of Rugby in Dr. Arnold's day. Take the plaster on happy hours, which are in fact three hours long—5:00 to 8:00 P.M.—on Fridays, almost as if one might not be happy after eight. And I believe that further revision of the rules is in the works and that even the undergraduates think it a good thing.

The ultimate truth is that the university should need no more regulations than would go on the backside of an old envelope. Neither should the Pennsylvania Department of Revenue, Washington, or the New England Wildflower Preservation Society. All that is needed is that people be sensible. Good luck.

Yet here and there a hotel party might prove the beginning of wisdom. You don't need to go from room to room; myself, I began to grow up in the delightful patio of a home out Pinewoods Avenue in Troy.[2] What happened, my host ran out of manhattans and regretted that nothing was left but martinis. In those days, though, my career as a tosspot was based upon cooking sherry served in a demitasse every six months or so, and on my unpracticed constitution the amalgam was disastrous, as became evident during dinner at the Troy Country Club, where I believe I am still remembered. The next morning, predictably, John Cage was conducting a bagpipe Voluntary in my head, and in my mouth a sow had not merely littered her farrow of nine but devoured them too.

It is not that I am proud of this chapter from my *enfances* nor that I think it cute. The point is that being quick to put two and two together, though I have made many mistakes in the past 50-odd years, I never made that one again. I am supposing that the average Lehigh undergraduate is, if not so smart as I am, smart enough to quit mixing them after being concussed for the first time. It is comforting to know that there is a reliable fall-back in plain, monochromatic imbibition, as anyone who spends the evening on Black Velvet will discover. It's expensive, but you know that it's nourishing.

This brings us back naturally to journalism, for the same issue of the *Brown and White* contained both an editorial and a column on the hotel party problem as well it might.

Broadly speaking, the editorial policy of a college journal is to oppose the college administration and to assume that Mr. or Miss Average Undergraduate is at the same time omnicompetent and helpless. I remember that at College X one time, the administration was editorially chidden for its draconian policy with respect to undergraduate automobiles—"if a man is legally entitled to a driver's license, he should be allowed to operate a car on this campus"—and two weeks later chidden again for its laxity, for one of the licensed drivers had just flattened himself versus a tree 20 feet

[2]Troy keeps cropping up in any account of my intemperate youth. It was on River Street one night that a friendly bartender gave me an infallible remedy for the hiccups: fill an Old-Fashioned glass with plain, ordinary water; thrust into it point down a plain, ordinary pencil (#1 if you have it); holding this in place between fore and middle fingers of the (preferably) right hand, drink the water. Surefire. I don't know why.

off the roadway—"it is the obligation of the college to see that its roads are safe."

The Lehigh editor points out accurately that if liquor is around, people are going to drink it and (as a rule) make fools of themselves if not worse. "Nor is the banning of these parties the solution to the problem." Does he imply that there *is* a solution to it? And he may be in more trouble when he says that Lehigh students "should be treated like responsible adults," for unless the phrase is very loosely used, they are not responsible adults, however much they like to think so. Yet it is otherwise a fine editorial. Come right down to it, even most adults are not responsible if we mean willing to accept responsibility for the consequences of their own behavior, and (in the glory of young manhood and womanhood) still fewer undergraduates are.[3]

Responsibility is a treasure, and scarce any man hath enough of it. If a drunken undergraduate, fresh from a hotel party, playfully burns down a dormitory, I think he ought to pay for it. Or suppose that like me in 1960 he is struck by ice sliding off the roof of Packer Hall and unseam'd from nave to th' chops: he may accept free stitching at the health service but let it go at that. Self-reliant to a fault, I did not even sue the university for my blood-drenched shirt and the new J. Press cravat I was wearing.

I am pleased to see that the *Brown and White*, as an alternative to miscellaneous intoxication, exhibits a softer mood in the article entitled "Bethlehem Parks Offer Relaxation and Recreation." Without mentioning hotel parties, the article calls attention to the pleasances and golf courses of Bethlehem: football, soccer, rugby, tennis, skiing, skating, picnicking—world without end. Who needs a hotel party?

The writer raises a curious question, though, for the article begins, "If you're looking for an escape from the tedious drone of

[3]"Any man over 40 who thinks 18-year-olds are just as smart as he is, is probably right." —Al Capp

campus living . . ." This is long-sanctified but not really acceptable language, suggesting as it does that the normal undergraduate grinds at his books by day and night because he cannot think of anything else to do. Anyone in a residential college who suffers from the "tedious drone" of living there is, so far from being a responsible adult, a subadolescent. Maybe the writer was being satirical, but I just thought I'd mention it.

Well, the hotel party issue seems now to have faded off inconclusively in the usual way, at least for the time being. The last I read, hosts are now holding down the number of their guests by requiring a visa from everyone. "...The new regulations are good because unwanted people can be excluded while keeping the quality of the parties the same as before." If the quality of the parties is the same as before, this suggests *solutio a non solvendo,* a solution so called because it doesn't solve anything. I thought the idea was to *change* the quality of the parties, but let it go.

Other local disturbances include a flap affecting the Marching 97 and an arrangement called Coed-by-Room Housing. I am not quite clear as to its operation, but the latter does promise to discourage the shyness and diffidence natural to the young. As usual the journalistic treatment is more fascinating than the plan itself. Adult responsibility is stressed, of course. "I think all the students would be adult enough to deal with something that could arise," says one male member of '85, ignoring the history of human behavior throughout the past 5,000 years. "Especially in this dorm, the guys and girls don't mix. I think room-by-room there would be a lot more interaction," says a female member of '86, qualifying for the Raised Eyebrows Department. "So many schools have it, why shouldn't we?" asks another '86 lassie, employing the limpest, most mischievous travesty of reasoning yet discovered.

Remembering Genesis, it is clear that the cohabitation of the sexes—fatal to two human beings created perfect; how much riskier then for the rest of us—is fraught with peril. And many other cases can be cited, Antony and Cleopatra, Catullus and Lesbia, and in medieval times the most famous coeducational experiment of all, that of Abelard and Heloise, which turned out catastrophically, especially for Abelard.

Mention of the Middle Ages brings us full circle to the hotel party theme, for the same problem existed at Bologna, Oxford, the Sorbonne, and so on, six and seven centuries ago. Many will recall an informal statement of undergraduate policy in those days, the one that goes

Meum est propositum in taberna mori,
Ut sint vina proxima morientis ori.
Tunc cantabunt laetius angelorum chori,
"Deus sit propitius huic potatori."

That is to say

It's my wish to die at a hotel party
With several kinds of drink handy to my mouth.
Then joyfully the angelic choirs will sing,
"May God be merciful to this drunkard."

Fine for informal chorusing. Use the air of "O Tannenbaum," though some prefer that of "Good King Wenceslas." There are 25 stanzas in the version I know.

But the rich pattern of higher education kaleidoscopically presented by the Lehigh Family tires the eyes in a little while. 'Tis time to close the five ports of knowledge (as Browne puts it), and each of us returneth, I to Shalott, you to . . .

Sub Ulmis Atrox; or It's Dire under the Elms

Winter, '81

There was this teacher I once had at school who believed invincibly in the civilizing power of "culture." "Maners makyth man," he used to quote, meaning that folks that know Shakespeare, Ancient History, and Counterpoint get on well and kindly with each other, unlike folks that don't know them. He believed this, I say, in spite of spending his whole life among the cultured.

I wonder what he would have thought if a few years ago he had read in the *Brown and White* a news item out of Wadham College, Oxford,[1] the president and fellows of which were replying to a list of "nonnegotiable" demands from a group of Angry Young Men:

> Dear Gentlemen:
>
> We note your threat to take what you call "direct action" unless your demands are immediately met. We feel that it is only sporting to let you know that our governing body includes three experts on chemical warfare, two ex-commandos skilled with dynamite and torturing prisoners, four qualified marksmen in both small arms and rifles, two ex-artillerymen, one holder of the Victoria Cross, four karate experts, and a chaplain. The governing body has authorized me to tell you that we look forward with confidence to what you call a "confrontation," and I may say even with anticipation.

[1]Here President Deming Lewis was once an undergraduate.

DBX house after the fund drive.

J. K. Frolick.

Deadwood College administration building.

At Lehigh, where culture is particularly strong and high, such belligerence is hardly thinkable, but I am afraid that the agapemone we enjoy here is very rare, almost unique. Consider a selection from some random papers once belonging to James K. Frolick, one of my wife's innumerable cousins, a longtime member of the History department at Deadwood College and for several years head of it. After his funeral they were found lying around[2] on the floor of his study, and my wife told me to pick them up and dispose of them. I am disposing.

#1. Frolick was for a while advisor to one of the Deadwood fraternities and in that capacity no doubt acquired the following item:

> Dear Brothers—
>
> At the risk of some slight tediousness I am responding (in one sense) to the fund-raising appeal that reached me yesterday. Because of our formal relationship I ought to make clear to you why my response is merely verbal.
>
> For one thing, since I graduated from college myself, I have regularly paid my dues to both the national and the alumni association of my undergraduate chapter. This may be no proud boast, though it is more than many can make, but it tells me that I am doing my bit already and need not feel a slacker if I let it go at that.
>
> But the real point arises from the moving paragraph where you allude to the bonds of friendship first forged in youth and growing ever closer as the years pass. I have found that true as a general proposition, but I wonder whether you have done so or whether you just picked the words out of an old Compleat Speechmaker and thought they sounded pretty.
>
> Shortly after I joined the Deadwood faculty, I wrote informally to the president of the DBX chapter to let him know of my arrival. I thought only that it might be pleasant once a year to visit the house on some festival occasion and that in my faculty position I might now and then be of some slight usefulness to the membership.
>
> As it turned out, I never received any acknowledg-

[2]Or, as *Lehigh Horizons* would put it, "laying around."

ment of my note; and in the 21 years of my stay here I have been with you precisely once, when at my own instance I dropped in at an open house after a ballgame and, having helped myself to a glass of inexpensive water and even more inexpensive scotch, stood around for ten minutes as isolated as a typhoid carrier, admiring the view since there was no one to talk to. After thus reveling, I went back to the parking lot, where I discovered that some hotspur had put a conspicuous dent in one of my fenders.

My only other contact with the chapter has been this present invitation to contribute to the cost of a new lodge.

Some way I can't cudgel myself into caring whether you build a new lodge or just burn down the old one.

Fraternally,
/s/ Daniel R. Fream[3]

#2.-3. These two papers are pretty clearly consecutive and must have been written during Frolick's tenure as chairman of his department, a period when the teaching of history at Deadwood was unusually ineffective.

Marblehead, Mass.

Dear Professor Frolick—

Your letter came last week, but I was too busy till yesterday to pay it much mind. I'm sorry you had such a hard time finding my summer address. I know I meant to leave it with Deirdre in the office, but I guess I forgot to. I'm glad she remembered that Mother lives in Ogden, so the

[3]Fream taught literature. An American specialist, he is remembered for his studies of Bryant's "A Meditation on Rhode Island Coal," Lowell's "Ode Written for the Celebration of the Introduction of the Cochituate Water into the City of Boston," &c.

letter can't have been held up more than a week or ten days.

About next fall, I don't know that I can help out the department in the way that you suggest. A 12-hour load is par for an instructor, and I really must decline to take on any more than that. I ought to add too that I have been trained as a historian, and I do not mean to give up my course in the Age of Reason for the sake of teaching what is no more than high school Civics.

Sorry to be brief, but I am thinking of buying this 24-foot sloop, and my days are pretty well occupied. I want to be sure I like the way she handles in a chop before I put any money down.

I don't know where I'll be the next three or four weeks, but this address will probably get me sooner or later if I can help out in any further way.

In some haste,
/s/ Pet

Manchester, Vt.

Dear Frolick—

Go pour milk on your ulcer. Very likely the Norumbega Yacht Club were dilatory in forwarding your diatribe; that's not my fault. And there is nothing in my contract that says I have to stay tethered to a hitching post throughout my summer holiday.

I guess I didn't make myself clear last month. Let me try again. If you think you can lay a 15-hour schedule on me in the fall, you are living in Cloud Cuckoo Land. I have as yet made no plan that would prevent me from returning to Deadwood in September, but please understand this: 12 hours of peonage are all I shall accept, I expect to keep the Age of Reason course, and I want to move into a private office (with telephone) as soon as possible, say by Columbus Day. This being settled, I don't much care how you deploy the rest of the department.

I'm staying here for a few days with relatives. The weather's been beautiful; I've played the Old Course every day and done my short game a lot of good. Maybe I forgot to mention that my grandfather's estate was finally settled early in June, and I should get something over $800,000 after all the pimps are paid off: not a great fortune these days, but enough to affect my lifestyle, and I have begun to wonder whether teaching is my vocation after all.

Let me know by the middle of the month that you have adjusted the scheduling and the office space as I have requested. I shall be on the move again, but the Trust Department of the Chase Bank in New York will always be able to reach me.

Yours,
/s/ Peter H. Lamb, III[4]

P.S. I almost forgot to tell you that I will not meet any eight o'clock classes.

P.L.

#4. Frolick was some kind of dean at one time. For a while Deadwood had more deans than faculty.

Dear Dean Frolick—

I am writing to express to you—and through you the whole administration—my heartfelt gratitude for your beautiful message of condolence on the occasion of my husband's death. I don't suppose that so much feeling has

[4]Lamb left Deadwood at the end of his second year, but not before letting the air out of the tires of Frolick's car.

been compressed into 11 words since Simonides composed the Thermopylae epigram.

Indeed David had a fine record at Deadwood: 35 years without a leave, and, except for that time the student shot him, he missed only seven days by reason of health and only three because of the weather.

It is gratifying to learn that the administration valued David so highly. I understand that the flag was lowered for a whole day in his honor. How wrong we are to rest our judgments on external and quantitative bases! During his last year David's salary was only about the median for an assistant professor, and I don't believe he ever realized how greatly his contribution to the Deadwood community was appreciated.

I am well and keep busy. With the pension of $250 a month I'm living rather quietly. But of course with David gone, I have fewer expenses.

Sincerely yours,
/s/ Martha S. Bowditch

#5. Another of Frolick's distinctions was to serve for a term as the thankless chairman of the Honorary Degrees committee.

Dear Professor Frolick—

I am in receipt of the invitation over your signature to accept the offer of the honorary degree of LHD from Deadwood College at its Commencement exercises next June. In declining I wish to make it clear why I do so.

Some researcher at Deadwood must have stumbled on the fact of my employment there as instructor many years ago. And recognizing that since the recent award of the

Nobel Prize in Economics I am now a person of brief eminence and briefer solvency, your committee has thought to dignify your Commencement with my presence.

You yourself are of course too young to know anything of my Deadwood days. The full recital would detail a vulgar exploitation as gross as anything since the Emancipation Proclamation; but let me touch on one or two salient features, saying nothing of the economic pressure that drove me against my will to Deadwood in the first place nor of the pettifogging incompetence of most of my colleagues.

I was greeted in September by the news that thanks to the imbecility of Professor Wastrel (now dead, I am happy to learn) the course offerings were in total disarray and that all my careful summer's preparation had been in vain. And that my classes were to be held in a ramshackle sheepfold over a quarter-mile from my so-called office. Later I found that desk copies of textbooks were deemed the property of the department and that smoking on the campus was a felony. Since my wife and I were "living" in college housing—and I wish I had time to dilate upon that, especially the plumbing—we might not admit alcoholic beverages to our domicile, and I had to smuggle them in after dark.

When I was drafted into the Army at the end of my first year—I was engaged for a three-year hitch—the college raised the rent of our hovel to my wife's distress. A year later it evicted her on the specious grounds of wartime exigency. And when, the war being over, I was separated from the Armed Forces and returned to Deadwood with a view to resuming my work, I found that I had been replaced and was jobless.

In other words, Professor Frolick, with regard to Deadwood my nostalgic feelings are inverted. The pangs of death would not compel me back to your shabby leprosarium for any reason, least of all for an award that could only depreciate me in the public view.

I do not, of course, hold you individually responsible for the behavior of the Deadwood "family" 40 years ago. So in closing I wish to make it quite clear that my contempt extends to all the members of your committee, the faculty, and administration, the student body, and the entire secretarial and custodial staff.

Cordially yours,
/s/ M.J. Vindex

#6. This, as will appear, is a carbon copy. I suppose that Frolick made and retained it because in his muddled way he thought it might protect him in the case of some statutory frame. Thus particularly the allusions to a higher morality than he in fact could justify for himself. He would have been smarter not to write anything at all; but so far as I know, he was in luck, and the Gloria episode died on first.

Dear Gloria—

I acknowledge the receipt of your report on Shays' Rebellion, which was over a week late, and also that of the nonacademic note included therewith. If I understand the rather elliptical language of the latter, you suggest that we spend the weekend of the 12th prox. in Atlantic City at your expense.

I have always tried to be on good terms with my students, but this is carrying it too far. Let me try to explain.

At the age of 41 I am over two decades your senior. No doubt I should take your invitation as an encouraging compliment if you were not failing History 7-8.

Anyway you ought to know that I was married according to an old-fashioned formula that required me to abjure adultery (even for scholastic purposes) during the whole of my married life.

And I do not engage in gambling, which is nothing more than a particularly irresponsible form of theft.

And did you consider, Gloria, that there would be hours and hours when we were not—shall I say—sentimentally engaged? If you could take your spade and bucket and play on the sands while I remained in our hotel room to grade hour tests . . . but, great heavens, we should have to *talk* together. I don't know how this hits you, but it terrifies me.

With best wishes,
/s/ James K. Frolick

P.S. While I think of it, your next report for 7-8 is due two weeks from today. Your present standing suggests that you make every effort to get it in promptly.

JKF

#7. Frolick had evidently published a statement ill-advisedly supporting some student protest or other. Mavon, though in Fine Arts, was less the dreamy aesthete than the vigorous partisan.

Dear Frolick—

Forgive me if I must dissent from your understanding of today's undergraduates taken *en masse.* In their capacity as students they might as well be so many Neanderthals "who don't want to be taught, having already decided what they prefer to believe."

Everything they dignify as social protest is sound and fury that they enjoy because being mindless, it's effortless. Especially unattractive is their failure to understand not merely courtesy but the nature of Implied Contract. If you don't want to put out your lights by midnight, then get the

Wadham College.

hell to some college where you don't have to put them out. If you chose Deadwood out of 2,000 possibilities, you did so because it appealed to you, I suppose. Then behave yourself.

Finally, Frolick, I am surprised to find even you saying, "It's about time we changed a rule that we adopted in 1903." People like you would revise or repeal the Decalogue if they had the chance, on the grounds that it was adopted even earlier than 1903. The utility of a rule, Frolick, is determined by its righteousness and its common sense, not by the date of its promulgation. Surely even you, a man with an eighth-grade education, ought to be able to see that?

/s/ Edward S. Mavon[5]

[5]Mavon's monograph on ceramic figurines, *Of Meissen Men*, is treasured by collectors, a classic in its field.

These few selections are sufficient to convey the "feel" of the Deadwood community, I fancy, and I need not dig deeper into the cornucopia for documents touching on aggravated assault, arson, vandalism, mayhem, and so on. But the concentration of this material gives one a view—no doubt too highly colored—of Deadwood as combining the worst features of Sodom and Gomorrah, Peyton Place, and Philadelphia; and if I have not met cannibalism, I suppose that's just because it didn't happen to enter Frolick's correspondence.

At all events, that's why I don't believe in the refining influence of culture.

Little Victims

Reunion, '76

Dear to my heart is this passage from Samuel Butler's *Notebooks:* "*Medio tutissimus ibis.* A boy in examination translated it thus: 'In the middle of them all stalks the ibis, most cautious of birds'; and he put a note, as follows: 'By this translation I have endeavoured to give the full value of the superlative.'" That hapless child of a hundred years ago gives a dreadful joy to the humanely nurtured. Other readers, familiar once with *Fractured French,* have lived purer, sweeter lives ever since they met *J'y suis, j'y reste* as translated, "I'm Swiss and I'm spending the night."

These considerations give me a kick-off into pupillary solecism, which is the heart of the florilegium to follow.

The happiness of the subject lies much in its innocuousness, for there is little disgraceful in the blunders of a tyro—especially since his elders and betters, though less exposed, make equally egregious blunders too, with less excuse. Excepted only the practitioner that takes himself too seriously or (worse) fancies himself an authority, as one or two do below.

This casual icing on the academic cake is one of the unsought yet beloved fringe benefits of the teaching profession. In some disciplines, that is: the Math people have no chance at it; the Sociologists, perhaps, wouldn't recognize it; but English, Languages, and History are in a strong position.

The thesis of this compilation—produced unedited from undergraduate writing, largely in my own classes 1946-1975—is that in this area of amiable eccentricity Lehigh is right up there with its competitors. *Eamus in antiquam silvam*; let us stroll through some of the evidence.

Creative spelling, of course, is too common a trap to be very interesting. Yet many a gray-haired College Board reader recalls with undiminished happiness the candidate who wanted to write something about a vessel: *vessal,* he began; disliked it and substituted *vassel*; still dissatisfied tried *vesal*; and at last in desperation set down *bote.* Locally we cannot match that, yet may admire our own Lehigh man who wrote of "the advantageous of reviseing the spellin system to its simplilest form."

Proper names produce their rewards, as when we meet *Swift's Family Robinson*; a synthetic universal language called Espionage; a dictionary published by Funk and Wagtails; a miracle of Oriental architecture, Tasma Hall; and *Promiscuous Unbound,* a symbolic epic by Shelley.

Sometimes we roam along the byways of Fancy:

> The background on which I take my stand is unsubstantiated.
>
> In my childhood I used to love to read tales of giants and knomes, strolls and orgies.

Or we soar into the empyrean:

> What can I say—I search for sentiment, feeling no an abundance of emotion—I look and examine my psyche and a paragon of scrutiny is the tantamount.

Or we fail to tuck in our shirttails:

> The average church attendance dropped considerably while I was going.

Readers of Chaucer will welcome the observation that

That's A Lot of Bulletin:

> January was dissatisfied to find his wife in a tree with Damian.

And the more widely read will enjoy a ramble into literary criticism:

> Captain Ahab became enraged, and determined to hunt down Moby Dick on account of him having bitten off his leg at their previous meeting.
>
> His sentences were long at times, but in many places they were also short.
>
> The *Londonderry* bound for Capetown appeared in the play *Agatha Christie,* the name of the author eludes me.
>
> Steinbeck wrote in hopes that the reader would get an idea of what he was trying to say.
>
> The call of nature is no longer a passion to Wordsworth as it was in his younger days.
>
> . . . and finally, when her husband dies, he turns up later to marry her. Things just don't happen that way.

A discussion of *The Return of the Native* tells us:

> Naturally anyone who looked at the title would conclude that the setting of the story was in the jungles of Africa, where genuine natives run through the forests giving horrible yells at the sight of a stranger. But when Hardy tells about some heaths

> and barrows in England the reader is amazed and wonders just how a native is going to return to that land which has been inhabited by white men for centuries.

This tactician was, presumably, unaffiliated with ROTC:

> The eskirmish line breaks into an advance by inflirtation at some designated line in the combat aera.

And the Music department would disown the critic who wrote that

> Tschaikovsky in the 'Nutcracker Suite' makes use of the bassoon, french horn, strings, clarinet, flute, and ovaries.

These novice athletes were doubtless all linebackers:

> This was his first year out for football so a few sophomores were to help these new players learn the fundaments.

History is another spacious field:

> Washington at the early age of sixteen became a souvenir.

> Though Germany subjected England to unmerciful air bombardments, she failed to bring the perfidious Albumin to her knees.

> In spite of his wealthy heritage, Kennedy was not content to live a life of idolatry.

> Is this the same type of patriotism as that which was displayed by George Washington or Nathan Hale? In my humble opinion it is more like that of a scoundrel like Matthew Arnold.
>
> In Jonson's poem the use of *thee* indicates a similarity the father gives his son. (When this poem was written, *thee* meant *me* or *I*.)
>
> Faulkner blames much of the troubles of the South on the abortionists.
>
> 'A house built on rock will weather any storm,' stated Christ almost two centuries ago.
>
> England (or Gaul, as it was known in those days) was . . .

Though not within the meaning of the act, the following confession is poignant:

> Mr. Armstrong: Due to an unfortunate an costly happening I was unable to read the article assigned for today. On my way home Saturday I carelessly dropped my English and math books from the New Street bridge into the water.

A good writer will always be sure that he and his readers know the meaning of the words he uses:

> To be alone, as Webster describes it, is to be apart from others; to be by one's self.
>
> To be afraid, is, as Webster defines it, to be fright-

> ened or terrified; the act of fearing someone or thing.

Violence on TV is often corruptive, but not always:

> When a boy reaches the age of four or five often what he wants most is a toy gun or knife to kill his friends with. This in itself is all right, but . .

> He told her to pull the trigger, but she couldn't and dropped the gun. This weakness of not being able to shoot at someone you know is common to all of us.

Imagery must be handled with gloves:

> . . . but I found that lies, like boomerangs, always come home to roost.

> Readers, like sheep, read what they are told is good.

> Teddie, having no seat in the public eye . . .

> An athlete's standing rests squarely on his own shoulders.

Sociology might claim these pretties:

> These men working hard all week, Saturday is the only day they have to ease themselves.

> The new highway, of course, has been built for more modern automobiles than those which are used today.

That's A Lot of Bulletin:

Until the latter part of the 19th century, reproductive processes can hardly be said to have had an existance.

Women, as a whole, are indispensable.

Of the four riders of the Apocalypse, three have been subdued by man: Famine, Pestilence, and Death are no longer serious problems to mankind.

The manner in which our social structure is arranged makes a partnership of one man and one woman a necessity if the off spring are to be bred in a satisfactory manner.

Pousse café:

When we enter the indiscreetly lighted ballroom ...

There are instances where a woman is responsible for caring for her aged parents or is the widow of a large family. [Cf. Mark xii, 18-23.]

[From the heyday of the twist] I disapprove of public oscillation in the parks.

Broad meadow lands filled with sturdy apple trees, lie all about.

I like to fish and haunt, especially on the mountains.

Let us be gay.

> Take a typical couple—let's call them Don and Bill—who . . .

L'amour the merrier:

> . . . the best method yet devised for handling so erotic and unpredictable a group as college students.

> Fathers are considered among my great men. They are propagating our race in an enviable manner.

> I look forward to every holiday because my boy friend comes down from New York to see me, and we do make the most of our time—as we did over the Christmas and New Year week. I am not the only one, everybody does it, and that's what makes the holiday season such a gay one.

> These new-found romances blossom into bloom as soon as the ground is dry enough.

> The mothers think their daughters are still to young to marry, and so they send them off to school to delay the issue for four more years.

> They had been in love, but the embers were no longer glowering.

> Unlike the ape, man can talk and sing more efficiently. And by learning how to whistle he has discovered another way to call his mate.

> The highlight of the vacation was visiting my steady girlfriend. We went to movies, dances, and attended to some other activities.

It seems fitting to complete the flower arrangement with a spray of anticlimax, part succinct, part fully orchestrated:

> Tennyson expected to see the face of Jesus, or God. Browning expected to see Mrs. Browning.

> The thought of graduation brings back memories of beautiful and sacred graduation exercises, palm trees lining processional paths on the green grass of our football stadium, proud parents sitting reverently in the grandstand, a warm summer evening climaxed by a gloriously colored sunset, and the choked feeling of pride and honor in being one of some four hundred students to graduate from Wilkinsburg High School.

NOTE: Not all of my material is precisely suited to such a publication as the *Bulletin.* For the wealthy bibliophile a culling of the AAA-rated spectaculars is available on rag paper and delivered by United Parcel.

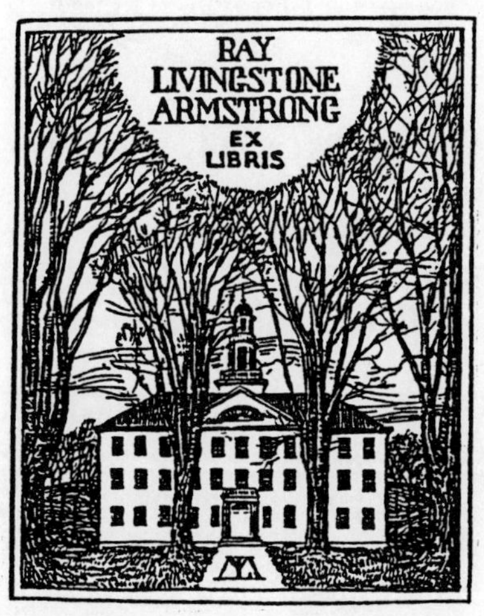

Wistful Vistas

914 Vernon Street

Spring, '76

"To my astonishment I was informed on leaving college that I had studied navigation!" wrote Thoreau—"why, if I had taken one turn down the harbor I should have known more about it." Thoreau was not writing in anticipation of English 198, but the passage will serve to introduce the 15 toilworn undergraduates and their yet more toilworn preceptor presently laboring at 914 Vernon Street, three blocks (in a sense) from the Lehigh campus

> *English 198. Self-Reliance in a Technological Society.* Theory and practice of self-reliance in today's world. In addition to reading and discussing several pertinent books, the students will become members of a legally registered corporation set up just for this class. As members of the corporation they will get a bank loan, purchase a south-side house, work on redesigning and remodeling the house, then sell the house and divide the profits (if any). Not for cowards or cleanliness freaks. Both men and women welcome. Limited to 15 students. Four credit hours.

The project, celebrated in the Bethlehem *Globe-Times*, the Allentown *Call-Chronicle*, and the Philadelphia *Inquirer*, has (I understand) engaged even the attention of ABC and CBS and bids fair to run second only to the Winter Olympics in dominating early 1976.

Arising out of the university's program called Humanities Perspectives on Technology (HPT)—"to encourage students to look at traditional subjects in nontraditional ways"—the course fell readily upon the shoulders of Peter G. Beidler, associate professor of English, not merely because he is literate, frequently reading books, but because he is ardently familiar with the construction of dwellings.

For 198 is not merely an exercise in manual training, as the statement shows. The philosophical side of it is based on a syllabus

Beidler and his disciples.

Beidler extrapolates.

that includes not only the inevitable *Walden* and Emerson's "Self-Reliance" essay, but among other titles *Brave New World* and *One Flew over the Cuckoo's Nest.* The complete group is together once a week for a two-hour class, and at the end of the semester there will be an examination executed with pens, not with hammers.

The purpose of all this is perhaps best defined in large part by negatives. The course essentially is not

a) preparation for membership in a carpenters' union, though the students will learn how to use a saw without hurting themselves;

b) a step toward solving the housing shortage;

c) an invitation to Lehigh graduates to live by themselves in the woods;

d) nor even a study in the manifold intricacies of the real estate business.

But it must be true—it seems to a thumb-fumbler—that anyone who has built even part of a house with his own hands must entertain the concept *house* as no one else can; and far more widely, anyone competently engaged in any such combined operation—it needn't be house building—becomes more himself: the principle is that since man was designed for freedom (and seldom enjoys it), the more areas he is at home in, the freer he is.

For the project a house (of course) was necessary. It must be in a fairly convenient location; it must be fairly cheap—meaning that it must also be in fairly horrid condition, though not irreparable; it must be potentially salable. After a futile exploration via normal commercial channels, Professor Beidler found his house in the old-fashioned way of walking around and looking for it.

When this *Bulletin* appears, the February situation will be medieval history; but right now the time to visit 914 Vernon Street is either Wednesday afternoon or either end of Thursday, when operations are going on. The visitor must be prepared for certain challenges of his own, for Vernon Street, on the breast of old South Mountain, rises like the cog railway on Mt. Washington. Residents when parking their cars up there chain them to nearby trees, or should; and if you are overweight and short-winded like me, you will reach 914 on your hands and knees. But not without reward, for from the site the views to west and north in the thin air are rewarding, especially if you like Bethlehem. And since Vernon Street is not a thoroughfare—or I guess it isn't; beyond 914 and above the timberline it turns into a lane that disappears around a corner—no resident will be harassed by hot-rodders blasting past his house at all hours of the night.

Approaching the house, the visitor ducks a board flung from a gable window, passes beneath a lean-to that will be replaced by a patio later in the season, and enters to find Professor Beidler and five helpers looking like so many courteous troglodytes. If anyone still thinks of academicians as living in a *tour d'ivoire* and thinking beautiful thoughts for eight hours a day, he should see Beidler in action, especially on a damp morning in midwinter.

The floor area of the house is about 28' x 12', and it is true but hard to believe that the original house was even smaller. It is still harder to believe Beidler's assertion that a family of 13 was once reared in it, for—if you count their parents—15 human beings unaccustomed to the Broadway subway in rush hour could hardly stand in it, let alone grow up in it.

When all is done, though, the house will be a perfectly reasonable dwelling for a couple who have simple tastes, who don't expect many overnight guests, and who don't host square dances: kitchen, bathroom and living room on the ground floor and two bedrooms upstairs, yielding the extensive views aforementioned.

Many "before" photographs exist. I am sorry that it is too early to provide an "after." The contrast will be impressive.

Externally the house should be modestly attractive when its old brick is decently revealed. Its simple design is in refreshing contrast to the South Side Transitional that dominates the neighborhood.

A word as to the untenured workers. Beidler could accommodate only 15 in the course; he could have had at least 60. Taking the first 15 as they came, he wound up with 8 males and 7 females, a fortuitously satisfactory distribution at a time when the Girl Scouts of America are refusing membership to boys. ("Women Are Welcome," read the original statement of the course, a challenge removed at the behest of the university for some subtle reason.) I hear that the enthusiasm of the personnel is such that some of them have begged to be allowed to work on Saturdays, a request reluctantly discouraged by Beidler, who is something of a homebody and likes to visit his family on weekends.

The workers are not supposed to be omnicompetent. They do not frivol on the roof, a fall from which could be disabling. And some of the advanced features—notably the plumbing, which calls for exotic implements and operations and which must ultimately be sanctified by public authority—have to be created by pros.

There are frustrations. Hardly had the old roof been removed in mid-January when the area was stricken by the worst rains since Sadie Thompson's time, the contractor could not show when he was supposed to, and operations came to a standstill until a dove was sent out and the waters subsided.

No one knowing Beidler, though, will doubt that he is more than a match for the weather. The son of an architect, he early found himself more interested in constructing things than in designing them, and he has not failed to improve his bias. For a year after completing his doctorate he worked as a carpenter; the house he lives in testifies to his preterpractical skill; and it was inevitable that having entertained the concept of the course, the Steering Committee should tap him for it.

"The house he lives in," I was saying. It began as a grist mill in 1762 and was still functioning in a humbler way (grinding fertilizer) in the thirties. When Beidler acquired it in 1963, it had long been deserted and is said to have looked like Old 97 after the wreck. Now remodeled, largely by Beidler with his bare hands, it is a dwelling so combining the unusual with the attractive that fortunately for the Beidlers' peace, no one knows where it is. The Beidlers are among the very few faculty families at Lehigh to have waterwheels hung in their basements. Below, the millstream complete with trout still lies at the bottom of a pit, and it must be thanks to either remarkably good behavior or lack of enterprise that none of the children—there are four of them—has yet fallen into it. In other ways somewhat more conventional, the old stone building is set against a background of stream and hillside and demands inclusion in any celebration of picturesque Pennsylvania.

Mr. and Mrs. Beidler are both products of the Lehigh graduate school, having proceeded *paene pari passu* (almost side by side) since they commenced simultaneously at Earlham in 1962. In a burst of speed Beidler drew briefly ahead of his wife with an M.A. in 1965, beating hers by a year. On the third lap she came even, however, and in 1968 they were one of the rare couples to receive doctorates at the same exercises, she in Education, he in Philosophy.

None of the children has a degree as yet.

The demands of her family prevent Mrs. Beidler, a lecturer in Education at Lehigh, from working more than part time. As for her husband, he is on paper a medievalist. His dissertation was written on Chaucer's edifying Merchant's Tale, and, a younger man, he meets those courses in the area that Professor Albert E. Hartung '47, an older man, can no longer keep up with. He has a powerful secondary concern with American literature and has written significantly on *Huckleberry Finn* at a time when it seemed—wrongly—that everything possible had been said about that.

Still further—and this is part of the extramural urge—he is devoted to the American Indian; and taking a year's leave in 1973-74, he moved his family to the University of Arizona at Tucson for anthropological study. There one of his children was stung by a scorpion, "but," Beidler told me apologetically, "it was only a small one." (That is, it was a comparatively small scorpion that stung the child.) This study resulted in a course on the American Indian in literature from Cooper on down. If there is danger in getting into a rut, Beidler is one of the safest people on the campus.

But I return to Vernon Street in a kind of way.

Around a hundred years ago John Ruskin inspired a group

of undergraduates—including various names of future distinction, Andrew Lang and Oscar Wilde among them—to experience the dignity of labor by constructing a road that led down to the Thames near Oxford, and he himself did not shun participation: "Thus, when I had to direct road making at Oxford, I sate, myself with an iron-masked stone-breaker . . . to break stones beside the London road...till I knew how to advise my too impetuous pupils to effect their purpose in that matter, instead of breaking the heads of the hammers off (a serious item in our daily expenses)." The result, however successful on the spiritual plane, was otherwise less distinguished. "When enthusiasm had died, the surveyor sent by the landowner reported on the project 'the young men have done no mischief to speak of.'" One counts on something better from Project Beidler since it proposes a higher end than the dignity of labor and since I suspect that a slipshod piece of work testifies to imperfect motivation in the workers. I think that we can look forward confidently to the middle of May, when the first "after" photographs can be taken.

Will English 198 become a feature of the Lehigh curriculum or even be offered again at all? Unanswerable, at least till the end of the semester, when the 15 practitioners wrap it all up and decide whether it was worth their while. It seems from here that at best it would properly have to remain a small operation, dependent upon the limited supply of Beidlers and of practical idealists. But unless it results this year in such disaster or disillusionment as is most unlikely, I hope that something like it will be with us for years to come.

These notes opened with a citation from Thoreau and so may appropriately close with one from his friend Emerson, a lesser yet sometimes interesting writer. "It is easy to see that a greater self-reliance must work a revolution in all the offices and relations of men; in their religion; in their education; in their pursuits; their modes of living; their association; in their property; in their speculative views." Whatever good comes out of English 198, it is good that the university is willing to find out.

Sweatshirt and Dust Jacket

Winter '79

Fifty-odd years ago *College Humor* published a drawing that impressionistically interpreted a large midwestern university—Minnesota or Wisconsin, I can never tell the difference. Dominating the campus was a stadium the size of the Astrodome; on its flanks were the field house and the gymnasium, each on the same heroic scale. And wedged off in one corner was a shingle cabin like a fish-shanty, a sign over the door proclaiming "Book-larnin', Sums, and the Like o' That."

No doubt this was a fair comment on the educational climate of the twenties; indeed in Mittelamerika it may not have changed much, from what I hear. But the last half century has wrought many a mutation at least at Lehigh, where the cerebral aspect of college life has become more and more prominent—even important—as displayed by many visible symptoms. Of these the university bookstore is not the least significant.

The early history of the bookstore is lost in the deeps of Time; but Miss Edith Seifert, retired bursar, tells me that in the twenties it occupied a very small area in the basement of Drown Hall, in the bursar's office kind of but not exactly, along with other amenities, a barber shop, and a bowling alley. It had a candy counter, Miss Seifert recalls, some books (of course), and little else.

In September 1930 Stanley Heffner came to Lehigh to begin his incredible 47-year association with the bookstore—or Supply Bureau, as it was called, suggesting a stock of Redi-Mix cement, roofing material, and garden tools. By that time it had moved to the basement of the Alumni Memorial Building and into the room where Sam Connor's Public Information outfit now functions—an area of about 2,000 sq. ft., I judge, though it was hard for

Ed Fehr, Bob Bell and the bookstore.

me to pace it accurately because of all the partitions and things.

It went on growing and was badly impacted when I first saw it, in 1946. So when the University Center was revised, around 1958, the books and electric razors and such went into 3,000 sq. ft. on the second floor, more or less in the area now called the Neville Lounge. Yet even this spaciousness proved too confining, and in 1971 it came down the hill again to spread out over 10,000 sq. ft. in its present location on the ground floor of Maginnes.[1]

Getting out growth figures for the past 30 years would be too much work, but at present the operation does like $1.5 million of business a year, and the end is far from being in sight: $2.5 million is a reasonable projection for 1985. So I am told by the director, Robert W. Bell, who kindly spared me an hour of his time, which he could ill afford.[2] Mr. Bell, an alumnus of the State University of New York at Albany, has been in the bookstore game ever since he graduated in 1952—barring two years in the Armed Forces—at his alma mater, at American International in Springfield, and, since 1969, at Lehigh. He has a dazzlingly fluent grasp of his complex responsibility, and when he tells you that he is devotedly fond of running a college bookstore, you believe him without effort.

It is perhaps superfluous to say that the bookstore handles the innumerable textbooks called for by the instructional staff. This is not always as easy as it sounds, as when a publisher lets you know on August 20 that the text you ordered the previous April is out of print. But I understand that this happens less often than it used to do, and you seldom now find, for example, an English instructor inscribing *Paradise Lost* on his blackboard in lieu of printed copies.

The non-textbook side is fairly massive too, for it includes around 9,000 titles. Faculty suggestions, student requests, best-seller lists, and common sense play large parts in the awful job of making the selections, and some way the system works. The day I fanned the shelves, I found a good range of authors from Euripides[3]

[1]That is, ground floor if you approach it southwards, basement if northwards.

[2]Again Mr. Ramsey's *verdammt* tape recorder didn't work for me. The next time I borrow it, I shall borrow a technician too.

[3]480-406 B.C., more or less. Greek writer: *Iphigeneia at Aulis; Iphigeneia in Tauris; Iphigeneia at Miss Porter's; Iphigeneia, Student Nurse,* &c.

to Eliot, let alone Edgar Rice Burroughs and other kapok.

Though not a bibliolater's paradise, the bookstore sometimes comes up with delightful surprises when a dealer sends it a crate of miscellanea to be offered at reduced prices. I was electrified one day to find several Norman Douglas items for pennies apiece, as the saying is, especially a copy of *In the Beginning*, privately printed 1927, limited, uncut, and signed—all that for $.50.

A few books and magazines—*Playboy, Penthouse*, and suchlike—are available for the soft-core porno trade, undergraduates still bedazzled by the discovery that there are two sexes.[4]

Special orders are accepted. Unfortunately the 10 percent faculty discount was discontinued as of 1971, mainly because the faculty made too much of a nuisance of themselves in collecting it, as when one of our solons might hold up a check-out line by demanding a penny return on his $.10 candy bar. Bell thinks the discount was unreasonable anyway, on the grounds that the faculty have (for the time being) more money than the undergraduates. There's an answer to that one, but I don't have time to get into it here.

Now and then there may be a problem of communication, as in every other coign of university life. Suppose yourself, Alert Reader, to be a clerk coping with some slack-jawed undergraduate in search of a book of whose identity he has but an imperfect grasp: "...that *Evil and War* book," he seems to be telling you, "It was supposed to be in on Tuesday." Would you have been able to help him? Or would you have sold him *War and Peace*?[5]

Non-books account for about 45 percent of the total operation. Especially conspicuous are clothing and gifts, which are competently overseen by Donald Byington, an old associate of mine since the forties, when we collaborated in making money for Esso (as they used to call it), he representing the producer, I the

[4]The *desperately* insecure must repair to Copenhagen West at the Five Points for their emotional cholesterol. No connection with the University.

[5]The student was seeking *A Handful of Dust* by Evelyn Waugh.

consumer. The buying, Don tells me, is a matter of adjusting the starry-eyed fancies of salesmen to the expressed demand of the clientele. It generally works out well, especially because undergraduate taste is not very volatile: today's T-shirt is built on pretty much the same lines as yesterday's. The bookstore, by the way, has a whole Greek alphabet to appliqué on the spot to your camisole if you wish to fraternalize it.

Anomalies do occur from time to time. Back in 1972, when there was actually a problem of *filling* space, the bookstore experimented with a variety of suppliers, one of whom was supposed to ship a gross of T-shirts with LEHIGH on the bosoms thereof, just the way you'd think. What turned up, though, was LE HIGH, identifying the wearer as a student at the high school of Le, Pennsylvania. For some reason these *lusus naturae* went like hotcakes and, Bell tells me, are still treasured as collectors' items. Who understands customers? Again there was a shipment of spiral notebooks bearing not the LU seal but that of the University of Massachusetts. Not only was the demand feverish; when the lot was exhausted, the clientele badgered the management to restock in the same kind.

Everything's up-to-date at the check-out. Charging a purchase is now as elaborate as being confirmed: you need not only your ID and a state of grace; you need a special charge card as well. This bears a design like the spectra of hydrogen, yttrium, &c. as illustrated in the *Book of Knowledge*; and just before the benediction the clerk massages this thing with an illuminated wand—they really call it that—which some way records the article, the price, the customer, the weather, and a lot of other information.[6] A fascinating process, and I find myself charging things just for the fun of it. Bell says that the system gives almost complete and infallible control over accounts receivable.

This is not to say that the bookstore has always been immune against "shrinkage," as it is euphemistically called. This is partly a

[6]There's no sense in giving a technical description. You wouldn't understand it. I do, of course.

matter of plain, old-fashioned pilfering, for apparently throughout a wide segment of today's society shoplifting is seen not as theft but rather as picking up a few afterdinner mints when leaving a restaurant.[7] And customers are exhorted not to leave calculators, stereo equipment, or family jewels in the book drop while they're shopping. Nevertheless, Bell thinks that shrinkage is at least equally due to a spasm of migraine now and then somewhere in the computer.

Probably so. For clarity let me dramatize the experience of a colleague of mine a couple of years ago. "X" is my friend, who has charged merchandise worth $11.32. "Z" is the bookstore.[8] X approaches Z, fingering his bill, which he does not understand.

X: Don't I owe you something?

Z: No, no. You have a *credit* with us. See? $11.32 CR. But just leave the bill with me, and we'll check it.

(A month later X's bill still says $11.32 CR)

Z: You see? It's like we said. It's a credit.

X: But I thought . . .

Z: So that's all straightened out.

X: (*aside*) Oh, what the hell.

Later on X charged a ream of typewriter paper and some paperback mysteries that he had hitherto been unable to afford.

It is "uneconomic," as they say at the Business College, to give away $22.64 instead of taking in $11.32. Presumably it cannot happen under the new charging system.

Another Business College term is "competitive." The bookstore charges competitive prices. Yet in November 1976 a gunslinger for the *Brown and White* wrapped himself in the mantle of Lincoln Steffens and in a searing article alleged that we consumers were being ripped off black, blue, and simple on toiletries. At Muhlenberg, Cedar Crest, Lafayette, and places like that, he said, we could have bought for $.79 the tube of Crest that Lehigh wanted

[7]In 1929 I stole a teaspoon from the Whale Inn in Goshen, MA. Though I returned it (anonymously) in 1937, I still suffer from remorse.

[8]"Y," the merchandise, does not sustain a speaking role.

$1.19 for; and so on through a list of 14 items. Without actually saying so, the article implied that the director and key figures in the administration were reveling in guilty luxury on the profits of the scam. In the next issue, though, we learned that the writer, in too great a hurry for his Pulitzer, had dreamed up his own figures: In fact a $26.02 bill at Cedar Crest would have been but $26.37 at Lehigh, a trifling discrepancy probably attributable to the high quality of our personnel.[9] The writer in question, if not with the Washington *Post,* is probably no longer in Journalism.

The bookstore, incidentally, warm, bright, and attractive, is a mecca when we have large numbers of visitors on the campus—Upperclass Parents' Day, Proletarian Parents' Day, and so on, especially if the weather is like that of the Davidson game on October 14.

Et puis après? Where do we go from here? After a mere seven years the bookstore is feeling too big for its britches, and Bell would love to have more floor space, something like 20,000-25,000 sq. ft.

Where is he to find it? He admires Maginnes because it is frequented by over 110 percent of the Lehigh population every day and, handy to 4th Street, by many noncollegiate types, as well. He would not like to go back up the arduous hill. He is sure that a dual operation—splitting the books from the shaving cream and haberdashery—would make everything far more troublesome. Perhaps, he feels, the development of new library facilities between Mart and Maginnes may offer an opportunity. Perhaps, I feel, clearing the present riffraff out of the second floor of Maginnes would allow for vertical expansion.

The only certainty seems to be that we, even more dependably than Resorts International, are faced with an implacable growth situation.

[9]In rush seasons the bookstore employs what Bell calls "temporary adults"—a somewhat tactless phrase, I thought.

Within a Budding Grove[1]

Winter, '78

Attentive readers will doubtless remember that in my nonage my acquaintance with colleges—as opposed to "girls' colleges," of which I had not yet learned—was based insecurely upon the fiction of Burt L. Standish, Owen Johnson, and a stable of writers for the *American Boy*. Women played a modest, indeed generally decorative, role in this area, so far as they entered it at all, and they were supremely unmemorable except that it is impossible to forget the name of Inza Burrage, who finally married Frank Merriwell. Equal (academic) Rights had to wait till I reached a more sophisticated cultural level and encountered the works of Lynn and Lois Seyster Montross and other contributors to *College Humor*. The setting where I now found myself was commonly a good-sized coeducational university in a nameless Midwestern state, where it appeared that sex was as important as football.

Among other things I picked up a good deal of misty information about sororities, more or less as follows: (a) If a girl didn't make one (preferably a good one) she might as well cut her throat. (b) Her membership (if she achieved it) assured her that she was of finer clay than the rabble around her and entitled her to a full and elaborate social life whose object, implied rather than stated, was a prosperous postgraduate marriage. (c) The system might reach its finest flowering in a totemistic relationship that would have pleased the matriarchal heart of Robert Graves: a given sorority might ally itself by understanding to a given fraternity to the

[1]As so often, trouble with the limited horizon of my editor, Mr. Ramsey, though for his sake I was careful to use the English version of Proust's otherwise well-known title. Expanded it might run: "In association with several nice young women at a heartwarming stage of their development."

Lasses at home (above, left). Doris Campbell and Ann Sotzing study in Alpha Phi dining room (top, right). Presidents Karen Talheim, Sharon Trost, Debbie James, l. to r (above, right). Susan Schmider, Nancy Reynolds, Lianne Kraushaar, Ruth King, l. to r., happy that AGD is No. 1 in intramurals (bottom).

point where the two societies were in effect equal subsidiaries of the same metaphysical corporation, and exogamy, before graduation at least, was virtually heretical.

Like most of my youthful perceptions, this one bears no resemblance to the current situation at Lehigh, whatever may have been true in the Dark Ages out at Winnemac. I began to smarten up about two years ago when preparing a memorable account (Winter 1976) of the establishment of the three pioneer sorority chapters on this campus; and now that I return to issue a progress report, I see a radically different if less exotic picture.

Last fall the sororities moved into their own quarters in SMAGS, as Saucon Married and Graduate Students is euphoniously known;[2] and now that they were effecting local coherence instead of being spread thinly across the countryside like autumn leaves, I wanted to check up on them. Thus I trespassed on the time of Mlles. Debbie James (Alpha Gamma Delta; Northfield, NJ; Urban Studies and Economics); Karen Talhelm (Alpha Phi; Hellertown; History); and Sharon Trost (Gamma Phi Beta; Huntington Valley; Geology) who this year head their societies. The first two responded to my solicitation; but from Miss Trost I didn't hear and I didn't hear, which gave me the exciting notion that either she had something to hide or (worse) that Gamma Phi Beta did. Unfortunately it turned out that she had simply lost my letter in her "In" basket. I am more than grateful to all these ladies, and I may add that if we were in the sixth grade together, I should be glad to let any of them carry my books home after school or to borrow my roller skates. I congratulate their respective societies.

My first call was on Debbie James, who kindly invited me to view the AGD premises. Miss James, *en petite tenue* featuring a well-cut pair of brown and white shorts sororally embossed,[3] hospitably

[2]Since the sorority girls are neither wives nor graduate students, there must be something wrong here. I don't understand it either.

[3]Mlles. Talhelm and Trost, who visited me in my office, were more formally outfitted: shoes and all that. Miss Talhelm reminds me of Lois Moran.

conducted me through the entire dwelling and added an excellent cup of coffee.

SMAGS, you should know, is a demilune of buildings located well off whatever that road is that leads from the Saucon Valley fields into Hellertown. I was rather worried over it at one time, for it is only half a mile or so from the site where the Convocation Center is to rise to the tune of $3,700,000, a region that on October 28 Professor Don Ryan (Geology) suspected of sinkholes. Whatever happens to the Convocation Center, though, SMAGS is safe enough, he added, because *it* is built on a flood plain. I asked Professor Larry Whitcomb (Geology, retd.) what that meant, and I learned that a flood plain is a plain subject to flooding. Indeed there was a time last spring when you could have held a regatta on the SMAGS parking lot, but they tell me that something has been done about it. So SMAGS, if sometimes under water, is founded on solid, though humid, territory, and a very handsome complex it is, with a graciously landscaped area out front and a cornfield stretching north toward South Mountain in the rear. Miss James wished that the agriculturalists of the neighborhood would confine their harvesting to daylight hours but agreed that the racket they made was no more than a seasonal nuisance.

The sororities—on five-year leases with option to renew—occupy the three central high-rise (three-story) units in the complex. Judging by AGD—the units are almost identical—each group has remodeled the ground floor of its lair so as to provide a spacious living room, dining room, and kitchen. AGD has a TV room, an office, and a guest bedroom. There are ten apartments above, consisting of living room (complete with kitchenette), two bedrooms, and bath. Forty members could be squeezed in altogether, Miss James said, but 36 is a comfortable maximum, and she hopes it can be kept that way. The remodeling was supposed to be finished by November 1, but no one took that deadline very seriously—when I was there a few days earlier, workmen were still smearing a black glop on the dining-room floor—but no doubt it is more or less done by now and the inhabitants can arrange their furniture. In the end everyone expects to do her own cooking over the weekends and to employ a pro during the week. In the meantime, which may last into February, the problem of cuisine is fluid and inconvenient. Thus Gamma Phi Beta had a cook lined up for early November. But would the cook have a kitchen?

Practically AGD has a washer and dryer room, greatly in requisition: let the hum of the washer cease, and in 30 seconds the next applicant, her arms piled high with camisoles, shirtwaists, and petticoats, is at the door. Aesthetically this house is lucky in possessing a virtuosa in macramé, whose work—I especially admired an almost life-size giraffe—adds a lively interest to the decor of the common rooms.

I can assume that the other two houses are generally similar to AGD, except, perhaps, for the macrame.

The sororities have suffered no such harassment as has victimized Apt. 55 in RH-11, which complained last fall of mysterious noises in the walls and which a year earlier had been afflicted by bees, or that's what they said.[4]

Bus service to and from the campus, an important consideration to those who do not own their own Porsches, is now deemed generally satisfactory, following a period of early squabbles. Miss Trost felt that though parties on the other side of the mountain tend to be over around 1:00, a 2:15 special would get a good play. And she added that more than a minicar is often needed at the closing of the library—somewhere about midnight, I think—when earnest students have sometimes found themselves three miles from home in mountain country, learned but disconsolate.

Nevertheless the amenities immeasurably outweigh the trifling drawbacks, not least because SMAGS has brought the sororities together into essential communities. *The Brown and White,* ever on the alert to discover a Cause to make a fuss about, presented (September 30) the sororities as awash in grievances yet unwilling

[4]I think that Apt. 55 is in bigger trouble than it knows. It may have nothing but a poltergeist, but I'd call in my friendly neighborhood exorcist.

to discuss them: a view firmly rebutted by Miss Talhelm (October 7) and still more firmly rebutted by all three presidents (October 21).

No doubt all three groups have gleams in their eyes as they fantasy homes of their own—equal rights and so on. At present with building costs soaring like the express elevator at Radio City, this is a long-term ideal. A plain but comfortable dwelling could be thrown together, they tell me, for about $1,200,000 no doubt. But next year? And the year after that? It seems to me that an alternative solution might be to take over some of the redundant floor space already in existence, e.g., the president's house, which is absurdly large for Dr. Lewis, who could easily be accommodated in a cozy suite in the Alumni Building, right next to his office.

The sororities are not concerned exclusively with housing. Each one is enjoined by its national organization to justify itself by engagement in Works of Corporal Charity, supplemented by any local project that commends itself. Their beneficiaries are many: the mentally retarded, YMCA swimming classes, the multiply sclerotic, the hospitalized children at St. Luke's, a camp for the underprivileged, the residents of homes for the aged, the Heart Fund, and more besides.

Some of their methods come as novelties to me. I am not surprised at their selling chrysanthemums, stadium-type, during the football season. Nor at their peddling lollipops, though surely this must be a slow mover among those of college age? But I am stirred by the singing valentines available at $.50 in February, especially because I believe they are delivered vis-à-vis, not telephoned. And still more by the romantically entitled Slave Day, on which you can hire eight hours of a young woman's time for $10.[5] Within limits, no doubt. I see such an Abigail as sewing on buttons, dusting, or emptying wastebaskets, but not processing the garbage and still less spraying her employer with rose water after his bath or being thrown into a piscina to fatten his pet lampreys.

[5]Or ten hours of her time for $8. My notes are somewhat jumbled.

As of even date the men have not moved to reciprocate this servile accommodation, though it looks to me like a sure money-maker, a new Xerox.

Harking back to the times I know best, I recall that individual houses often developed their own stigmata. KA, for instance, were restrained, gentlemanly men with a bias toward academic excellence; at DKE you could throw a paper airplane in no direction without hitting an athlete; and Alpha Delta Phi were sophisticated, beautifully dressed, well-connected, effortless in small talk.[6] I asked Miss Trost whether the sororities had begun to produce any such recognition symbols. "Not at all," she felt. Gamma Phi Beta certainly, and the others so far as she had observed them, exhibited a happy product mix held together by congeniality, not by humor (in the Jonsonian sense). She did add that Gamma Phi Beta had three Phi Betes last year, underlining my suggestion of 1976 that Phi Beta Kappa is going to be a girls' club sooner or later. Far from raising restrictions, her sorority affiliation had virtually demolished them. "I wouldn't have met half as many girls or got to know them any other way," she said.

Miss James felt that AGD's successes—the intramural championship plaque, for one—are due to reliability rather than to flair. "We show up," she said.

I am delighted to learn that pins remain a significant feature of the social operation, for though they remain very pretty things, I see them today far less frequently than I did when men wore vests. I had got the mistaken impression that pins were now merely a bijouterie laid away in a box somewhere, like a fire insurance policy. Not so in the brave days of old. It is understood that then the hardy members of St. Anthony—always an austere society—would attach their badges firmly to their epidermis when taking a bath; and even in the times that I remember, they tended to hold them in their mouths during overall ablutions. That's loyalty! It reminds

[6]Never mind what Psi U was noted for.

me of one of my uncles by marriage, a Yale man, member of Skull and Bones. It was a regular diversion in his family to mention Bones in casual conversation just to make Uncle Walter leave the room. We don't find that kind of integrity these days!

Anyhow, as I was starting to say, the pins continue to be sacramentally important and are duly honored. A candlelight ceremony distinguishes the lassie who has won her trophy in the field, and if she proceeds yet further to an actual engagement I believe that music is added to the candles.[7] I wish I could think that the male undergraduates are equally gracious in recognizing achievement.

Preceded by open houses now and then during the fall, formal rushing for freshmen is conducted in the spring, following the holiday. Each girl who has exhibited interest must visit all three groups, and through an adjustment of preferences on both sides the bidding takes place at the end of a week. Upperclass rushing may take place informally throughout the fall semester.

Now that the sororities are no longer a novelty and have found themselves in visible, desirable headquarters they are rapidly falling into an accepted feature of the landscape. A welcome feature, too, for everything I have seen and learned about them shows them as socially and academically valuable units of this community, freely associated, devoid of fantasy, conscientious, and competent in ordering their proprieties.

I'm only sorry that you have to sell so many chrysanthemums to raise $1,200,000.

Vivan le femmine! as Don Giovanni put it.[8]

[7]If she is actually *married,* I extrapolate at least a fireworks display followed by a kitchen shower.

[8]I realize that he came to a bad end, but surely you could say that his fault was an excess of good will.

When Expensive Icicles Hang from the Wall

Fall, '79

As I sat last August in the chequer'd shade, idly leafing through the reminiscences of Frances Hill, pausing now and then to admire a passage of particularly fine writing, and sipping a Pepsi Light, a black walnut struck me a glancing blow on the temple and knocked my glasses off. Like Newton's apple it redirected the thought processes of its victim, and after my head stopped ringing, I realized, not a new hypothesis in kinetics, but that it would soon be autumn, that the Stanley Cup might be decided any day, that the Phillies had ritually blown it again, and that before long, Kirks Inc. of Pleasant Valley, distributors of heating oil, would be dispatching the tank truck that would soon be as familiar a sight at my door as the milkman.

The spring of '79 was horrid enough to satisfy T.S. Eliot, the summer was straight out of Dante, and according to my goose bone, next winter is going to be the White Hell of Pitz Palu all over. We shall be ready for it here, though. For one thing we are absolutely going to close the 24-hour cat window and keep it closed.

But although my domestic situation is inherently interesting, Lehigh alumni are probably more concerned with their university as it faces higher energy costs and an unspeakable winter.

In the following discussion I have tried to touch on what we have done and are doing, and to embody certain suggestions—some practical, some visionary—to supplement the effort. I see our challenge as facing the entire community—the Family—not just Buildings and Grounds. And if my somewhat involuted method reminds you of Henry James, reading whom always gives me the

bends, all I can say is that it came out that way.

Let it be granted that the university is aware of possible fuel shortages, inevitable price boosts, and cold weather in January and February. Now consider the magnitude of its operation.

I don't know how many buildings the university has. I started to count them on the map in the catalog, but the phone rang when I was somewhere in the twenties and I lost track. Anyway, there are quite a few, say 75, some of them fairly large. You can best get the picture if you calculate from a single unit, in this case my own house for convenience. In 1965 it cost $225.53 to heat Grendlesmere, as it is known; in 1975 $479.49; in 1978 $776.41; and for 1979 I just don't want to know. If the university has 75 times more buildings than I do, it cost at least $58,230.95 to heat them in 1978, and even that figure may be an underestimate.[1]

All right, then. During the last fiscal-type year (July to July) we got through 1,300,000 gallons of oil and 21,000 mcf of gas, according to Mr. Bergeron of Buildings & Grounds, who kindly

[1]Indeed it seems so. According to Miss Lusardi of the *Bulletin's* research staff, there are 94 buildings. According to B&G, the fuel bill is more like $644,430. In reaching her total of 94, I suppose that Lee Ann properly omitted the fraternity houses, which heat themselves.

filled me in on many of these details. The university sensibly burns gas during the summer, when there is too much of it, and oil from November to April, when UGI grows costive. Also some electricity, which we get about $.035 per kilowatt-hour because we do all the hard work ourselves and step it down from some absurd voltage like 12,600 to a potential more suitable for desk lamps, power-driven pencil sharpeners, and the like.

Not indifferent to contemporary developments, B&G is always working on prudent modifications of its function. It replaces insulation with heavier insulation; it installs storm windows lavishly. Recognizing that our classrooms have often been prodigally overheated, it attaches here and there clever little valve things that maintain an even temperature, no matter what. During the Christmas holidays it shuts off everything in sight and pulls the plugs on the Coke machines and water fountains. One December 23 I found that it had left just enough power in the Maginnes elevator to carry me to the fifth floor, but none at all to open the door. Ringing the alarm bell in the empty building got me nowhere, and I might have been incarcerated till Epiphany had I been unable to extricate myself, like Allan Quatermain escaping from King Solomon's Mines.

Since the 1,300,000 gallons of fuel oil consumed in 1978-79 was down from 1,700,000 the year before, these economies are clearly worthwhile.

Pursuing the subject further, I consulted the Transportation office. This is a comparatively new aspect of the administration, formally inaugurated only last year, when it seemed desirable to establish a spiritual home for the buses that go over the mountain to SMAGS, the 15-passenger vans for geological field trips, and so on. It is under the direction of Christopher J. Christian '78.

I do not want to be diverted into the bus transport operation for its own sake, but it constitutes the umbilical cord linking the campus with SMAGS and runs hourly from 8:00 a.m. to 12:25 a.m. most days, to 2:25 a.m. Fridays and Saturdays.[2] A formidable fleet of vans, buses, and plain ordinary cars are at the university's disposal, and they consume a great deal of spirit.

Well, the total consumption runs about 40,000 gallons per year, the price is going up, and Mr. Christian's chief comfort is that there is apparently no problem of supply. He thinks it would be handy for the university to develop some gasoline storage capacity. I fancy it would then be unnecessary to run down to a service station every two or three days, and we could take advantage of any fluctuations in price. More important, he hopes eventually to wangle an allocation from the state. The present position is that anything less than 86,000 gallons per year is peanuts in the eyes of Pennsylvania Department of Energy (DOE). It would be simple, Mr. Christian said, to win the allocation by doubling our annual consumption, but in a way it would be self-defeating too. So he hopes that in time the DOE may sober up and lower its sights.

As far as I can see, all this is most commendable. I wonder, though, whether I may make a couple of diffident suggestions.

For one thing, I believe that President Lewis is a director of PP&L. Suppose that within the privacy of a board meeting he could negotiate a special bargain for his university, a kind of gentlemen's agreement. Nothing big; say 10 percent. I feel sure that PP&L could easily cover it under Depreciation or Miscellaneous in the quarterly report. If Dr. Lewis is also on the boards of Exxon, Atlantic Richfield, and UGI, he might be able to work it there, too.[3]

Failing that, I take a leaf from the book of an artful friend of mine. His annual electric bill runs around $275, and he has bought enough common stock of PP&L to take in more than that in dividends. He giggles up his sleeve, he tells me, when he makes out the monthly check because Billing at PP&L think they're making money on him, while Disbursements are returning him 117 percent. Does the university's portfolio include enough PP&L to get free electricity this way? Or Exxon, Atlantic Richfield, and UGI?

Then it seems to me that the university used to burn coal. I

[2]My wife says I mean Saturdays and Sundays, really.

[3]It would be dishonorable to offer an honorary degree except *honoris causa*, but I thought I'd just mention it.

know what must have happened, because the same thing happened to us when we first moved into fashionable Bucks County. We burned coal too, and it was very satisfactory, and dirt cheap by modern standards. But after two or three years my wife began to complain about it. The shoveling was raising hell with her back, she said (though she is very wiry for a woman of 110 pounds), and lugging out the ashes was even worse. Nothing would do but that we convert to oil—clean, effortless, and above all, modern—and we could even have a rumpus room in the cellar. I imagine that roughly the same thing happened at Lehigh, and that is why we have to raise the tuition to keep Islam in more-than-Oriental splendor.[4] Has the university considered a humiliating but frugal reconversion? Mr. Bergeron tells me that you can now get coal so artfully processed that far from polluting the atmosphere of a neighborhood, it is smokeless, rather bracing, and tending to clear the sinuses. Even its ash is some way useful down at the Steel Company.

Now, by way of turning to other options. I want to dramatize two relevant principles, one ethical and one psychological.

I think the ensuing narrative is a solar myth and thus probably familiar, but my great-uncle Alfred Haswell said it happened to him in 1910. Those days he lived up in the hills beyond West Hoosick, New York; it's a densely unpopulated region even now, and because Uncle Alfred lived farther from the village than the road commissioner did, midwinter communications were often unsatisfactory. The winter of 1909-10 was a perfectly beastly winter, he said, using a livelier epithet than mine, and never more so than after a three-day blizzard that began around January 10 and went on for three days, more or less. By that time there wasn't any countryside left, nor any sign of life for another week or so. Finally one morning Uncle Alfred saw somebody fighting his way along where

[4]My sister-in-law is so annoyed with the Middle East that she has poured acid on a profusely illustrated gift edition of the *Rubaiyat* and canceled her subscription to *The Chic of Araby*, a fashion magazine published in Baghdad.

the road should have been, and in time recognized his neighbor Luther something—I forget his other name—and called to him to turn in and set a spell.

". . . weather," said Luther, a plain-spoken man, no mealy-mouth. "I got to . . . store."

"What's the trouble?" said Uncle Alfred.

"Trouble," said Luther. "Snowed in for ten . . . days and not a . . . speck of . . . nutmeg in the house."

This experience teaches us several things, principally that some people make unreasonable demands of their environment;[5] few would be so upset by this particular deprivation. Perhaps it is not too soon for epicures at Lehigh to lay in a supply of condiments or resolve to do without them.

My second idyll comes from a piece of melodramatic fiction that I encountered long, long ago at a time when it was already out of date. Somebody in an automobile was pursuing somebody else for some reason or other, and my heart was supposed to be in my mouth as I read that, "Five—ten—fifteen miles an hour the great car roared through the night." What this proves is that people are adaptable. During the early forties, when we had gasoline rationing thanks to the war and I was classified A (or negligible) because I then had no discoverable purpose in life, I used to drive slowly as a conservation measure—the folklore of the time said that 25 mph was the most economical of speeds—and I was surprised to find that after a week or so 25 came to seem like a perfectly reasonable mode of procedure. And when some urgency forced me to throw discretion to the winds and rev up to 35, I found the pace almost frightening: houses, telephone poles, hot dog stands, cut-rate furniture outlets became a mere blur as I scorched through Middlesex County, fighting to hold my '37 Ford on the road.

Another words, as the freshmen frequently wrote, even an

[5]I said "unreasonable." If Luther had run out of oregano or capers, I could see it.

undergraduate does not need all the luxuries he is accustomed to and can easily reshape himself to a less demanding lifestyle. If we're thinking of cars particularly, and I am, the faculty of course are no problem, for all they do with them is jam them into the Maginnes parking lot and leave them there. But what of those *in statu pupillari?* I don't suggest that everything was infallibly superior in the colleges of the twenties; but where I went, only juniors and seniors could have cars at all. And though the nearest girl was 65 miles away, we were no more psychologically maladjusted than folks generally are. Last year about 1,567 students were registered with the Motor Vehicle Office at Lehigh, though girls were all over the immediate campus like a mulch.

Several of my advisors, not very originally, counsel more clothes and lower room temperatures. One of them is purchasing the French Creek sweater he heard of on TV; it would keep him cozy, he figures, even on Ellesmere Island, let alone in the Valley. Another was touting psychological suggestion: He has a trick thermometer that he can set to record the temperature that *he* would like, never mind how cold it is really. He says it works like a charm. And that, he adds, is just why you shouldn't get a Celsius type, which would keep you shivering all winter. A third party commended the example of Gerald Tsai. To keep his head clear, Tsai always set his office thermostat at 55, and at the age of forty he cashed in a stack of chips for $30,000,000.[6] We should take as our ideal, my friend said, the savages of Tierra del Fuego, those who, clad exiguously if at all, perspired freely at some distance from the fire that barely warmed the mobled Europeans hovering over it.

I believe in togetherness myself. Mr. Bergeron tells me that if you start with Grace Hall at 55, a wrestling crowd sends it into the 70's in a matter of minutes, and he doesn't see why twice the number of warm bodies won't do the same in the Convocation Center. Nor is it necessary to gather together 6,000 or even 3,000 people to

[6]It won't work *all* the time. Louis XIV was both a fresh-air type and one of the biggest nincompoops of his day.

produce this effect, not since we introduced coeducation.[7]

A more original thinker told me last week that a great deal of gasoline would be saved if we drove a tunnel through South Mountain, halving the distance to Saucon Valley and more than halving the expenditure of fuel. Professor Ryan (Geology) tells me, however, that South Mountain is composed of what he calls granite gneiss, about 1 billion years old, a recalcitrant substance and one of no great commercial value when extracted. A very costly venture, then, and one that would take years to pay for itself.

The suggestion that we exploit our hydraulic resources seems to me even less promising. There is no significant water-power on South Mountain, only a trifling dribble barely sufficient to electrify a dollhouse.

Finally: Has B&G checked the windows in Room 318 of Christmas-Saucon? (I haven't been in there since the English department was extruded in 1970.) The 25 years I occupied that room, an east wind would turn the plastic pinwheel on our bookcase, let the sashes be closed ever so firmly.

Any way you look at it, it's going to be a tough winter.

[7]I remember a freshman about 20 years ago who wrote a theme on "My Roommate." He was lucky in having a congenial one. As he put it, ". . . and after three months I know that I couldn't have a nicer bedfellow." He was a wholesome, well-balanced young man, and I think that his good will simply outran his command of diction.

Wistful Vista

Remembrances of college years past

Spring, '86

First of all, the historical background, if not precisely essential, is colorful and exciting. Wistful College was founded in the eighteenth Century by a prominent colonial citizen greatly interested in both real estate development and the perpetuation of his name: his will provided a then-substantial sum for the establishment of a "free school" in a then-nameless township on condition that the area be dubbed Wistfulville.

Unfortunately the founder, an Army officer as well as other things, did not live to see the consummation of his wishes as he would have preferred to do. There was no problem about the name, but the school was long held up by the exigencies of international politics, for the French and Indian War was more or less going on at the time. Familiar with British tactics as exhibited in America during the previous 150 years, Major Wistful was understandably pessimistic when the British set out to dislodge the French from Crown Point.

Indeed his pessimism was all too well justified, for the British on their last day found themselves marching in parade formation, band playing martial airs so loud that they were heard in Albany—at a time when they should have been going on tiptoes. Anyway, the British proceeded in perfect order into a ravine with the foe in the woods to the right, in the woods to the left, and behind a breastwork right ahead. I have never understood why there were any survivors at all. It is a comfort to know that the founder, a smarter man than Sir William Johnson, would not have led an army into a trap like that.[1]

But I digress. After the French had blown it in the Northeast and the Indians were more a bother than a menace, the college was actually founded in the sense that a building was built, a faculty of three or four—they had failed to get tenure at Yale—was collected, and a student body large enough to fill a one-room schoolhouse turned up from somewhere. (The free-school notion, by the way, was dropped early, as you know if you are paying tuition at Wistful today.) Wiseacres around there said that Wistful would never amount to anything, situated as it was in the wilderness and not even on the way from anywhere to anywhere else.

W.C. Bryant spent most of a sophomore year around 1811 at Wistful, but, unable to satisfy the rigorous academic requirements, transferred to Yale, the occasion for his composing "Thanatopsis."

Things went on like this till after the War of 1812, as they say, somebody noticed that Wistful had *no Traditional Rival.* Thus arose the establishment of Aimless College, designed for those less-robust students and faculty members who were tired of climbing the mountains whenever they wanted to go to Boston and who, though the Indians were becoming a spenter force every day, felt safer when on the east bank of the Connecticut River.[2]

The founding of Aimless made possible a traditional Big Game every autumn; and so Wistful introduced football as a major sport. The longest trip in my life was my return from Aimless after one of these contests with four helpless but not inactive drunks sick to the stomach in the rear seat.

Wistful grew but little during the nineteenth century, indeed as one graduate put it, it consisted of but two men, the

[1]In order to attack the French, established a long way *north* of them, the British and Colonials were marching *south.* I never got the hang of it myself. Many Wistful undergraduates, otherwise bemused, have too easily assumed that the founder was fighting *against* the British some 20 years after his death on the field of battle and in a different war. It is all too easy to lose perspective.

[2]The defecting president, eastbound, carried in his saddlebags most of the Wistful library.

president on one end of a log and a student on the other. Even at the turn of the century it could be described by G. Santayana as an "unassuming little college among the hills."

But when the Indian menace was finally laid to rest at Wounded Knee in 1890, Wistful was free to develop, and during the first decades of the twentieth century it did so. When I entered as a freshman in those Dream Days, the student body had swelled to an unwieldy 800.

So much for the background. We come to the present day via a letter that I received last spring.

> *Dear Wistful Alumnus,*
>
> *I wonder if I could trespass on your time for a few minutes.*
>
> *I am a member of the Class of 1985 at Wistful, and I should like to elicit your help in a project that I am currently engaged in connection with my major in Sociology.*
>
> *I have chosen to write my major essay this spring on the social developments at Wistful during the last 50 or 60 years; and I should be glad of any help you can give me with my work.*
>
> *For example, as you look back, what do you choose to emphasize as regards the fraternities* [now more or less destroyed], *cars, drinking, religious observance, and athletics? Has there been a sexual revolution? What about the quality of college life in general?*
>
> *I would greatly appreciate the favor of an early reply, as my paper is due during the last week of April.*
>
> *Sincerely yours,*
> */s/ Bosworth Field*

Naturally I did not do what *Bosworth* wished me to do. I answered his letter, of course, but I pointed out that he was asking for not fewer than 25,000 words in a little over three weeks, that I was a professional and did not hand out Oakleys, but that if he could hold up his deadline for a while I would—for the sake of Wistful—

make him a bargain price of ten thousand dollars.

I added a few useful notes (*Vide infra*) for his benefit, but I never heard from him again, and whether he produced an acceptable paper last April I shall probably never know.

As regards the fraternities... well, *Bosworth*, more nonsense has been written on this subject than on any other except maybe religion. They were voluntary associations of more or less congenial young men living on land and in buildings that they owned and maintained. Resenting their quasi-independence and recognizing their vulnerability—like that of a Sears branch in Moscow—Wistful inexpensively acquired the virtual possession of a great deal of valuable real estate by expropriating them and proscribing their membership. I don't read much of the alumni magazine except the obituaries, but I believe that though Wistful boasts a Young Communist Club, a Gay Community, a branch of the Camorra, and an Ophiolaters' Circle, the fraternity menace has been stamped out.

A freshman of unusual promise, I had no difficulty in making a desirable affiliation, especially because Father had been a founder of the chapter. No matter what you have heard, *Bosworth*, such membership implied no nonsensical nor hazardous hardship for its participants. Any hazing was stimulating rather than harmful. A tough-minded generation, we withstood the branding iron whimperless, and indeed the scars soon faded to a rather attractive rosy tint, and mine today is hardly legible.

It is true that our lives were subject to certain stringencies: reasonable quiet in the evening; jackets, clean shirts, and neckties at dinner. But since most of us had learned these lessons at home, we did not feel them as impositions. Indeed I get the impression that we were somewhat repressed by modern standards. No case of rape, no assault and battery occurred in the fraternal atmosphere; nor did any brotherhood amuse itself by defiling the property of another. Still and all, we had a good time.

Cars... juniors and seniors could have them, but—just as today—they were a great trouble and expense. In the first place, there was plenty to do right in Wistfulville. Then if you had to go somewhere, it was easier to get a free ride with someone else. It was more important to own a coonskin coat, or so I thought, feeling that my baccalaureate would be tarnished if I were without one. My coat is still around in a closet somewhere, having gone a second time to college when my daughter took it along as a kind of status symbol when she entered Smith; she could not have done that with a 1928 Chevrolet. Cars were most important during rushing season, when some of the more costly ones, parked in front of the houses, suggested sophisticated opulence within.

No cars at Wistful were jalopies with funny phrases painted on them. Anyone at Wistful would have died rather than use the word "frat."

Drinking. . . on account of Prohibition there wasn't by recent standards much drinking, no matter what you have heard, *Bosworth*; the nearest dram was too far away. There was some, of course, especially on festal occasions, and anyone who wanted to make a pig of himself could do it by taking some trouble. It seems to me now that a little went a long way. For a houseparty weekend, a fifth of unleaded gin was deemed adequate to support the élan of an undergraduate and his guest through two nights of revelry.[3]

Drinking, in other words, was peripheral to a Wistful education, not vital to it, though one met the usual disposition to see excess as both manly and hilarious, as it is not. On Sunday mornings the campus was not snowdrifted under plastic cups.

Religion . . . Wistful was very religious when I went there, conducting 8 services per week and taking attendance. I did not find anything very awful in this disposition. I like going to church, and at 7:45 a.m. on weekdays I might as well have been in chapel as anywhere else. The Sunday services, too, were wholesome as requiring those present to have washed and shaved and to conduct themselves with propriety. Few, though, went so far as to attend in

[3]A frugal man, like myself, invited to a houseparty only a girl who he knew did not drink, a substantial saving.

cutaways.

Thanks to petitioning and mild unrest, the rules were somewhat relaxed in my later days. The annoying thing about the petitioners was their sanctimoniousness, for they protested that the attendance policy was *ipso facto* antireligious, that true religion had to be spontaneous, and similar blather. I used to wonder why the petitioners hadn't gone to a college that let them sleep all morning.

Athletics... I am sure that they are much more sophisticated today. Athletics spelled prestige in our small community, but mainly folks engaged in sport because they enjoyed it; nobody hoped to base a career on it. (I was several years out of college before I learned that professional football existed.) Indeed the athletic program was conducted with a great deal of barnyard informality: one of my least-happy recollections is of being haled from a hot shower at 10:30 one January evening so that I might spend the next two hours with a garden hose putting the frosting on some tennis courts for the sake of a hockey match the next day. Other winter sports, too, were still in the barrel-stave stage of development: The one ski jump had been prepared by a village carpenter, and why no one was killed on it wonders me to this day.

Wistful graduates wanted to go into law, letters, banking, and real estate, not into the NFL. I myself had little to do with the athletic program after two years of compulsory PT. No doubt I could have achieved distinction on the gridiron, the rink, and the diamond had I chosen to take the trouble. But being physically immature at my rather early age—I entered Wistful at 14—I was advised against varsity competition until I should have filled out and gained my strength. The varsity W that I sometimes wear in cold weather I did not exactly *earn*. It goes back to the time when my daughter, dissatisfied because her father seemed to her to have no distinction of any kind, awarded it to me by way of a custom-executed pullover.[4]

Sexual revolution . . . not in those halcyon days, for coeducation at Wistful, I am happy to remember, still slept in the womb of Time, and a very good place too. (If you wanted girls all over the place and in the way, why didn't you go to NYU?) To be sure, men and women in their vigorous youth—from 10 to 55—have always been prone to make fools of themselves in following their hearts. But if I can believe half of what I hear today, and I don't—for much of it is bound to be gutter boasting—Mr. and Miss Modern Collegian, far from being emancipated, are trapped, did they but realize it. You might as well say that a hophead is emancipated when freed from the demands of prudence and personal hygiene.

At Wistful in the twenties—that era of jazz and Babylonian excess, as everyone knows that didn't live in it—there was far less of that foolishness in college than I am told there is now. (See, for example, Percy Marks, *The Plastic Age*, 1924, for a picture of the erotic situation at Brown in those days, and consider that this rather tame and often silly book enjoyed a considerable *succès de scandale.*) Undergraduates often talked as big and vulgar as anyone else; much of the dialogue at Wistful would have raised blushes in a Welsh coal mine; there was a little choral bawdry about Wearing a Purple Ribbon. But not very many garters were actually snapped. The nearest girls were 65 miles away, and it was easier to take a cold shower.

I do recall that at the May houseparty of 1930 one of our guests—Phyllis Carrington—was discovered to be wearing no stockings. This exhibitionism excited some comment but no real scandal. Phyllis had a figure to rival Stupefyin' Jones's, but she was no more wanton than Abigail Adams, and she and her host survived the weekend without disaster of any kind.

Phyllis was wrong, though, in going barelegged, for the back-seam stockings of those days did more for a girl's legs than any

[1]There was the time when I ran the 440—uphill, mind you—in a trifle over 36 seconds; but the occasion was unofficial, and I was clocked on a Big Ben alarm; the record would probably not stand up if challenged. As for my lack of distinction, I was elected to Phi Beta Kappa, which meant nothing to my daughter at all. Actually I was elected because someone on the committee miscalculated my scholastic average. Not wishing to embarrass him, I did not trouble to point out his error.

The well-dressed college man of the 20's.

Chapel of Wistful College.

subsequent hosiery.

Not much of a revolution.[5]

"What about the quality of [your] college life in general?" It was immeasurably superior to yours, *Bosworth.*

[5]Mount Holyoke required that an orchestra have at least one violin and not more than one saxophone.

Afterword: The French and Indian War

Most people—judging by responses on "Jeopardy!"—think that the French and Indian War was fought between the French and the Indians, and indeed it sounds like that. But such was not the case. The French and the Indians were *allies*, fighting shoulder to shoulder against the British and the Yankees. But, admittedly confusing, there were also some *nice* Indians—Chingachgook and Uncas spring to mind—on *our* side, fighting *against* the French and the *other* Indians.

The French and Indian War was really just one of a series of Wars that made life burdensome in America for a hundred years or so. Some are known as King William's War, Queen Anne's War, King George's War, and then finally the French and Indian War (proper), so called because by then there was another King George and the repeated denomination might have been misleading.

In Europe, where there were no Indians to speak of, these Wars had to have other and still more confusing names like the War of the Spanish Succession, the War of the Austrian Succession, and so on.

Many find this period incoherent, but the way to understand it is keeping track of Louisburg on Cape Breton Island. The French began the whole sorry business by building an impregnable fortress there. This irritated the British, who captured it in the first of the Wars, but gave it back, according to the terms of the treaty that they signed at the close of hostilities. Then the French rebuilt it even more impregnably than the first time, and so it went on for a long while. The British and the Yankees would pregn Louisburg, generally under Sir William Pepperell, and then give it back the next time they signed a treaty, so that it could be rebuilt in anticipation of the next War. Finally William Pitt, perceiving that Louisburg was the key to the whole situation, refused to recede it to the French after the last of the Wars, and the whole era came to an end around 1760.

The French being no longer bothersome without Louisburg, the stage was set for the American Revolution, which began about 15 years later and which Louisburg played no part in that I remember.

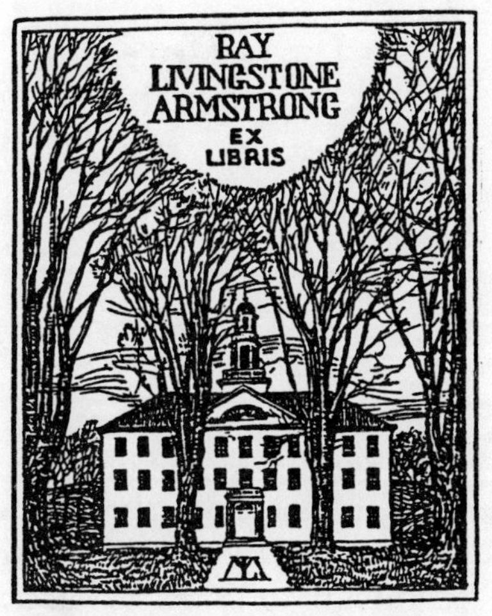

Commencement Week

Vive La Difference

Sylvia the fair, in the bloom of fifteen,
Felt an innocent warmth, as she lay on the green.

—Dryden

Once upon a time there was a magazine here called the *Lehigh Burr.* Why *Burr* I don't know.[1] Recently we could have commemorated its ambiguous decease, which took place about 50 years ago.

But somehow or other 1984 closed at Lehigh, and so did 1985, before anyone thought to honor (or at least mention) The *Lehigh Burr* a half century after its death. The *Burr,* in case you didn't know it, was a more or less humor magazine, a type of publication then deemed essential to a college, like football and a faculty. It was founded, like everything else at Lehigh, by R.H. Davis, back in 1898, and unfounded by Dean McConn shortly after the December 1934 issue appeared. Peace to its ashes; for whatever you as a subscriber might have thought of it, it was second-class matter according to the Bethlehem post office, and never mind the wide-open comment.

"When the September '34 issue of the *Burr* was being prepared Dean C. Max McConn called a meeting of the staff and stated that he really didn't approve of a publication like the *Burr* to be a money maker for the editors and the business manager when they usually divided up $3,000 and he also said keep sex out of the magazine.[2]

"This last statement of course was bait [?] for the brainy

[1]A jealous rival once referred to it as the *Lehigh Ho Hum.*

[2]He didn't say what they were to replace it with. . . . I take it that the barbarous idiom in this passage is Whitney's, not the dean's.

editors so they went to work for the 'Keep Sex Out' issue.

"As soon as the magazine hit the street the dean threw the publication out of the university. Today we would have probably hired a lawyer, but in those days we did what we were told."[3]

So Sumner B. Whitney '35, who ought to know, for he was business manager in his senior year.

I disapprove of public oscillation in the parks
—Student theme

Back in the thirties, when a Viennese-type musical called *White Horse Inn* appeared in New York, someone asked someone else what the music was like. "Characteristic," was the laconic but adequate response. Characteristic too was the college humor magazine of those days, inspired chiefly by the original *Life* and by *Judge* (for though *The New Yorker* had been around since 1925, most folks knew better than to compete with it). Those collegiate counterparts that I retain any impression of, barring perhaps *The Lampoon*, resembled my performance upon the piano when my mother compelled me to "entertain" a luckless guest by playing "Träumeri."[4] A college ought to have a funny paper, and a child ought to play a musical instrument. Never mind the lack of talent.

The college humor magazine featured short satiric pieces of grimly lighthearted prose, cartoons of startling ineptitude (often illustrating a two-line gag), and a lot of other twoliners unillustrated.

Prof: *What's a skeleton?*
Frosh: *A stack of bones with all the people scraped off.*

As a great deal of the material was exchanges, content was fairly easy to come by.

The humor did indeed tend to be pro-sexual. It assumed carnal attraction as a powerful and omnipresent feature of the

[3]It was a more mannerly world in those days.

[4]"Träumerei" was ideal for me: short and very slow.

collegiate adolescent and thought it a good idea.

Soph. *I think we could make those two girls.*
Frosh: *Make them what?*

Sometimes these japes were no more inflaming than the love passages in *Tom Sawyer.* Sometimes they were tougher and remind me of children who invite each other to go out behind the barn so they can say swear words; young men exulting in the freedom to publish improprieties that would not have been countenanced in their homes: all good fun and maybe not much more antisocial than chalking slogans on box cars.

Well, then, this necessarily brief analysis can afford to look at only three broad considerations: Society and the Free Press; Human Sexuality Considered as Musak; and particularly the scarlet misbehavior of *The Burr,* LIV, 4 (December 1934).

I haven't bothered to look it up, but I feel sure that when the dean's lordly veto became known, various libertines wrapped themselves in the toga of Voltaire or the apron of Peter Zenger and cried aloud that any inhibition of anything whatsoever in print violated the provisions of the Twelve Tables, the Magna Carta, the Code Napoléon, in denying the freedom of the Press, without which no free man, etc. etc. All this (if it happened as I suppose or even if it did not) is a handful of gurry. Folks that clamor the loudest for such and such a freedom are commonly the ones least likely to extend it to anyone they disagree with. "*Auspicia nefas prohibent,*" as Ulpian (or one of that crowd) said: i.e., your behavior is more or less under the control of the circumstances wherein you find yourself. Thus when Father manually chastised me now and then and long ago for smoking cigarettes or throwing apples at my (female) cousin, he was not infringing my rights as a freeborn American. He was asserting his own rights as the one that sheltered and fed me and made the rules. Same with *The Burr.* Lehigh loves to call itself a Family—a very poor image, I think—and its Executive had a perfect right—somewhere short of the *Patria Potestas* (which allows the death penalty without any time wasted on tedious prosecution)—to insist on *its* judgment upon naughty children. Publish your flatulent obscenities, your daring allusions, if you must, but not under the shadow of our good name. Sounds reasonable.

> *Until the latter part of the nineteenth century*
> *reproductive processes can hardly be said*
> *to have had an existence.*
>
> —Student theme

If Moral Responsibility is difficult enough, Sex is hopelessly intractable; no one can really make *sense* out of it. What you can try to do is ignore it now and then. I remember Dr. B. I. Bell about 60 years ago saying in the course of a sermon that "in the beginning God created two sexes, and the human race is still behaving as if this were a novelty." At all events, 45 percent of us are boys and 45 percent are girls, so created, I am told, that we can perpetuate our race, a motive that must be one of the Deepest Things among the Deep Things of God, and in the process defile our planet, exterminate the more attractive inhabitants from the Aardvark on down, and of course generally outrage each other.

> *They had been in love, but the embers were*
> *no longer glowering.*
>
> —Student theme

Be that as it may, boys and girls tend to notice each other and often to get excited about it, ignoring *pro tem* the two fundamental aspects of such passion, its manifold inconvenience and its foolishment. We are endlessly fascinated by it less because we can't sleep at night than because we are subliminally ashamed of the extravagance it leads us into—or at least did so lead us in days when a decent formality laid a veneer over basic passion: the movie date followed by a banana split at the naborhood pharmacy, the $.25 valentine, and in some areas the May-basket; later the pathetic ring with a fire-sale diamond in it. The hopes, the fears, the ambiguities, the nightmares, and the rejections—hours and hours of time wasted while the real world demanded that the car be washed, the external woodwork painted, the trash put out.

> *I counsel you to avoid . The*
> *is momentary, the*

is ridiculous, and the is damnable.[5]

—Chesterfield

So much for sex. Now let us look upon *The Burr* in its last days. Surprisingly a money-maker on a small scale, its libertinism (as it might be called) attracted the unfavorable attention of the administration, as noted *supra.* Disaster ensued.

Why not? (A) The administration thought the contents of *The Burr* undesirable. (B) *The Burr* responded with a final number like firing on Fort Sumter, and reaped Appomattox.

Let us see.

The front cover, I guess it is, shows a stork on a rooftop holding a newborn infant in the conventional, pre-Pampers breech-clout. So far it might as well be *Parents' Magazine* or *Babies, Just Babies.*

Especially striking within are altogether four full-page ads for tobacco products; today they would be regarded as more obnoxious than any amount of pornography. When I saw the pitch for Lucky Strikes, my heart stood still, for there was the girl I dreamed about all that winter; it was clear, I felt, that if I were to find happiness in this world, I should have to find it with her. I knew, of course, that my then annual salary of $900 would not have bought her elbow-length gloves, and I had to spend the next year and a half smiling at grief like Viola's sister.

Shall I wasting in despair,
Die because a woman's fair?

—Geo. Wither

[5]That is, I *think* it's Chesterfield's; at least he might have written something like that to his natural son Philip. I know it perfectly well, but I couldn't check it in any of my three dictionaries of quotations. Professor Dilworth (Emer.), who is supposed to be familiar with the eighteenth century, said that he had never even *heard* it. I asked Professor Hook who was the eighteenth century trouble-shooter in the present English department; Hook hemmed and hawed and said that he wasn't sure but that there might not *be* one just now . . . . A Society of learned men, my foot.

Half a dozen pages are filled with exchange reprints. I am sorry to see that the one from my own ivy-covered academy is just as lame as all the others.

Do humor magazines abound on campuses today? I have no idea. If they do, I wonder whether they've grown up in the past 50 years.

An entire page is occupied by the following bitterly satirical epitaph: boxed in black, it proclaims "Sacred to the memory of a clean joke: we hope you have better luck finding one than we did." This sentiment is credited to the *Voo Doo.* I remember that name, but wherefrom did it issue? Union Theological? Any way you look at it, it proclaims a staggering lack of sophistication.

Inevitably a selection of japes is directed at departments and instructional personages. One suggests as a Christmas gift to a Dr. Sell: "A half dozen juicy worms for Dr. Sell to dissect and a female hippopotamus to perform an appendectomy on." It were laudatory to call this material ephemeral.

A full-page poem entitled "Sex." One stanza will do:

> The cystoms [sic] officials stopped being sissies
> And allowed the importation of Joyce's *Ulysses.*
> Damsels began doing their best
> To emulate naughty, sexy Mae West.

This illustrates the principle that though a versifier with a tin ear may get away with a monody on Death, he ought not to attempt light verse, which is rigorously demanding.

Enough yet. Anyone who is still interested in *The* ultimate *Burr* can find a copy around somewhere; probably in the Adult section of the rare books.

So then, why bother? Because *The Burr* was a fact in the history of our little community. It had something to say and said it again and again. (Ah, Youth!) It got into trouble as it deserved to do, and the majestic ship of the university sailed on through its wreckage. I am sure there is a lesson in it somewhere for all of us.

Chairete, Adelphai

Winter, '76

Back in the Golden Age of musical comedy—early in September 1927—*Good News* opened in New York and went on to run for years. Its setting at fictitious Tate College was so ruthlessly collegiate that George Olsen and his band, who provided the music, were more than suitably dressed, Olsen himself wearing a red crewneck sweater with a white varsity "T," awarded for what I have no idea. The plot was as silly as a musical comedy plot ought to be; the music was delightful—and still is, if you have forgotten the words—and the point at present is that the *Tribune* reviewer next day said that despite all his experience he had never expected to hear in the midst of an obvious Broadway hit a young woman singing a number called "A Girl of the Pi Beta Phi."

I caught *Good News* the second night—I developed mumps the next day, but that was a merest coincidence—and the girl of the Pi Beta Phi made me wish I could transfer to Tate. Mary Spargo, a Pi Phi from UVM in those days, told me later that her sisterhood had legitimately adopted the number, and I daresay that Pi Phi has been happily singing it ever since.

This brings us to Lehigh, where (until a little while ago) like the *Tribune* reviewer, I did not expect to hear sisterly lyrics in an erstwhile incongruous ambience.

Yet they are to be heard. That is, there are all of a sudden three sorority chapters at Lehigh, and no doubt they have songs of their own, as well as quiet, beautiful, and intelligent girls who, like Mary Lawler in *Good News*, could coach an athlete through an hour test and so preserve his eligibility.

This development was inevitable as soon as in 1971 Lehigh admitted the first women for better or worse (for I still think the question fairly moot). Safely on the sidelines now, I almost wish I

Soft lydian airs.

could have heard the *Geschrei* arising from Title IX if Lehigh, having coedicized, had prohibited sororities. Nothing of the sort occurred. Not at all: when these days a new body of undergraduate women comes into existence, the national sororities, ever watchful, gather around it to recommend themselves. And a fine, busy time they must have had of it over the last 15 years in American education.

Here at Lehigh, then, have been three groups of young women brought together by congeniality and a wish to turn it to some kind of account. Desiring and approached by national affiliation, they consider what is offered in terms of repute, stability, and helpfulness; and they make their choice accordingly. The result is the three Lehigh sororities, chapters of Alpha Phi, Gamma Phi Beta, and Alpha Gamma Delta. Two of them are of considerable antiquity, for what that honorable claim may be worth. College sororities began in a kind of way before the Civil War—upsetting to recent freshmen of my acquaintance who supposed that women were first taught to read and write in 1946. Alpha Phi was founded at Syracuse—as were the two others—in 1872, Gamma Phi Beta in 1874, and Alpha Gamma Delta in 1904. In my copy of *Baird's Manual,* published in 1927, Alpha Phi had 28 active chapters and one deadhead, while in Dean Quay's 1968 edition the figures are 89 and 9. Similarly considered, GFB was 33 and 1 (1927) versus 88 and 1 (1968); AGD 37 and 1 (1927) and 97 and 7 (1968). I conclude that they all must have been doing something right for the last half century. Add that all three have admirable records in public service and miscellaneous charitable activities.

There has been no fraternity hostility to the appearance of these women's organizations, as witness Paul Leitner '76, head of the Interfraternity Council, who kindly discussed it with me. Not surprising, for men seldom object to women as long as the women can be depended on not to get in the way of anything important. The IFC was purely receptive, Mr. Leitner said, when the formation of the women's societies came to its attention, and it has done everything that it could to promote and encourage them. It was not clear—this was back in November—whether the women would become members of IFC; they may find their own panhellenic organization more satisfactory. But recognized by IFC they currently are, and when they are ready for it there is no reason why they shouldn't be able to profit from the ministrations of the Fraternity Management Association.

Yes, Mr. Leitner thought after being pressured into it, girls do seem to be more "public spirited" than men are—a woman's group is more likely to put real zest and efficiency into Causes—though he pointed out quite rightly that the fraternities at Lehigh have not been precisely backward in this area. But female activity, perhaps for mildly competitive reasons, might very well stimulate greater extroversion in all of the social organizations here, that is, cherish more orphans, subsidize more EKG's, visit more hospitals. The sororities are more than a matter of us girls getting together to make black walnut fudge on Saturday night.

What of their chapter organization? For at present they are roaming about the mountainside without a fixed focus. I enjoyed the privilege of talking with Miss Robin Eeckhout '77, head of Alpha Phi, an attractive young woman with a Veronica Lake hairstyle and a manner that carries complete conviction and suggests a prosperous future for any group that she's connected with. On the assumption—which Miss Eeckhout tells me is a fairly valid one at this stage—that what is true of any one of the three groups is true of the others, I take Alpha Phi as representative.

It has at present 17 members and looks forward to a maximum of around 45, which Miss Eeckhout thinks is about right. (I think she's wrong; I think 32 is about right if you can make it financially viable; but it's her problem, not mine.) It would like to have a home of its own, but it is aware that unlike Camelot and Thebes a sorority house will not rise from the ground to the tune of anyone's harp. A likely pattern toward a prosperous future is the rental, then perhaps the purchase, of a suitable property as near the campus as possible; X number of years spent in exploring the joys and sharpening the angles of sisterly domesticity; and in the end, all going well, another lordly mansion on the heights, where, I believe, there is still room. The national organization is at hand with precept and advice; it even has money to lend. But any chapter will demonstrate its competence and integrity for a significant period of time before its national will help to subsidize Valhall at a price that a few years ago would have built Buckingham Palace. The newest society house on South Mountain cost around $500,000. Today it would cost perhaps $650,000. And tomorrow?

As the history of the national shows, Alpha Phi has a powerful bias in favor of eleemosynary activity. But the genesis of the chapter lies, as it should do, in friendship and congeniality.

Rushing, less protracted than the male version, should normally occupy one week in the late winter. Innumerable details remain to be worked out, but the bidding will probably be controlled by matching the preferential lists of aspirants.

The university, I need hardly say, has not been unaware that all these things have been burgeoning. Indeed its vigilance and sensitivity are, if anything, excessive, for almost a month after Alpha Phi's initiation in mid-November the *Brown and White* was complaining that final university approval is overdue. (It has since been granted.) The historian of this era is referred to a memorandum to Dean Quay over the signatures of Assistant Dean Drager and Assistant Dean Reeves, dated November 5, that presents a finely detailed pattern of the administrative view. *Inter alia,* any group to win approval would have to satisfy the following four conditions, which I abbreviate:

> 1. Adherence to all applicable regulations as stated in the *Handbook.*
>
> 2. Membership subject to no ethnic or credal disability.
>
> 3. Internal stability committed to long-term function at Lehigh.
>
> 4. Acceptance of "all the financial responsibilities that accompany sorority life."

It is clear that university approval is not lightly given and that the groups that it ultimately descends upon are going to be with us for a while and then some.

I might add that the memorandum finds the women's nationals comparing in general rather favorably with the men's in exhibiting closer organization and greater direct responsibility for their chapters.

Under current circumstances—and I mean the total of 800 women undergraduates—there is no thought of encouraging the foundation of further chapters than those that we have spoken of. The university, rather, will be interested in seeing how the three pioneers fare. It seems probable that they will provide an enduring enhancement to the coeducational establishment and an enrichment of the whole pattern of Lehigh social relationships.

And yet.

I do feel finally obliged to say that I see certain problems bound to obtrude themselves in the future of these hopeful and enthusiastic beginnings.

1. Alpha Phi pronounces the second element of its exoteric title as *fee.* I think that the girls may find themselves in the irritating fix of a Mr. Smyth, forced to contend lifelong for the orthography that he loves. The Department of Classical Languages, to be sure, confirms my impression that in the fourth century B.C. in Athens *Phi* would have sounded something like puh-hee iambically stressed. But we are on the so-called threshold of the so-called twenty-first century of the so-called Christian era.

2. The Allentown *Call-Chronicle* of November 16 described the initiation into Alpha Phi of 16 Lehigh undergraduates. If you can call it an initiation. It sounded to me more like a committee of the Junior League getting together to lay plans for a benefit musicale. Far from being held in a dank subcellar by the light of a corpse candle, it took place at the Hotel Bethlehem in broad daylight. The activities showed a similar lack of propriety: nobody had to carry a red-hot ploughshare for ten paces; nobody even had a garter snake dropped down the neck of her middy blouse. I can only hope that when Alpha Phi got away from all the deans and the parents it got down to business. (The other sororities will initiate their pledges this semester.)

3. This one is broader and longer. It came to me two days after the aforesaid initiations, when I first saw "Alpha Phi" pasted on the rear window of a car with a Lehigh parking sticker, and it may have sinister implications for the entire university community. "Sex Quota Kept but Abolishment is a Possibility," trumpets the *Brown and White* of December 5. Anybody knows what that means in the climate of today: the ceiling of 800 women may hold for next year, or for the year after that, but sooner or later... Did anyone but me notice that of the four members of 1976 initiated this fall into Phi Beta Kappa, three were women? I'm not saying it's good; I'm not saying it's bad. But does anyone hear the far-off whisper of a trend?

And now I ask you all to join me in the singing of the Almus Pater.

That's A Lot of Bulletin:

NOTE: Not for the first time I learn that a title of my choosing perplexes the editor, Mr. Ramsey, whose formal education exhibits curious lacunae. As every schoolboy knows, my title means, "Welcome, Sisters," and I thought it obvious as a cordial greeting to a trio of Greek-letter societies composed of young ladies. . . RLA.

Vexilla[1] Regis

Fall, '77

In a word, Religious Truth is not only a portion, but a condition of general knowledge. To blot it out is nothing short . . . of unravelling the web of University Teaching. It is . . . to take the Spring from out of the year; it is to imitate the preposterous proceeding of those tragedians who represented a drama with the omission of its principal part.

—John Henry Newman

Back in the Dark Ages I knew a man at college who, faced by the need to choose a topic for a term paper in the survey course, selected "The Influence of the Classics on English Literature." (He was only a sophomore.) His preliminary investigation revealed, however, that a really worthwhile job would take him about 50 years more than he had allotted, especially because he knew very little about the Classics either, and in the end he wrote on a more manageable, specialized theme, the imagery of Emerson's "Concord Hymn," a poem of some 16 lines.

Similarly I have found that my initial determination to survey the entire scene of religion at Lehigh—all its subdivisions, infiltrations, and implications—would require as much work as *The Golden Bough*, and I do not have time for it now. The physical problems of the chapel alone would fill a thesis. If I confine myself, therefore, to only a small region of Christendom, I trust that there may be imputed to me no sectarian indifference, let alone malice.[2]

Well, anyway, the relation between collegiate education and

[1]"The banners of the King advance." The great hymn of Venantius Fortunatus (fl. 6 c.).

[2]Some of my best friends are Methodists.

Chaplain Flesher and students.

Chaplain Flesher observes his daughter's art work.

religion has always been uneasy: you will find tension between administrative piety and pupillary fractiousness in any era—think of the sixteenth century—mainly, I imagine, not so much because of Pelagius, Abelard, Calvin, or Darwin, but because young men around the age of 20 are temperamentally at the lowest ebb of their spiritual sensibilities. Someone told me once that if he ever saw a truly pious and devoted body of undergraduates, it would scare the pants off him.

Thus in the mid-thirties when Bennington College was shiny and new, painfully aware of its prophetic voice while fearful that its slip might be showing, a pair of prospective parents—prospective in the educational sense, that is—were being shown about the place, and having seen everything else—the Dry Point Etching department, the Sociological Dance lab—they asked for the chapel. "We have none," said their bright young cicerone. "God has no standing on *this* campus."

Only a short time earlier God had a great deal of standing at the crossroads lyceum that I was then attending, for chapel services were held eight times a week, six of them at 7:45 a.m.[3] and twice on Sunday; there was a reasonable allowance of absences, but the system was basically compulsory and the turn-out in consequence good.

So much has been changed in recent years that Bennington may at present resemble a *béguinage*; while at my own alma mater, which I have been rather out of touch with, they may now flood the chapel in winter for intramural hockey.[4] In other words the emphasis changes with the climate and is not at all *quod ubique, quod semper, quod ab omnibus creditum est,* as St. Vincent memorably puts it, accepted in all places and at all times by everybody.

To the casual and thus mistaken observer, Lehigh considered as a religious community or at least as a community with some tincture of religion, may well seem to be sunk in a sloth reminiscent of the eighteenth century. Far from that. He is wrong who supposes our chapel filled with a dim religious light but little else, its chief function being to house the Bach Choir in May, now that the baccalaureate service has been demoted to a voluntary occasion.

[3]This was tough on Delta Phi. A new chapter at the time, they lived in an abandoned farmhouse three miles away.

[4]I wouldn't put anything past them. I heard last month that Andrew Young was one of their speakers in June and received an honorary degree. Since then, when asked where I got my schooling, I say that I was "privately educated."

The chaplain has demonstrated that the building can fairly vibrate with appropriate activity, and if he can further his aspirations, it is going to vibrate a great deal more.

There is the chaplain himself. The Reverend Hubert L. Flesher is well and favorably known to all readers of the Spring 1972 issue of the *Bulletin.* I had a hard time reaching him, for he left Bethlehem for a month's holiday on hearing that I wished to speak with him; others, I feel sure, find him more accessible. Be that as it may, he occupies a commodious office in the infirmary building, cheek by jowl with Motor Vehicle Registration: His bulletin board advises of opportunities in Yoga for the fall semester, and a fine study of Raggedy Ann by his daughter distinguishes the wall within. The chaplain himself, in addition to *being* chaplain, is director of all religious activities on the campus and is yet further a multiform functionary attached to the office of Dean Preston Parr '43, dean and vice president for Student Affairs. Since even further he may be called upon for almost any labor in the material sphere, he is a hard-working clergyman in the ghostly.

There is also a department of Religion Studies with four members on its staff and 22 courses listed as its offerings. Headed by Professor A. Roy Eckardt, it lives peacefully in Maginnes.

It may be true that the Lehigh scene seems virtually paralyzed when contrasted with the cultures and faiths elsewhere testifying to lively spiritual commitment: Northern Ireland, the Jordan Valley, and Kashmir come to mind. Not a single bombing nor even selective assassination has fractured the calm under the spreading chestnuts.

But as the Lord suggested to Elijah, the biggest things don't always make the most noise.

Getting back to the chapel, I repeat that it is a far less somnolent structure than my ill-advised casual observer might conclude. As the chaplain tells me—having returned from his holiday—it is developing into a more and more functional aspect of the campus.

The first section of pews in the nave, for instance, have been replaced by chairs designed with some reference to the human form. They are unadhesive, too. Many will remember the baccalaureate when, a spell of damp weather having succeeded a revarnishing, the university hymn brought the faculty to its feet with a mighty rending as it wrenched itself loose from the pews; many a gay academic hood bears to this day a stippled memorial.

The chaplain sees the building as properly open to a considerable variety of activities, as its recent history will show. Music and the drama particularly, within the bounds implied by its being a consecrated edifice.[5] To encourage that end, he hopes that it may be renovated so as to include such devices as selective lighting, curtaining, and so on, that will allow its adaptation to the demands of any given occasion, a dance group, appropriately framed and thus separated from the distracting vista of the chancel and sanctuary.

There are other possibilities and desiderata. Professor Robert Cutler, our chief organic practitioner, dislikes the acoustics, which have been ravaged by the installation of acoustic tile—a modern improvement—and anyway he feels that he would like a concert organ, that is, an organ not buried in the fabric but out in the open where he can cut loose and shiver the windows with it. More prosaically the chaplain wishes that the leaks in the roof might be discouraged and, more prosaically still, that toilet facilities might be added. A mere $1,700,000 would do it all, I understand: $1,250,000 for revamping the whole works, $300,000 for deferred maintenance,[6] and $150,000 to please Professor Cutler.

The catacombs, or more elegantly the undercroft, is still used sometimes for folk-singing and other questionable pastimes, but the chaplain both hopefully and confidently sees it developing

[5]Forgetting difficulties of production, I should suppose that *Giselle*, *The Long Christmas Dinner*, and the Siegfried Idyll would be acceptable and that *Can-Can*, *South Pacific*, and "The Stars and Stripes Forever" would not. *Waiting for Godot* should never be presented anywhere.

[6]The chapel has no budgetary allowance.

into a broader kind of student drop-in and lounge with an ecclesiastical implication if intramural access to the chapel above may be provided.

The chaplain continues to see, as he saw in 1972, a growing concern with religious orthodoxy, by which I mean no rigorous Athanasian dogmata but a return from beads, label buttons, and other bizarrerie, a trend confirmed by the consensus of a national study that an era of experimentation is closing and that a reversion to the historical churches is in process. Locally it appears that a greater number of undergraduates are attending the churches of their choice in the extramural community and—though the congregation is not yet dangerously large—the university chapel as well.

The truth is, I think, that human beings are incorrigibly religious: even to tend a potted geranium is an act of worship. And there is right progress when an individual relates that act of worship not merely to that of each of his contemporaries but to the experience of centuries of his predecessors.

The chaplain's generally sanguine views are echoed by Father Robert G. Cofenas, M.A. '67, Ed.D. '77, who has represented the Roman Catholic Church at Lehigh since 1975. Father Cofenas is an immensely likable, frighteningly energetic and ubiquitous young man to whom I should gladly take my troubles if I had any and who did not depart on a month's holiday when he heard that I wished to speak with him. Like the chaplain's his activities would produce vertigo in any normal creature: In addition to his purely sacerdotal function, he counsels, he visits, he conducts retreats, and, a strong believer in "visibility," he appears at each living group at least once a year. And as if all this were insufficient, he does the same across town at Moravian as well.

Father Cofenas too finds a renewed interest in religion, and again he is backed up by nationwide testimony as well as by his observation of the Lehigh campus. In at least a shapeless way everyone searches for a meaning in life; trends and emphases vary cyclically, but at present the foibles are losing some of their appeal and traditional response is gaining.

Right this minute Father Cofenas's chief pride and joy is the new Newman Center on the campus, where the work of renovation is going on briskly to be completed long before the appearance of this *Bulletin.* The three-story, nine-room building, long a private residence strategically located between Grace Hall and the gym, was acquired by the university in 1976 and has been leased to the Diocese of Allentown rent-free for 30 years. It is being regenerated to the tune of over $100,000[7] originating in the Diocese and in private contributions. When completed it will house two resident clergy and will include a library with audiovisual equipment, a chapel (of course), and rooms for miscellaneous social activities. Like the ministry of the university chapel, the Newman Association is open to all men—*homines, non viri*[8]—to all men of good will, no matter what label they wear.

I was interested in the product mix at Lehigh but met with only indifferent success in establishing it. I understand that the forms used here at registration include a space where a student may if he wishes indicate his religious or irreligious bias. A visit to the registrar's office, however, was fruitless, for I was there informed that these results are not available; apparently the registrar first collects them and then throws them away, just as if he were in the Army. For my breakdown, then, I am reduced to the chaplain's rough figures, which estimate 62.5 percent some kind of non-Roman Catholic Christian, 22.5 percent Roman Catholic, 14 percent Jewish, and 2 percent who may be pure atheists or animists or undecided or just people who are sick and tired of filling out forms.[9]

[7]Allowing for fluctuations in the value of money since the thirteenth century, about the cost of Salisbury Cathedral, which took longer, of course.

[8]This raises the question of whether women have souls. Disregarding St. Ambrose's uncertainty, note that c. 1600 Donne—who *liked* them, you recall—thought they didn't. By 1630, though, he had changed his mind, no one knows why. The federal government says that they do, and I suppose that settles it.

[9]In the face of probability I like to believe in the freshman who wrote in "Druid (Reformed)."

Lehigh in the past, by the way, has given pretheological training to many a clergyman. Mr. Ramsey has kindly presented me with a printout distinguishing the clerical persons among the alumni. I did not have the time to count them, but the printout vertically is 22 inches long and that must add up to a good many names. Soon perhaps, if the present trend continues, it will reach two feet or more.

Though I have regretfully had to unmention the important Jewish community and others—who may be just as well satisfied—I conclude that religion at Lehigh is alive and as well as can be expected. Since the world is going to come to an end in 23 years, probably in April, this is a Good Thing. There is still time to fix the roof of the chapel and to install the lavatories.

Mundus Alter et Idem[1]

I was taught long ago that pretty much all writing fell into the two grand divisions of narration and exposition. The way to begin the first, I learned, is to plunge *in medias res*: "Bang! Bang! Bang!" for instance, or "Call me Ishmael." Only some while later might you let on to who was shooting at whom or introducing himself, as the case might be. But in exposition you ought to provide a background. It didn't necessarily do any good, but it showed that, no superficial trifler, you were making like a writer of substance. Like William Harrison (1534-1593), who, beginning a work on Elizabethan shipping, advised that, "It shall not be amiss to begin at the navie of Xerxes." (Xerxes' *floruit*, you recall, was the fifth century B.C.)

Since I am examining college yearbooks—really just one college yearbook—I am sorry not to go before the Christian Era or indeed much earlier than my subject, the Lehigh *Epitome* of more or less 1886.[2] I believe that earlier American annuals, following the New England prototype, were printed on a single sheet displaying the faculty (5 names), the graduating class (17 names in order of social standing), and the statement that in the year previous we had or had not defeated Yale. That is, I do not really know the steps that led from Xerxes to the 1886 *Epitome*, the fraternities, the Civil War, and the discovery of football.

[1]I have borrowed this title from Joseph Hall (1574-1656). I thought I would give some class to the monograph by putting in a little Latin.

[2]This *Epitome* is dated in the exasperating and misleading way that yearbooks have traditionally exhibited. I graduated from college in 1930, but you will have to read me up in the 1931 yearbook. The book under immediate consideration is named 1886 and features the classes from '84 to '87.

Let us be clear about two details. The word itself, *epitome*, includes four syllables and is antepenultimately accentuated, sort of rhyming with *anatomy*, not with *metronome*. And it does not mean high point or summit or any of that: It means (these days) abridgment. I cannot count the times when I have advised lyrical freshmen not to write, "Making the first team was the *epitome* of my high school career." Unless indeed they meant something very curious.

Well then, it shall not be amiss to look at the *Epitome* of 1886. It is 6 " x 9 ", it is paperbound, and the binding is coming apart. It comprises 103 pages of text proper and 25 pages of ads, including one for the university itself. The cover, amidst conventionalized sunbursts, tells us pictorially that the then Lehigh man was interested or supposed to be in eating, in drinking (fermented and *gebraut* beverages only), astronomy, physical culture, chemistry, surveying, and—to my surprise—criminology, that is, if a deerstalker and a calabash have any symbolic value at all. In short, a Renaissance man, barring the lack of any interest in rhetoric.

The book is unselectively dedicated to the trustees, to the alumni, to the faculty, to the undergraduates, and to anyone that buys a copy of it—in short, to almost everyone this side of Tibet. It cost $.25 and boasts, no doubt truthfully, that at that price it's a steal.

Although superficially a world apart from the *Epitomes* of the 1980s—the 1983 book weighs about six pounds on my bathroom scale while 1886 has no weight at all—all the *schmalz* is merely accidental, not substantial, as Aquinas would have put it, and the contrast is more interesting than significant.

Lehigh in 1886 had an instructional force of 24, including 9 instructors, or "helots," as they were known in those days and in fact are still; and an undergraduate body of 216, a very fine ratio. There were 25 trustees, 10 of them genuine, 15 honorary. The class distribution must mean something, for I find 26 seniors, 29 juniors, 57 sophomores, and 104 freshmen. This attrition must be eloquent of rigid academic standards in some contrast to those of the present day, when nothing but aggravated statutory crime interferes with undergraduate residence.

Socially speaking, there were five fraternities beginning with Chi Phi and including Phi Theta Psi, which seems to have turned into Psi U if I have understood the footnote on page 51; and ATO, which in those days must have suffered from a strong *furor gallicus*, for it speaks of *Membres Absents* (Absent Members), *Etudiants de Première Année* (Students of First Year = freshmen, I daresay), and shows a lyrical disposition evidenced by a vocal trio, two tenors and a bass. I wish I understood, by the way, why Delta Phi was founded at Union in 1827 according to the 1927 Baird's *Manual* and at Norwich in 1856 if you trust the 1983 *Epitome.*

Total fraternity membership was around 58, for in those simpler days the groups were so small that members could recognize each other and even become congenial.

Commencement Week receives its meed of prominence in 1886. There was a merciless lot of it, as always, but it had the (presumed) merit of displaying the talents, such as they were, of the graduating class. Commencement in 1883 featured "orations,"[3] no fewer than seven of them, ten musical selections, and only after all this were the degrees conferred. Significantly I see that 22 of the 29 members of 1883 were "excused from speaking on University Day." Could there have been a black period in Lehigh's history when *every* graduate had a piece to recite?

Indeed a rationally designed Commencement has never come into my experience, though President Harvey Neville made a fine try at it. It is not long since every name of every kind of graduate at Lehigh was read aloud from the bema, though already plainly recorded in print. I don't know what others did, but I had crossword puzzles between the leaves of my program; and for kicks I would wait to see what the lector did with a name like Pradhjiwicz or MacAmhalghaidh.

The high point of Commencement Week must have been the "Sophomore Cremation," the program of which appears in

[3]An oration differs from a mere speech or address in being far more pretentious and bombastic.

these pages. As you see, the Latin is more pretentious than difficult: the only far-out terms are *Olneii* and *Doolitli.* Someone named Olney must have written the textbook used in Second Year Math, and C. L. Doolittle, was professor of Mathematics and Astronomy. No doubt the sophomores felt that they had had a lot of trouble with calculus[4] and that it was largely the fault of the textbook and of their instructor. Clearly they burned something, a copy of the textbook or an effigy of Olney or Olney himself, and everyone had a hilarious good time of it.

Extracurricular activities may be simply stated. Base Ball and Foot Ball came in separate syllables, and the former of these sports was played by a nine. (Shades of Frank Merriwell.) Hares and Hounds was more or less Cross Country; on one of their jaunts that year they covered 20 miles. But my favorite aggregation is the Saucon Hall Orchestra, which comprised piano, four flutes, a harmonica, a "tin flageolet," cornet, violin, and a magerian [*sic*], whatever the hell that is. It can't be a typo for *manager.*

In addition the editors provided both verbal humor and graphic art. In kindness to their ashes I do not quote the one nor reproduce the other. Never deal unkindly with anyone that is doing his best. . . . But if I, God forbid, ever addressed a graduating class, I should tell them, "The day after you get home, take all the undergraduate work that you are proudest of and burn it. Even reading it to yourself in later years is like being broken on the wheel or burned at the stake along with Olney's *Calculus.*"

Little remains to be told, but the advertisements are not wholly without interest. We learn that "one of the best hotels in New York" Earle's, was located on Canal Street: "Rooms, $1 per Day and Upwards." We older boys will feel a twinge at the full-page assertion

[4]Calculus. Probably the well-known branch of mathematics. But it may mean a pebble; in days of old, folks did their ciphering with pebbles as I still do. Or a stone (pebble) in the kidney or the bladder or one of those places. When we read of Browning's Grammarian that "*Calculus* racked him," it does not mean that he had a hard time with math.

that the Lehigh Valley Railroad is "The People's Favorite Line." Correct spelling was required for entrance to the university, and Charles W. Welsh at Fourth and Wyandotte ran not so much a barbershop as a Shaving and Hair Cutting Emporium. The university did not charge tuition, it boasts: a fine policy regrettably outdated.

Now I wanted to get hold of the 1985 *Epitome*, but I might as well not have bothered; it wasn't available, they told me. The Alumni office had lost its copy of the 1984 version. But I am looking at 1983, which has to be good enough. It has a lot of photography in it, not always advisedly, while 1886 has none, Daguerre in those days being shunned as just another crazy Frenchman. But the traditional stigmata are still with us: intemperance and other anti-social behavior are still by implication deemed amusing, manly, or womanly, as they are not, not really, even though they are collegiate; and I feel sure that if indeed we could go back to Xerxes' time, we should find ourselves in a familiar environment.

Just one thing more. On page 328 of the 1983 book, among the acknowledgments, I find Rhonda Stone and Rhonda Stoner. How many wags, I wonder, phoned the *Epitome* to find out what happened to Rhonda Stonest?

Back to the Abacus

Late in 1976 Professor Edward Gallagher of the English department courteously asked me whether I would submit to him any thoughts of mine suitable to *HPT News*, a publication whereof he was at that time the editor. Like a character in "Another World" or like Thoreau I wanted to get away by myself and think things through, and I did. My considered view is just what it was in 1927, let alone 1976, namely, that the humane perspective on technology is that there is too much of it (of technology, I mean) and that—supposing we care for the well-being of humanity—we ought to scrap it, as the Erewhonians did, and spend our efforts on something sensible. Since this opinion is (roughly) at least as old as Plato, it does not come as much of a novelty except to people who have not read Plato.

What people need in the practical sphere are not more sophisticated computers with the power to make mistakes on an unprecedented scale but homely amenities like roofs that do not leak, windows that you can open and shut without risking hernia, and can-openers that stay sharp for more than two weeks.

(On a higher level what people need is to be good, happy, and comfortable. Wish us luck.)

Before going further, however, I have heard that it is important to distinguish between Science and Technology because they are always getting mixed up.

Science, as has been explained to me, is concerned with the discovery and enunciation of great big broad Truths and is not necessarily interested in what anyone does with Them afterward. In fact sometimes this is true and sometimes it is not.

Some scientific discoveries are all right as far as they go. Thus, we honor Galileo for telling us that if you drop a sash-weight off the downside of the Leaning Tower of Pisa, it will hit the ground. A bit later Newton explained that a moving body will go on forever

Rain/cpf

unless an outfielder or something interferes with it. Somebody else made a big production of the Second Law of Thermodynamics, which says, e.g., that if you fill a bathtub with hot water, it will cool off after a while. Our modern understanding of the universe is said to be based on these and other such pronouncements, though I am bound to add that they sound to me like nothing more than ordinary common sense, and I think that a lot of people knew about them long before Galileo.

Some science is simply claptrap. Einstein says that if you drive your car fast enough, your wristwatch will run backward, which I personally do not believe for a minute, and even if it were true, who needs it?

Anyway, technology is when you take one of these big principles and do something practical with it. So starting with Galileo you may drop a paper bag full of water from the mezzanine at an Elks' convention, or a bomb on Coventry Cathedral. It is clear on the one hand that neither of these actions is socially constructive, and on the other, that they would happen just the same if Galileo had never been born.

As for people, the one thing you can be sure about with

them is that they will misuse anything they discover. A timeless paradigm was provided during the Second War by some aborigines on the west coast of Ireland. They found a floating mine by the shore, and in the spirit of inquiry that has made man what he is, they began to unscrew the bolts and things and take it apart. They found out what it was, but too late to benefit from the knowledge. "Whether we should live like baboons or like men, is a little uncertain," wrote Thoreau, who was a matchless observer and analyst but a hopelessly optimistic prophet. No baboon yet born would have been ass enough to fool around with a mine.

Fortunately for this generation the consequences of our unassuageable itchiness are not always immediately lethal. Sometimes they are only pretentious and silly.

I was sure that we had hit bottom for the decade when, watching some pro football toward the end of the 1976 season, I found that measurement was being made not by a couple of acolytes but by a laser from the sidelines: if something in the referee's hand lit up or did not light up, the offense had either made a first down or had not made it or *vice versa.* This innovation struck me as a blessed example of modern technology in action, being troublesome, expensive, meaninglessly accurate, and irrelevantly seductive.

1. I am not sure what a laser is, but I am sure that it gets out of order like any other gadget; and if the referee needs a receiver, that means *two* things to get out of order (while the Rose Bowl waits for somebody to find the old sticks). Furthermore, the referee, who has enough on his mind anyway, now has one more thing to fret about, all mixed up in his pants pocket with his colored handkerchiefs, his spare whistle, and such.

2. I have no idea what a football-sized laser costs, but let us say $150. A couple of broomsticks and 30 feet of toilet chain you can get new for about $10, and it will last you a lifetime.

3. On a pile-up through the line the referee never knows anyhow where the ball ought to be after seven or eight athletes have been prodded off it. His guess is maybe one and one-

half feet wrong. So he needs a split millimeter cosmic ray after that to tell him what down it is.

4. Though the laser has charm as a novelty, it is probably like the hand calculator that my daughter, meaning no ill, gave me when she went to college and clipped me for a far more costly model. I used this thing for a preliminary study of my income tax liability for 1977 and found that my charitable contributions—before the end of the year, mind you—totaled $32,016.47, an absurdly misleading figure, as anyone acquainted with my lifestyle can testify. The calculator is a cute shiny device, and I love the way it lights up, but when I get serious with the IRS in January, I shall have to go back to reckoning on my fingers as usual.

My wife said maybe the laser saves time on the gridiron since the help no longer have to run (like) 75 feet out on the field and then back again; and that would make some sense if time were important. But everyone knows that the last 2 minutes of any half take 25 minutes to play. So much for that suggestion.

As I said, I thought the laser as applied to football was the last word for our time, but that was before a few days ago. That is when I learned from Vance Packard's latest book that a recently devised surgical procedure exercised upon infant girls will render them permanently flat-chested and thus enhance their competitiveness as "foresters, jockeys, acrobats, soldiers, and mechanics."

The state rests.

Thundering Heard

Fall, '78

> *Noise, the grand dynamic, the audible expression of all that is exultant, ruthless, and virile . . . We will make the whole universe a noise in the end. We have already made great strides in this direction as regards the Earth.*
>
> —*The Screwtape Letters*

One of the greatest strides was made on August 29 in Grace Hall at the Freshman-Alumni Rally. If the building was not literally as noisy as hell for over an hour, it came close enough. Judging by decibels the Class of '82 and the band are off to a great season. . . . Hall Cushman '31 told me once that when he was with American Locomotive he knew a veteran employee who used to goof off by crawling into a boiler from whose exterior rust was being chipped and taking a refreshing nap there. I wished I had that kind of aural insulation. I was glad to read in the checklist in capital letters that at least the cannon—once injudiciously introduced to these ceremonies—was interdicted.

The uproar proper began around 7:15 when an array of bandspersons in undress uniform straggled into the building long after their approach had been heard ringing welkins up and down the valley. (It is interesting to note that in an enclosed space it makes no difference what the brasses are up to: the tympani have it all their own way.) In addition there were 12 cheerleaders—6 male, 6 female—to say nothing of the freshpersons—1,000 of them; I made it 10,000—who occupied Sections E, F, H and so on down to ZZ and who showed no signs of the poised continence that will be expected of them four years hence.

Banner with strange device.

Raise your ups and pose for photo.

Dominating the pandemonium was, of course, Professor John Steckbeck, showing for the twentieth time the *esprit* and the terrifying energy that have made him a legend at these affairs. When Steck was at the helm you could have cut the charisma with a knife if knives had been provided.

At intervals, fortunately, the hullabaloo abated for a little. For one thing there was the trooping of the colors for the first time in several years: 20 class flags paraded in, leading the alumni representatives.

Paul Wagner '57, president of the Lehigh Home Club, welcomed the neophytes. "The alumni love you just as Steck does," he said, though I don't know how he could tell. "When you get back here in fifty years, there'll be more chairs for you to sit in."

Bill Clayton '51, Alumni Association president, added his greetings and presented alumni clubs and class presidents or representatives, whom he had hosted earlier at the University Center dinner.

Harry Osborn, president of '32, then hailed his new children and introduced the other ten proxy parents present. He touched also on the stirring days of a half century ago and the periodical corruption of the fish in the Lehigh River by the prudential dumping of illicit beer.

Osborn then presented the '82 banner of red and blue to the class representatives, Elizabeth Maginnes and Richard A. Pearsall. Both recipients come from a long line of loyal Lehigh forebears. A daughter of Bristol Maginnes '58 and granddaughter of the late Albert B. Maginnes '21, for whom Maginnes Hall is named, Elizabeth is the niece of Nancy Maginnes Kissinger, L.H.D. '77, the first woman trustee. Richard's father, Mason '58, is a former president of the Lehigh Club of Texas. Young Pearsall is a grandson of Chester Pearsall '10. His great-grandfather Mason D. Pratt was a member of the class of 1889.

More salvoes and hosannahs welcomed Steck as he took over for the finale. "Every rally I've attended has been a memorable one," he roared. "Now there are two things I want you to do:

1. Raise your cups and pose for the photo.
2. Please do not rush down from your seats."

The liturgical phase of the evening was now over and was succeeded by the crunching of innumerable pretzels as '82 descended to the level of refreshment. I removed the Flents from my ears.

"It sure does something to you," I overheard from one freshman to another as we were leaving.

* * * * * * *

It sure does. When I got home a bit later I could have sworn that I heard from afar the imperious strain of a Chicago-style trumpet striding through the soft summer air.

"This is a switch," I said to my wife. "Since when do you like *China Boy*?"

"*China Boy*?" said my wife. "That's *Pavane for a Dead Princess*!"

Whatever a freshman rally does to you, I have a feeling it is permanent.

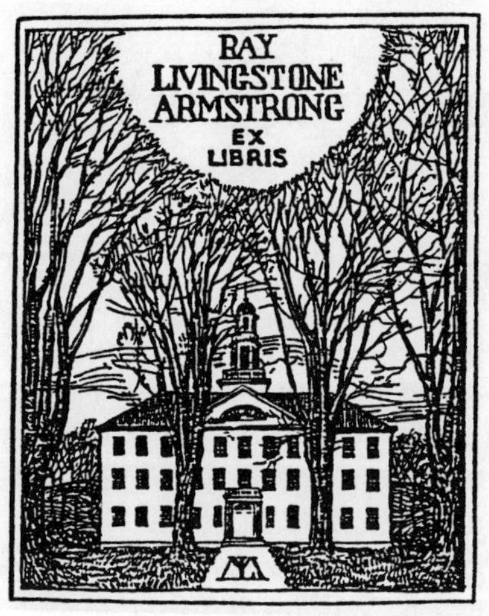

Posthorn

A Postlude
Beside the Still Waters

This "litel boke," as Chaucer would call it in his illiterate way, was supposed to be kind of about Lehigh University, not about me. I got into it now and then only because of my various involvements with the personnel and with the circumstances that bring it to its vivid liveliness. This final note, then, may not be entitled "Harvest of My Years," as so many final notes are, or "A Goodly Heritage." I just wish, for the benefit of those interested, to round out the Armstrong Legend while I can still hold a pen.

I retired (or was retired) in 1975, though still enjoying the plenitude of my powers. When I dropped in at the English office on July 1 that year, I found a workman changing the lock on the door of my (former) office, and the secretary asked me my name and business. Yet some of the amenities remained to me for a while, and even today their traces have not altogether vanished. It has been a gradual process. For some years I was allowed a desk in a corner where I wouldn't be in anybody's way. Later on I had to share the desk with someone I never met and didn't want to meet. More recently still I lost even that privilege and found the drawers cleared of my various supplies: old memoranda, a New England road map, and especially a short-handled hammer that Grandfather acquired just after the Civil War. I am glad that I took my valuable pictures home before the termites got to work on the walls. I still have a mail slot in the English office, where I get notices of scholarly meetings in Chicago, St. Louis, and New Orleans. How much longer shall I be able to retain even that?

Natural, nonadministrative influences tend to foster estrangement. It is now hardly possible for me to find parking in the Maginnes lot; and these days it's challenge enough to walk anywhere, let alone clamber about our tip-tilted campus. And many university functions, taking place around sunset or thereafter, are useless to me since I no longer drive when Old Sol has gone down.

My intellectual life has not flagged, of course, though it has not precisely flourished either. My extensive work on S.T. Coleridge came to an end when someone pointed out to me one day that a chap named Lowes at Harvard had anticipated me in around 1927, and I was left with a couple of shoe boxes full of index cards. I studied Icelandic for a while so that I might read the sagas properly, but Icelandic is a real gut-buster, and my eyes were threatened by cataract. I did, though, read all the way through the Vulgate Bible, yet when I finished it I didn't see but that it generally agreed with the Authorized Version.

As academic impulse weakens, I spend more and more of my time—now about 98 percent of it—at Grendlesmere, my retreat in the radon zone of Bucks County, accompanied by my daughter, for any heavy work, and by her winsome baby, little Locusta, whom she found under a gooseberry bush, I understand, though I take that account with a grain of salt.[1] Peace comes dropping slow, as someone or other puts it, except for this long-eared owl that ululates most of the night from only 100 feet away, and by day an occasional falling helicopter. My house is not by the side of the road, so I don't have to be a friend to anyone, and the man from UPS is instructed to leave parcels quietly, with no horn tooting. . . . Since I have three cats, I sometimes find a dismembered mouse in the upstairs bathtub.

The first Snowdrops will be out of the ground in a little over six weeks from the time of this writing.

Shantih Shantih Shantih

Grendlesmere, St. Lucy's Day, 1988

[1]My daughter also has a kind of now-and-then boyfriend—since he sleeps by day, I don't see very much of him—that she met in Atlantic City on a cheap, one-day excursion. She tells me that he is a dealer, but what he deals in I don't know.

Dr. John A. Hertz Becomes an Administrator

This is no journey over fractious seas
To parts that parboil or to parts that freeze,
No simple pilgrimage across the frantic
Reversible paths of the still-vexed Atlantic.
A deeper gulf debars, a wider ditch,
No traveler returns from the bourne of which:
The Hertzes now prepare a last translation,
To leave instruction for administration,
Quitting the threadbare classroom residents
To hobnob with trustees and presidents.
The linear distance may be picayune;
The moral stretches far beyond the moon.
"Yes," in ironic, reminiscent thought
The dean observes, "once on a time I taught."
"Yes, but don't mention it, I do beseech;"
His wife admits, "my husband used to teach."
"Yes," says some grizzled drudge, "I well recall
He worked right here, in Christmas-Saucon Hall.
This very Hertz, now numbered 'mongst our betters,
Once gave his youth and strength to Business Letters.
It seems but yesterday when he was seen
Spatt'ring with Suncrest milk his new grey gaberdine.
Not many of us, true, he knew by name,
But treated every one of us the same.
Now what we once supposed was warm regard
Has dwindled to a five-cent Christmas card."

The Lehigh World According To Ray Armstrong

The butterfly, aloft, no longer rubs
His shoulders 'gainst the uncomplaining grubs.
To you, dear John, and to you too, dear El-
eanor, without remorse a true farewell.
Your humble friends, whose world is hencforth colder,
Tomorrow to old woods and pastures older.

Clerihews

"Let's see," mused Professor Dilworth;
"Just what is John Stuart Mill worth?"
"Why should anyone care?"
Snickered Voltaire.

Professor Carl Moore
Found Christian doctrine obscure;
But it was mastered easily
By Chaplain Fuessle.

Professor J. B. Severs
Never even finished *The Reivers.*
Nothing, he thought, was half so cool as
"The Parlement of Foules."

President Harvey A. Neville
Abjured the World, the Flesh, and the Devil:
All entities resident
In the average college president.

With regard to #2 *supra,* Ray Fuessle's name was pronounced *Feezly* as near as makes no difference.